The Way to
SHAMBHALA

The Way to
SHAMBHALA

Edwin
Bernbaum

Shambhala
Boston & London
2001

To David, who was born at the same time as this book,
and to Diane, his mother.

SHAMBHALA PUBLICATIONS, INC.
Horticultural Hall
300 Massachusetts Avenue
Boston, Massachusetts 02115
www.shambhala.com

9 8 7 6 5 4 3 2 1

FIRST SHAMBHALA EDITION
Printed in the United States of America

⊗ This edition is printed on acid-free paper that meets
the American National Standards Institute Z39.48 Standard.
Distributed in the United States by Random House, Inc.,
and in Canada by Random House of Canada Ltd

Library of Congress Cataloging-in-Publication Data
Bernbaum, Edwin.
The way to shambhala: a search for the mythical kingdom beyond the
Himalayas / Edwin Bernbaum—1st Shambhala ed.
p. cm.
Originally published: Garden City, N.Y.: Anchor Press, 1980.
Includes bibliographical references and index.
ISBN 1-57062-874-2 (pbk.)
1. Shambhala. I. Title.
GR941.S52 B47 2001
398'.42—dc21
2001042908

Contents

Illustrations

Unless otherwise indicated, all photographs are by the author.

Map
1. Central Asia and India (map by Joanne Callenbach), page 35.

Figures
1. Shambhala (sketch by Moira Hahn), page 7.
2. Tsilupa (redrawn by Moira Hahn from *A New Tibeto-Mongol Pantheon* by Raghu Vira and Lokesh Chandra), page 16.
3. The Tibetan system of mystical geography (diagram by Moira Hahn), page 32.
4. The mantra *Om Mani Padme Hum* (reproduced by courtesy of the Ewan Choden Tibetan Buddhist Center), page 114.
5. The psychic-energy system (diagram by Moira Hahn), page 118.
6. The structure of a mandala (diagram by Moira Hahn), page 120.
7. The Ten of Power (reproduced by courtesy of the Ewam Choden Tibetan Buddhist Center), page 125.
8. The Kalachakra deity with consort (redrawn by Moira Hahn from *A New Tibeto-Mongol Pantheon* by Raghu Vira and Lokesh Chandra), page 126.
9. The lotus shape of Shambhala (sketch by Moira Hahn), page 143.
10. The lotus shape of Shambhala and the nerves of the heart center (diagram by Moira Hahn, based on a sketch by Khempo Noryang), page 145.
11. The shape of Shambhala and the deeper levels of mind (diagram by Moira Hahn), page 147.
12. Dushepa (redrawn by Moira Hahn from *A New Tibeto-Mongol Pantheon* by Raghu Vira and Lokesh Chandra), page 163.

13. Sucandra, the first religious King of Shambhala (redrawn by Moira Hahn from *A New Tibeto-Mongol Pantheon* by Raghu Vira and Lokesh Chandra), page 233.

14. Manjushrikirti, the first Kulika King of Shambhala (redrawn by Moira Hahn from *A New Tibeto-Mongol Pantheon* by Raghu Vira and Lokesh Chandra), page 235.

15. Rudra Cakrin, the future King of Shambhala (redrawn by Moira Hahn from *A New Tibeto-Mongol Pantheon* by Raghu Vira and Lokesh Chandra), page 239.

Plates following page 172

1. The kingdom of Shambhala (Tibetan painting, Musée Guimet, Paris. Photograph from Musées Nationaux–Paris).

2. The hidden valley of Khembalung.

3. Tengboche Monastery.

4. Rudra Cakrin in the final battle against the barbarians (detail of a Tibetan painting, Rose Art Museum, Brandeis University).

5. Sucandra, the first religious King of Shambhala (Tibetan or Chinese painting, Museum of Fine Arts, Boston. Photograph by Shozui Toganoo).

6. The hermit Oleshe in his hermitage.

7. Padma Sambhava (image, Tengboche Monastery).

8. Tulshi Rimpoche reading his guidebook to Khembalung.

9. The title page of Tulshi Rimpoche's guidebook to Khembalung.

10. Kangtega, the horse-saddle snow mountain.

11. Takmaru, the red rock with the key to Khembalung.

12. Snow mountains above Khembalung.

13. Peach Blossom River (Chinese painting, photograph from the Asian Art Museum of San Francisco, the Avery Brundage Collection).

14. Olmolungring, the Bon equivalent of Shambhala (drawing by Tenzin Namdak. Reproduced from David L. Snellgrove, *The Nine Ways of Bon*, courtesy of David L. Snellgrove and the School of Oriental and African Studies, University of London).

15. Kalki, the future incarnation of Vishnu (Indian painting, National Museum, New Delhi).

Preface to the 2001 Edition

Since the original publication of *The Way to Shambhala* in 1980, there have been a number of interesting developments. In the course of writing the book, I decided to do graduate work in Asian Studies at the University of California at Berkeley. When it came time to start my doctoral dissertation in 1983, I was told that I couldn't use my book for that purpose; since it had already been published, I would be plagiarizing myself. So, instead, I took the opportunity to approach the myth from a different point of view, looking at how it evolved from earlier material in Hindu mythology. My dissertation, *The Mythic Journey and Its Symbolism: A Study of the Development of Buddhist Guidebooks to Shambhala in Relation to Their Antecedents in Hindu Mythology*, focused on examining the ways that underlying metaphors of the Buddhist path to enlightenment and ritual practices of meditation shaped the development of Tibetan texts describing the way to Shambhala. This involved doing a much more detailed translation of the basic itinerary to Shambhala found in the Tibetan Buddhist canon and analyzing how the Third Panchen Lama drew from that text and transformed it in his guidebook to the hidden kingdom—the one best known among Tibetans today.

One of the interesting things to come out of this study was the observation that the basic guidebook to Shambhala in the Tibetan canon, the Kalapavatara or "Entrance to Kalapa," hardly mentions the name "Shambhala" at all and that it has no clear-cut reference to the Kalacakra Tantra or Wheel of Time teachings that Shambhala is supposed to preserve. The text focuses instead on Kalapa, the capital of the hidden kingdom, and refers extensively to Buddhist teachings that developed in India well before the Kalacakra is said to have come there from Shambhala in the tenth century A.D. In addition, the guidebook's description of the realm of Kalapa differs markedly from descriptions of Shambhala found in the principal texts of the Kalacakra Tantra. All this suggests the intriguing possibility that the *Kalapavatara* may be a very old work that predates the introduction of the Kalacakra teachings and the development of the Buddhist myth of Shambhala.

Kalapa itself appears earlier in Hindu texts as an idyllic abode of sages in the Himalayas. The dissertation explores in much more detail than my book the links with this and other features of Hindu mythology and how they have been adapted and transformed in a Buddhist context. In particular, a number of places, obstacles, and magical beings in the Buddhist journey to Shambhala appear to have come from directions given in the Ramayana—one of the two great epics of Hindu literature—for traveling to a northern paradise named Uttarakuru.

The route by which the Kalacakra teachings came to India from Central Asia in the tenth century—the historical prototype, in reverse, for the mythical journey to Shambhala—may have passed through Ladakh, a region of India at the western end of the Himalayas and the Tibetan Plateau. Indeed, when I finally had a chance to go to Ladakh in 1981, shortly after the publication of *The Way to Shambhala*, a Tibetan monk told me of a monastery named Shargola that Ladakhis considered the eastern gateway to Shambhala. Perched in the middle of a cliff, the temple faces east along the trade route leading to Central Asia—and the likely historical site of the prototype for the hidden kingdom. A knowledgeable Ladakhi added that according to local prophecy the great war between the King of Shambhala and the forces of evil would take place shortly after an iron bridge was built across the Indus River just below Leh, the capital of Ladakh. In fact, the Indian military had recently constructed a steel bridge at precisely that spot.

I asked the Ladakhi if he happened to know of any guidebooks to Shambhala in Ladakh. He replied that he had come across one the year before in Zanskar, a remote region of rugged valleys and peaks just to the south of Ladakh. "It was in a house, not a monastery," he said. Following his directions, I went over the mountains and found the owner of the guidebook in his home. The man led meup to another house tucked under a cliff and began to dig through endless bundles of old texts. Just as I had given up hope, he exclaimed, "Here it is!"

The twenty folios of stiff yellow paper printed in Tibetan script turned out to be a longer version of the anonymous thirteenth-century text that a German scholar had translated and that appears in chapter 8 of this book. A few lines from it quoted by the Third Panchen Lama enabled me to identify the author as a certain Menlung Lama and solve the mystery of his missing guidebook to Shambhala. This text was of particular interest since of all the guidebooks it gives the simplest and most realistic description of the journey to the hidden kingdom, making it sound as though one could go there with a party of merchants in a camel caravan.

A few years later I was able to get even closer to Shambhala. On my first trip to Tibet in 1983, in the Potala Palace in Lhasa I found large wall paintings of the hidden kingdom and a three-dimensional Kalacakra mandala, or mystic circle, in the form of a small pagoda palace. When I told monks at Tashi Lhunpo Monastery—the seat of the Panchen Lamas, who had close ties to the hidden kingdom—of my interest in Shambhala, they took me to see a chapel dedicated to the Kalacakra. A long mural on one wall portrayed in great detail the final battle between the forces of good and evil.

The following year I managed to travel to the heart of Central Asia, to the region most likely to have inspired the myth of Shambhala. There, in the Turfan Depression of western China, at the foot of the Tien Shan mountains, I visited the ruins of the ancient kingdom of Khocho or Gaochang, the most likely historical prototype for the hidden kingdom itself. Gazing at the extensive walls spreading around me toward the distant mountains, I felt as though I had come to a place of particular significance on my own journey exploring the many different facets of the myth of Shambhala.

When I wrote this book, there was very little published or known in the West about the Kalacakra, Shambhala, and related legends of hidden valleys. Since that time, a number of lamas have given Kalacakra initiations in Europe and the United States, most notably the Dalai Lama at Madison Square Garden in New York. Tibetan monks have constructed intricate sand mandalas of the Kalacakra in ceremonies at major museums such as the American Museum of Natural History in New York and the Asian Art Museum of San Francisco. A growing number of publications have appeared on the Kalacakra initiations and on the teaching itself. The myth and prophecy of Shambhala have been the subject of books by various authors, both Tibetan and Western. The Shambhala Training program started by Chogyam Trungpa Rinpoche has spread and given greater visibility to the name "Shambhala." This program focuses on teaching secular meditation and the sacred path of the warrior who works to establish the golden age to come. Finally, Tibetan legends of hidden valleys have received attention in the West from publicity around expeditions that have discovered a remarkable waterfall in the wild gorge of the Tsangpo River near the location of the hidden valley of Pemako.

Chapter 3 of *The Way to Shambhala* opens with the story of a journey I took to the hidden valley of Khembalung, in Nepal east of Everest. As I was leaving the valley at the end of that story, I had an experience that I did not include in the book. I would like to conclude this preface with an excerpt from a piece I wrote about that experience many years later.

> In the middle of the night, I woke to hear the sizzle of snow striking our tents. If it didn't stop soon, avalanches would sweep the gully and steep slopes we had to climb the next morning. The only other way out, going down the valley, led into a narrow gorge completely blocked by impenetrable jungle.
>
> We were running low on food and had just enough to get back, provided we left right away. If we stayed to avoid avalanches, we would run the risk of starvation. From previous experience I knew that the agony of having to make a decision with terrible choices either way would be nearly as bad as what might actually happen.
>
> Lying in my sleeping bag with fear twisting in my gut, I remembered Urkien's stories of hunters and herdsmen who wandered into Khembalung never to return. Slowly, in the darkness of the storm, they began to take on a horrifying reality.

As panic rose to overwhelm my mind, I tried everything I could think of to calm myself down—imagining being somewhere else, focusing on my breath, even praying. But nothing worked. My inner turmoil and anxiety only increased, pulling me every which way. I could feel myself falling into a maelstrom of fear and self-recrimination with no possible escape.

My God, I thought, why had I come here? If only I had stayed home where I was safe and secure!

At that moment a thought, very simple and obvious, but illuminated with incredible clarity, flashed into my mind: I could as easily be killed there as here. I could walk out of my house and be struck by a car. No place was safe and secure. Whatever would happen would happen, wherever I was, whatever I did. There was no way to avoid it.

And with that realization, I suddenly saw that everything I had done in my life, culminating in the decision to come to the hidden valley, had led to this particular place, to this very moment. If I was fated to die here, it was my *own* fate—one that I had, in some mysterious and inexplicable way, chosen for myself. It was pointless to have any regrets. And with a profound feeling of relief—as if something opened in my chest and a cool breeze blew through me—I realized that whatever happened I would have it no other way.

An extraordinary sense of peace and calm came over me. I lay back in my sleeping bag, reveling in the sheer feel of it, flowing rich and creamlike through every limb and part of my body. All the fear, all the worry, all the agony of indecision, all the grim foreboding were gone—vanished in a night now strangely bright.

I had been listening intently to the sound of the snow, wishing with all my might for it to stop. Now it no longer mattered. It could snow as much as it wanted. After a long time, I opened the door of the tent and gazed out. The snow had stopped.

Early the next morning, taking advantage of the lull in the storm, we hastily packed up our things and escaped through the clouds.

Tibetan legends of hidden valleys such as Khembalung are related thematically to the myth of Shambhala. Like the hidden kingdom, these valleys preserve spiritual teachings and provide sanctuary in times of tempest. It was only a few years ago, long after I finished this book, that I realized that the experience of peace in the storm returning from Khembalung had given me a vivid glimpse of what I was seeking on the way to Shambhala.

Edwin Bernbaum
Berkeley, California
March 2001

Preface to the First Edition

Outside of Tibet and Mongolia, the Tibetan myth of Shambhala has received relatively little attention—certainly much less than it deserves. The idea of a mysterious kingdom hidden behind distant snow mountains has an intrinsic appeal that ought to make it of widespread interest. I have therefore written *The Way to Shambhala* for a general audience with no particular background in Tibet or Tibetan mythology and religion. The book itself presupposes no knowledge of these areas and avoids the use of technical terms that would make it difficult to follow. At the same time, it contains material that has not been published elsewhere and should be of interest to specialists in a number of fields.

The material in this book comes from a variety of oral and written sources. I first heard about Shambhala in 1969 from the Incarnate Lama of Tengboche, abbot of a Tibetan Buddhist monastery near Mount Everest. Two subsequent trips to Nepal in 1970 and 1972 on projects to preserve Tibetan books in the Himalayas gave me an opportunity to learn more about the hidden kingdom. In 1974 I began to do research on the myth itself and spent seven months in Nepal, India, and Sikkim in 1975–76, interviewing lamas and laypeople, gathering texts, and photo-

graphing art dealing with Shambhala. Back in the United States,
I was fortunate enough to be able to work with Lama Kunga
Rimpoche (Ngor Thartse Sheptung Rimpoche) on Tibetan texts
gathered from my trip, from his library, and from the PL 480
collection at the University of California at Berkeley. Unless otherwise indicated, material I have attributed to lamas and laypeople comes from personal interviews.

The book itself progresses from a description of the myth to an
interpretation of its inner meaning. The first four chapters deal
with Shambhala in general, its possible existence, and its relation
to other myths. Chapter 5 provides background on the nature of
Tibetan Buddhism and the mystical teaching kept in the hidden
kingdom. Chapter 6 begins the actual interpretation by looking
at what Shambhala symbolizes in the mind. Chapters 7 and 8
present stories of the journey to Shambhala and translations of
guidebooks describing the way to the kingdom. Chapter 9 inter-
prets the guidebooks as allegories for a journey into the hidden
depths of the mind. Chapter 10 looks at the prophecy of Shambhala in some detail and goes on to examine its symbolism.
Chapter 11 relates the myth to everyday life and brings the book
to its conclusion.

For simplicity and ease in reading, the Tibetan and Sanskrit
terms used in this book are written more or less as they sound,
without diacritical marks. I have avoided Tibetan transliterations,
in particular, because their formidable consonant clusters tend to
confuse the reader who is not familiar with their ungainly appearance. Since English does not use the umlaut mark, I have
also omitted the umlauts usually found in phonetic renderings of
Tibetan words. A few additional remarks will help the reader
with the pronunciation of Sanskrit and Tibetan terms found in
the book. In both, *e*, especially at the end of a word, is pronounced *ay* as in bay: Tengboche, for example, comes out as
Tengbochay, not as Tengboch. An *h* following any consonant
other than *c* or *s* indicates aspiration: Bud*dh*a is uttered with an
explosive *d*. In Sanskrit words, *c* is pronounced as *ch*, so that
Kalacakra sounds like Kala*ch*akra. Precise transliterations of important Tibetan and Sanskrit terms appear in the Notes and

Glossary at the end of the book. Since Sanskrit is more familiar to scholars and since the original texts dealing with Shambhala were translated from that language into Tibetan, I have tended to use Sanskrit terms rather than their Tibetan equivalents. The Notes and Glossary, however, contain Tibetan versions of some of these terms, such as the names of certain Kings of Shambhala.

In this book I have attempted to bring out the inner meaning of the myth of Shambhala, to help it speak to the concerns of people today. In order to do so, I have taken a view sympathetic to Tibetan Buddhism, trying to give some understanding of the tradition from which this myth has developed. This does not mean, however, that I advocate Tibetan Buddhism—only that I feel that it, along with other religious traditions, has many valuable insights to offer today. My purpose in writing this book has been neither to prove a thesis nor to make a definitive study, but rather to acquaint the reader with the myth of Shambhala and to suggest a way of approaching it—and other myths—that he or she may find both interesting and fruitful.

1

Behind the Ranges

Something hidden. Go and find it. Go and look behind the Ranges—
Something lost behind the Ranges. Lost and waiting for you. Go!

RUDYARD KIPLING

Behind the ice walls of the Himalayas lie the empty deserts and remote mountains of Central Asia. There, blown clear of habitation by the harsh winds of high altitude, the plateau of Tibet extends north over thousands of square miles up to the Kunluns, a range of unexplored peaks longer than the Himalayas and nearly as high. Beyond its little-known valleys are two of the most barren deserts in the world: the Takla Makan and the Gobi. Farther north more ranges—the Pamir, the Tien Shan, the Altai, and numerous others—break the horizon until they give way to the great forests and open tundra of Siberia. Sparsely populated and cut off by geographic and political barriers, this vast region remains the most mysterious part of Asia, an empty immensity in which almost anything could be lost and waiting to be found.

Deep in the deserts of Central Asia, explorers have come across the ruins of great civilizations that have flickered in and out of existence like mirages in time. Some have left records to identify them; others have simply faded out of history. East of the Takla Makan, archaeologists have uncovered caves at Tun-huang full of ancient scrolls and paintings that tell of early Buddhist empires. To the north, beyond the wastes of the Gobi, lie the ruins of Karakorum, the capital of one of the greatest em-pires of all—that of Genghis Khan. Sven Hedin, a Swedish ex-plorer who spent most of his life exploring Central Asia, found a lost city buried in the sands north of Khotan, a major oasis on the old caravan route between Europe and China, and wrote, "No explorer had an inkling, hitherto, of the existence of this an-cient city. Here I stand, like the prince in the enchanted wood, having wakened to new life the city which has slumbered for a thousand years."[1]

Over a thousand years before Hedin, a Chinese traveler had this to say of these parts: "You hear almost always shrill whis-tlings, or loud shouts; and when you try to discover whence they come, you are terrified at finding nothing. It very often happens that men get lost, for that place is the abode of evil spirits. After four hundred li, you come to the ancient kingdom of Tu-ho-lo. It is a long time since that country was changed into a desert. All its towns lie in ruins and are overgrown with wild plants."[2]

Many have sensed the presence of some mysterious influence hidden in Central Asia. Hindu mythology looks north of the Himalayas for Meru, the mystical mountain at the center of the world, where Indra, King of the Gods, is supposed to have his jeweled palace. The ancient Chinese believed that their Immor-tals—such as Lao Tzu, the founder of Taoism—had gone to live forever on a jade mountain somewhere west of China on the heights of the Kunluns. An old Buddhist legend holds that the King of the World will be born clutching a clot of blood in his hand; Genghis Khan was supposedly born in this fashion, and swept out of the heart of Central Asia nearly to conquer the world, creating an empire that reached from the Danube to the seas of China. The Muslims of Persia, whom he devastated, came to believe that he was the Scourge of God, sent out of the Gobi to punish them for their sins. Modern scholars, looking for the origins of religion, have turned to the spirit journeys of the Cen-tral Asian shaman, a sort of medicine man who goes in trance to other worlds to rescue the kidnaped souls of the sick and dying.

During the nineteenth century the British, who had taken over India, took an interest in Tibet, a mysterious country to the north that was ruled by lamas, or Buddhist priests, and isolated from the world outside. The Theosophists, members of an occult religious movement that became popular in England and America toward the end of the century, spread their belief that spiritual supermen with knowledge and powers far exceeding those known to science lived somewhere behind the Himalayas, where they secretly guided the destiny of the world. This and accounts of various explorers, whom the lamas tried to keep out, helped to establish Tibet's image as the ultimate mystical sanctuary, protected by the highest mountains on earth.

All of this probably inspired James Hilton to write *Lost Horizon*, his novel about Shangri-la, a Tibetan monastery hidden behind snow peaks in an idyllic valley where people live for hundreds of years without growing old. Only those who get lost can find the way to this sanctuary, concealed not in the Himalayas, as might be expected, but in the Kunluns on the northern rim of Tibet. There they lead peaceful lives devoted to the study and enjoyment of art, literature, music, and science collected from all over the world.

As the High Lama explains to the hero of the novel, the purpose of Shangri-la is to preserve the best of Eastern and Western culture for after "a time when all men, exultant in the technique of homicide, [will] rage so hotly over the world that every precious thing [will] be in danger, every book and picture and harmony, every treasure garnered through two millenniums." Then, when the wars are finally over and "the strong have devoured each other," the treasures saved in the hidden sanctuary of Shangri-la will enable mankind to emerge from the ruins of the past and build a new and better world.[8]

Something about the novel resonated so strongly in so many people's minds that "Shangri-la" became a common word for any kind of hidden sanctuary or earthly paradise. During his presidency, Franklin Roosevelt built a hideaway in the hills of Maryland and named it after Hilton's idyllic monastery; later on, after his death, it was given its present name, Camp David. During World War II, in a twist of unwitting irony, Roosevelt announced that General James Doolittle's bombing raid of Tokyo had originated in Shangri-la. Today, more than forty years since Hilton wrote his book, we still find thousands of Shangri-las all over the world—in the names of countless restaurants, hotels, and resorts. The lasting impression made by the novel raises an interesting question: Was *Lost Horizon* simply a romantic fantasy, or was it based on something deeper of which Hilton may or may not have been aware?

In the beginning of 1969, I happened to be trekking through the Himalayas of Nepal with the Incarnate Lama of Tengboche, abbot of a Tibetan Buddhist monastery near the foot of Mount Everest. Since the spectacular setting of his monastery invited the comparison, I asked him, as a joke, if he had ever heard of Shangri-la. When he replied that he had heard Westerners mention the name but didn't know what it was, I told him the story of *Lost Horizon*. After I had finished, he smiled and said, "Well, the old Tibetan books speak of a place like that—a land of great Kings and lamas called Shambhala. They say that the way there is long and difficult and that you can go only if you are an accomplished yogi."

While many Westerners have regarded Tibet as *the* mysterious hidden sanctuary, Tibetans themselves have looked elsewhere for such a place. Their sacred texts point to Shambhala, a mystical kingdom hidden behind snow peaks somewhere north of Tibet. There a line of enlightened kings is supposed to be guarding the most secret teachings of Buddhism for a time when all truth in the world outside is lost in war and the lust for power and wealth. Then, according to prophecy, a future King of Shambhala will come out with a great army to destroy the forces of evil and bring in a golden age. Under his enlightened rule, the world will become, at last, a place of peace and plenty, filled with the riches of wisdom and compassion.

The texts add that a long and mystical journey across a wilderness of deserts and mountains leads to Shambhala. Whoever manages to reach this distant sanctuary, having overcome numerous hardships and obstacles along the way, will find there a secret teaching that will enable him to master time and liberate himself from its bondage. The texts warn, however, that only those who are called and have the necessary spiritual preparation will be able to get to Shambhala; others will find only blinding storms and empty mountains—or even death.

The earliest references to Shambhala are found in the most sacred books of Tibetan Buddhism, a set of more than three hundred volumes called the *Kangyur* and *Tengyur*. These works, known as the Tibetan Canon, are for Tibetans what the Bible is for many Westerners; they include the sayings of the Buddha and commentaries on his teachings by later saints and scholars. The books themselves are made up of long loose-leaf pages of thick paper—many embellished with gold and silver letters—that are wrapped in silk and bound between two wood planks. The oldest volumes concerning Shambhala were first written down in Tibetan around the eleventh century A.D. as translations from older works in Sanskrit, the sacred language of India. The contents of the original books were supposed to have been kept hidden in Shambhala for over a thousand years before coming to India in the tenth century.

Since that time a number of poets, yogis, and scholars of Tibet and Mongolia have composed additional works on the hidden kingdom, many of which have been lost and forgotten. But the most secret aspects of Shambhala have never touched paper: They have been transmitted from teacher to initiated disciple by spoken word only. Lamas say that without these oral teachings many of the texts, which are written in obscure symbolic language, cannot be properly understood. In addition, laypeople have passed on numerous folk stories about Shambhala—some about the war and golden age to come, and others about the mystics who have gone there and the treasures they have brought back. A few artists have also painted rare paintings that show the Kings and their mystical kingdom surrounded by snow mountains.

According to the earliest texts, Shambhala lies north of Bodhgaya, a Buddhist shrine in northern India, but since the kingdom is hidden, they fail to specify exactly where or how far. Guide-books written later describe the route to Shambhala, but in terms so vague and archaic that their directions are extremely difficult to follow. As a result, most lamas are unsure of the kingdom's location and hold differing opinions as to where it might be, ranging from northern Tibet to the North Pole. Shortly after I had had an audience with the Dalai Lama, the exiled ruler of Tibet, another high lama, the Sakya Trizin, asked me what he had said and remarked, "You know, I was having tea with His Holiness not long ago and he asked *me* where I thought Shambhala was."

The texts are much more specific about the kingdom itself and give a remarkably clear and detailed picture of it.[4] According to their descriptions, a great ring of snow mountains glistening with ice completely surrounds Shambhala and keeps out all those not fit to enter. Some lamas believe the peaks are perpetually hidden in mist; others say that they are visible but so remote that few can ever get close enough even to see them. The texts imply that one can cross the snow mountains only by flying over them, but lamas point out that this must be done through spiritual powers —whoever tries to go by airplane or any other material means will meet destruction on the other side. To emphasize that spiritual powers are needed to cross the mountains, one painting I saw shows a group of travelers walking over a rainbow into Shambhala.

Inside the ring of snow mountains, around the center of the kingdom, runs another ring of even higher snow mountains. Rivers and smaller mountain ranges divide the area between the two rings into eight regions shaped like eight petals arranged around the center of a flower (see Plate 1, Fig. 1). In fact, the texts usually describe Shambhala as having the shape of an eight-petaled lotus blossom enclosed within a rosary of snow mountains. As we shall see in a later chapter, this shape has a symbolic significance that is relevant to the deeper meaning of the myth. Each of the eight petal-like regions contains in turn twelve principalities, making ninety-six princes or minor Kings who owe allegiance to the King of Shambhala. Their small kingdoms abound with cities of golden-roofed pagodas set among

Fig. 1 *Shambhala. A sketch showing the outer ring of snow mountains, the eight petal-shaped regions with their towns, the inner ring of snow mountains, and the King in the central palace of Kalapa.*

parks filled with lush meadows and flowering trees of all kinds.

The snow mountains surrounding the central portion of the lotus blossom have turned to ice, and shine with a crystalline light. Within this inner ring of peaks, at the very center of the kingdom, lies Kalapa, the capital of Shambhala. To the east and west of the city are two lovely lakes shaped like a half moon and a crescent moon and filled with jewels. Waterfowl swoop and skim over the scented flowers that float on their waters. To the south of Kalapa is a beautiful park of sandalwood trees called Malaya, the "Cool Grove"; here the first King of Shambhala built an enormous mandala, a mystic circle that embodies the essence of the secret teaching kept in the kingdom and symbolizes the transcendent unity of mind and universe. To the north rise ten rock mountains with the shrines and images of important saints and deities.

The jeweled palace of the King at the center of Shambhala shines with a glow that lights up the night like day, reducing the moon to a dim spot in the sky. The palace's pagoda roofs gleam with tiles made of the purest gold, and ornaments of pearl and diamond hang from the eaves. Coral molding carved with dancing goddesses decorates the outside walls. Emeralds and sapphires frame the doorways while golden awnings shade windows made of lapis lazuli and diamonds. Pillars and beams of coral, pearl, and zebra stone support the interior of the palace, which is sumptuously furnished with carpets and cushions of fine brocade. Different kinds of crystal imbedded in the floors and ceilings control the temperature of the rooms by giving off cold and heat.

In the center of the palace is the golden throne of the King, supported by eight carved lions and encrusted with the rarest gems. All around it, for miles in every direction, spreads the scent of sandalwood incense. As long as the King remains on this seat of wisdom and power, a magic jewel given him by the serpent deities who guard hidden treasures enables him to satisfy all his wishes. Ministers, generals, and countless other attendants surround him, ready to obey his every command. He also has at his service horses, elephants, and vehicles of all kinds, including aircraft "made of stone." In addition, the storerooms of his palace hold treasures of gold and jewels beyond conception. From the Tibetan point of view, the King of Shambhala possesses all the power and wealth that befit a Universal Emperor.

The inhabitants of the kingdom live in peace and harmony, free of sickness and hunger. Their crops never fail and their food is wholesome and nourishing. They all have a healthy appearance, with beautiful features, and wear turbans and graceful robes of white cloth. They speak the sacred language of Sanskrit. Each one has great wealth in the form of gold and jewels but never needs to use it. The laws of Shambhala are fair and gentle: Physical punishment, whether by beating or imprisonment, does not exist. According to one lama, Garje Khamtul Rimpoche, "There is not even a sign of nonvirtue or evil in these lands. Even the words *war* and *enmity* are unknown. The happiness and joy there can compete with that of the gods."[5]

Tibetans have, in fact, taken the Sanskrit name Shambhala to mean "the Source of Happiness."[6] But this does not mean that Shambhala is merely a paradise of languid bliss, as our description may have implied. Such places do exist in Tibetan mythology: If a person does good deeds and acquires enough merit, he will be reborn in a heaven of the gods, where he will have everything he desired on earth—youth, beauty, riches, power, and sensual delights. But there is a catch: After hundreds of years of blissful life as a god, he will exhaust his store of merit, and perspiration will begin to soil his clothes and make him smell. Then he will know that death is near, and he will suffer all the anguish he has temporarily avoided; he will die and be reborn again, but this time in hell.

According to Buddhism, good deeds, even those done out of compassion, are not enough; a person must also acquire the wisdom that will enable him to wake up to the true nature of reality and know himself as he truly is. When this happens, he will transcend all suffering and attain Nirvana, the ultimate goal beyond heaven and hell. Having thereby achieved enlightenment, he will become a Buddha, an "Awakened One," no longer subject to the vicissitudes of life and death.

Although many lay Tibetans regard Shambhala as a heaven of the gods, most lamas consider it a Pure Land, a special kind of paradise meant only for those on their way to Nirvana. According to the texts, the kingdom provides the conditions under which one can make the fastest possible progress toward enlightenment. Whoever reaches Shambhala or is reborn there can never fall back to a lower state of existence and will either attain Nirvana in that lifetime or very soon thereafter. Lamas add that Shambhala is the only Pure Land that exists on earth. When I inadvertently suggested to the Dalai Lama that it might be only an imaginary or immaterial paradise of the mind, he immediately replied, "No, definitely not: Shambhala has a material existence in this world."

Because of their focus on attaining enlightenment, the inhabitants of Shambhala devote most of their time to the study and practice of the highest wisdom known to Tibetan Buddhism—the Kalacakra, or "Wheel of Time." This is the most complex and secret of the Tibetan teachings; lamas will reveal its inner essence only to those initiated into it, and they add that even among initiates only a very few outside Shambhala can understand the deep symbolism of its texts and meditation. The Dalai Lama, who confers many of the initiations, regards the Kalacakra as one of the most effective and speedy methods of attaining enlightenment—provided one practices it correctly and with the proper motivation.

Later on, we will look more deeply into this teaching, but for the time being we need only examine how it relates to the lives of the people who are supposed to be living in Shambhala. More than any other form of Tibetan mysticism, the "Wheel of Time" is concerned with finding eternity in the passing moment, the indestructible in the midst of destruction. As a consequence, those who practice the Kalacakra seek the perfect state of Nirvana right here in the imperfections of the world. Rather than renounce worldly activities and interests for the asceticism of a hermit or monk, the people of Shambhala use everything, even the distractions of luxury and family life, as means of attaining enlightenment. They strive to free themselves from illusion through the very things that bind others to it.

Because of their positive attitude toward the material world, the inhabitants of Shambhala are supposed to have developed an advanced science and technology, which they put to the service of spiritual ends. Tibetan medical texts believed to have come from the kingdom describe human anatomy and physiology, so-

phisticated theories and methods of diagnosis, and ways to cure
and prevent serious diseases such as smallpox. Other Kalacakra
texts from Shambhala have provided Tibetans with their systems
of astronomy and astrology, as well as one of the calendars they
use today. According to descriptions of the King's palace at Kalapa, special skylights made of lenses act like high-powered tele-
scopes to reveal life on other planets and solar systems. The King
also possesses a glass mirror in which he can see scenes of whatever is happening for miles around; lamas familiar with modern
technology explain it as a kind of television screen that enables
him to monitor the events of the outside world. Descriptions of
"stone horses with the power of wind" suggest that Shambhala
has the technology to make aircraft of metal. Other texts describe techniques for transmuting one chemical substance into
another and ways of harnessing the energy of natural forces such
as the wind. Each region of the kingdom is supposed to special-
ize in a particular field of knowledge, such as psychology or
philosophy.[7]

The study of these sciences helps the inhabitants of Shambhala to master the highest science of all—the science of mind or
meditation, which is found at the heart of the Kalacakra.
Through its practice they develop a direct awareness and control
of their minds and bodies; these abilities enable them to cure
themselves of various ailments. As a side effect, they also acquire
extraordinary powers, such as the ability to read others'
thoughts, foresee the future, and walk at very high speeds. These
psychic powers protect the inhabitants of Shambhala from ag-
gressors: If someone tries to attack them, they simply either materialize exact copies of his weapons and turn them against him,
or they make themselves invisible. But they do not try to gain
these powers. Their overriding aim in studying the science of the
mind is to know themselves so that they can attain enlightenment and gain the wisdom needed to help others toward Nirvana.

The people of Shambhala are not immortal, but they do live
long lives of about a hundred years and die with the assurance
of being reborn in conditions at least as good as those they have

enjoyed in the kingdom. Nor are they fully enlightened: They still retain some human failings and illusions, but many fewer than people of the outside world. They all, however, strive to attain enlightenment and bring up their children to do likewise. Theirs is the closest to the ideal society that can be reached in this world.

Their Kings, on the other hand, are supposed to be enlightened, and Tibetans believe that each one is the incarnation of a particular well-known Bodhisattva—one who has reached the brink of Nirvana and need never be reborn but has chosen to do so in order to guide others to enlightenment. As Bodhisattvas who have stopped just short of complete Buddhahood, the Kings are embodiments of spiritual forces such as compassion and wisdom. As such, they have the power to dispense the blessings and insight needed to understand and practice the most advanced teachings of the Kalacakra. Tibetans believe that their high lamas are also Bodhisattvas and that one in particular, the Panchen Lama, was a ruler of Shambhala in a previous life and will be reborn as the future King who will come out to destroy the forces of evil and bring in the golden age.

The Kalacakra texts give us a detailed, but somewhat mythical, history of the kings of Shambhala, which some Western scholars think may be based on actual fact. Since these texts have very little interest in what happened before the advent of Buddhism around 500 B.C., they tell us almost nothing about the origins of the kingdom. The few lamas who talked about it said that Shambhala has existed since the beginning of the world but little is known about its early history. They guessed that it had Kings and a religion that made it a better place to be than elsewhere—but they added that the religion was not Buddhism.

The followers of Bon, the ancient pre-Buddhist religion of Tibet, claim that Shambhala is really Olmolungring, the source of their teachings, an invisible kingdom surrounded by snow mountains northwest of Tibet. Their texts trace a lineage of teachers and disciples back nearly eighteen thousand years to their first great teacher, Shenrab, who was supposed to have been born as King of Olmolungring in 16,017 B.C. According to these texts, he emerged from his kingdom to cross a burning desert and bring the religion of Bon to Tibet. After teaching for a short time in the region of Mount Kailas, he returned to Olmolungring and was followed by a line of Kings who have remained in their hidden sanctuary, guarding the essential teachings of Bon.[8]

The Buddhist history of Shambhala begins with the life of the Buddha, Siddhartha Gautama. According to the usual account, after many lifetimes of preparation, he was born as the prince of a kingdom on the border of present-day India and Nepal. Hearing a prophecy that his son would become a great religious leader if he were to see certain signs of sickness, old age, death, and renunciation, the King, who wanted him to be a world Emperor, quarantined him in the luxury of the palace and banned any mention of such things. After Siddhartha had grown up and enjoyed all the pleasures of life, including marriage and children, he grew restless and slipped out of the palace. The gods, seeking to remind him of his destiny, appeared before him in the forms of a diseased cripple, a decrepit old man, a rotting corpse, and a wandering monk. Stricken by the realization that he too would get sick, grow old, and die, he could no longer enjoy the transitory pleasures of life, and following the lead of the monk, Siddhartha left his wife and family in order to seek Nirvana, the changeless state beyond all suffering.

After years of trying every kind of practice and refined self-torture of asceticism, he realized that these extremes could end only in death by starvation, and after accepting some nourishing milk from a maiden, he sat under a tree and looked deep into his own mind to find what had eluded him for so long. Realizing that Siddhartha was on the verge of enlightenment, Mara, the god of delusion, sent voluptuous girls to seduce him, and when that failed, terrifying armies to deflect him from his goal. But Siddhartha remained unmoved, and when the dawn came, he had attained enlightenment and found the cause and the cure of all suffering.

At first he considered keeping what he had discovered to himself, thinking it might be too subtle for others to understand, but the gods implored him to teach it anyway. The Buddhists of Ceylon and Southeast Asia claim that he spent the rest of his life preaching publicly and that all of his teachings were recorded in the oldest Buddhist scriptures, known as the Pali Canon. The Tibetans, however, say that the wisdom the Buddha acquired was indeed too subtle for the general public and that he taught the deeper and more mystical aspects of it only to those who were spiritually advanced enough to make use of it. When he did this, he did it in a divine body that most people could not perceive, and for this reason these teachings were not recorded in the Pali Canon but were passed on orally until written down much later. According to the Dalai Lama, these sermons, which occupy much of the Tibetan Canon, took place in a spiritual dimension that is invisible to ordinary vision—but is as real as the everyday world we normally see.

Just before his death and final entry into Nirvana, the Buddha took on the form of the Kalacakra deity and gave this highest of mystical teachings to a great assembly of sages and gods in southern India. King Sucandra of Shambhala, the first King of any importance, was there and took the teaching back to his kingdom, where he wrote it down and composed commentaries on it (see Plate 5). He also built the great Kalacakra mandala mentioned earlier—a mystic circle enclosing a three-dimensional model of the deity's palace (see Plate 18). Sucandra was the first of a line of seven religious Kings who taught the Kalacakra to the inhabitants of Shambhala.

The eighth King, Manjushrikirti, had problems. A large number of sages found the Kalacakra teachings too lengthy and complex to understand and left the kingdom to follow another teaching. Realizing his mistake, Manjushrikirti drew these dissidents back to Shambhala through the power of his meditation and taught them a condensed and simplified version of the Kalacakra, which they adopted. At least one Western scholar, Helmut Hoffmann, thinks that this incident may reflect, in mythical form, an important clash between a foreign religion and Buddhism in Central Asia.[9] Through his unifying actions, Manjushrikirti founded a second line of twenty-five Kings that is supposed to culminate in the King who will establish the golden age throughout the world.

According to Tibetan texts, for over a thousand years after the death of the Buddha, the Kalacakra remained hidden in Shambhala. During that period Buddhism spread from India to Central Asia and China. By the time it reached Tibet, around the seventh and eighth centuries, it had incorporated the gods and beliefs of other religions and had turned toward increasingly ornate forms of mysticism. In the view of Western scholars, the Kalacakra, which made its first historical appearance later on in the tenth century, represents perhaps the most extreme development of Buddhism in this direction. Whether or not it actually originated at an earlier date, the teaching, as it has come down to us, certainly shows the influence of late Buddhist developments in India and Central Asia.

Tibetan texts relate the following story of how the Kalacakra was supposed to have returned to India from Shambhala. According to this account, sometime during the tenth century, an Indian yogi-scholar named Tsilupa learned of the existence of the hidden kingdom and set his mind on going there to get the teachings of the Kalacakra, without which he felt it would be impossible to attain enlightenment. On top of a mountain along the way, he met a stranger dressed in robes who asked him, "Where are you going?"

"To Shambhala in search of the knowledge of the Bodhisattvas," Tsilupa replied.

"The road there is extremely long and difficult. If you are eager to learn, you can acquire this knowledge even here."

At that point Tsilupa recognized the stranger as Manjushri, the Bodhisattva of Wisdom, and prostrated himself before him. Then Manjushri initiated him into the secrets of the Kalacakra and gave him much of the teaching, which he took back to India. A few years later another Indian yogi-scholar managed to go all the way to Shambhala and returned with a more complete set of commentaries on the Kalacakra. Whether or not these journeys actually took place, Western scholars think that the Kalacakra did enter India from a place of origin in Central Asia

Fig. 2   *Tsilupa, the first Indian yogi-scholar to seek the Kalacakra from Shambhala.*

around A.D. 960 and that it was practiced in the Indian provinces of Bengal and Kashmir.[10]

About sixty years later an Indian teacher named Somanatha journeyed up to Tibet and introduced the Kalacakra along with its system of measuring time. For this reason the Tibetan calendar begins with A.D. 1026—the year in which he brought the teaching of Shambhala to Tibet. A number of other Indian teachers followed Somanatha up over the Himalayas to help establish the Kalacakra as an important doctrine of Tibetan Buddhism. Not long thereafter Muslims from the West swept across India and destroyed most of Indian Buddhism, killing monks and razing monasteries. With that, the Kalacakra ended its brief sojourn in India and withdrew into the mountain sanctuary of Tibet.

Since that time lamas from all the major sects of Tibetan Buddhism have practiced the Kalacakra and written numerous commentaries on it. The main text of the Kalacakra found a prominent place in the first volume of the Tibetan Canon, and the teaching itself became the most important doctrine of the Yellow Hat, or Gelugpa, sect that ruled Tibet under the Dalai Lamas. Tsongkhapa, the founder of that sect, took a particular interest in the Kalacakra and reportedly went to Shambhala in a vision to receive instruction from the King himself. The largest and most powerful monastery in Tibet, Drepung, was named after Dhanyakataka, the place in India where the Buddha first preached the teaching. As all this clearly shows, Shambhala and the Kalacakra have had a marked influence on Tibetan religion and culture.

The kingdom has also influenced the political history of Tibet. Late in the nineteenth century, an Indian scholar-spy named Sarat Chandra Das visited Lhasa, the capital of Tibet, and reported a widespread belief that the Panchen Lama was going to retire to Shambhala in two hundred years. According to Das, Chinese officials had taken advantage of this belief to spread the conviction that the Russians and the British were the evil barbarians who were destined to take over the world and destroy Buddhism, even in Tibet. As a result, the Tibetan Government had adopted a policy of keeping these great powers at a distance through diplomacy and temporization. Das commented that the Chinese "are always busy in devising fresh plans for guaranteeing the safety of the country against all sorts of imaginary foreign aggression."[11]

Twenty years later, around the turn of the century, a Siberian lama named Dorjieff became an influential tutor of the Dalai Lama and persuaded him and other high Tibetan officials that since Russia and Shambhala both lay to the north, they must be the same country. Anyone who disbelieved this and denied that the Czar was the King of Shambhala must be a heretic and an enemy of Buddhism. As a result, the Dalai Lama made friendly overtures to the Czar and exchanged gifts with him, all the while snubbing the British in India. He even tried to visit St. Petersburg, a plan that his council squelched at the last minute. During this time Great Britain and Russia were vying for influence and control over the mountain ranges separating their Asian empires in a struggle of espionage and intrigue that became known as "The Great Game." When the viceroy of the British Empire in India heard what Dorjieff was up to, he became quite perturbed and dispatched the Younghusband Expedition to Lhasa in 1903 to force a trade treaty on Tibet. The Tibetans were puzzled by the strange Englishmen who invaded their country and attacked their army only to extract a piece of paper and return home. At any rate, there was—and still may be—a book in St. Petersburg, now Leningrad, that claims to trace the ancestry of the Romanov Dynasty of Russia back to King Sucandra of Shambhala.[12]

Even the Communists have made use of the myth for political purposes. Belief in Shambhala used to be as strong in Mongolia as it was in Tibet—in fact, it was probably stronger. Accordingly, during the struggle for independence from Chinese and White Russian control, Sukhe Bator, the modern national hero credited with founding the Mongolian People's Republic in 1921, composed a marching song for his troops that went, "Let us die in this war and be reborn as warriors of the King of Shambhala!" A few years later, in an attempt to end the line of Khutuktus, the traditional lama rulers of the country, the Mongolian Communist Party Congress of 1926 passed the following resolution: ". . . and as there is a tradition that after the Eighth Incarnation he will not be reincarnated again, but thereafter will be reborn as the Great General Hanamand in the realm of Shambhala, there is no question of installing the subsequent, Ninth Incarnation."[13]

The myth of Shambhala has also had a subtle influence in the West. At the end of the Middle Ages, a number of Catholic missionaries left Europe to convert the Tibetans and the Chinese. Two of them, João Cabral and Estevão Cacella, were looking for a way from India through Tibet to Cathay, or China, and heard about Shambhala, which they called "Xembala." In 1627, thinking it was another name for Cathay, they headed up to Tibet, looking for the road to Shambhala. When they reached Tashi Lhunpo, the seat of the Panchen Lama and the major monastery for lamas interested in the mystical kingdom, they discovered their mistake and returned to India. Their letters home mark the first mention of Shambhala in the West.[14]

Two hundred years later another Catholic missionary, Abbé Huc, journeyed through Tibet and heard what sounds like a garbled version of the prophecy of Shambhala. According to this version, the followers of the Panchen Lama form a society of people known as the "Kelans." They believe that someday in the future their leader will reincarnate north of Tibet in a country between the Altai and Tien Shan mountains—apparently Shambhala. After this happens, the Chinese will take over Tibet, and Buddhism will dwindle away to survive only in the hearts of the Kelans. At that time the Panchen Lama will summon them all to join him, and those who have died will come back to life. Then, with a great army of the Kelans at his command, he will conquer the Chinese, establish himself as a universal sovereign, and spread Buddhism throughout the world.[15]

Since James Hilton used the book written by Abbé Huc as his primary source of information on Tibet, this version of the Shambhala prophecy may well have provided some of the inspiration for *Lost Horizon*. In any case, Hilton did use Huc and other Catholic missionaries who traveled in Tibet as models for his High Lama of Shangri-la—a Capuchin friar named Father Perrault. In the novel Father Perrault stumbles on the hidden valley and sets out to convert its inhabitants, only to be gradually converted himself until he becomes nearly indistinguishable from a Buddhist lama. This, in fact, almost happened to some of the missionaries whose accounts Hilton read; one in particular, Father Desideri, entered a monastery in Lhasa in order to study and refute the doctrines of Tibetan Buddhism, but became so interested in his studies and developed such a respect for the practitioners of the religion that he failed to make many converts. Eventually he wrote, "I was ashamed to have a heart so hard that I did not honor my Master as this people did their deceiver."[16]

The first Western scholar really to write about Shambhala was the Hungarian Alexander Csoma de Koros. In 1819 he set out from Hungary with a knapsack on his back to search for the ancestral homeland of his people, believed to be somewhere in Central Asia. After a long journey on foot across the Middle East to India, he reached Tibet and spent the rest of his life studying Tibetan language and literature. Although he never found the homeland of the Hungarians, he did find texts on the Kalacakra and Shambhala and came to the conclusion that they referred to a fabulous kingdom north of the Syr Darya River in present-day Soviet Central Asia. Nearly a century later, two other scholars, Berthold Laufer and Albert Grünwedel, published German translations of two Tibetan guidebooks to Shambhala. These and the writings of Csoma de Koros aroused some Western interest in the kingdom, primarily in a small circle of Orientalists.[17]

Shambhala came to the attention of a larger audience through the beliefs of the Theosophists. During the second half of the nineteenth century, a Russian named Madame Blavatsky founded the Theosophical Society, a widespread mystical movement that provided the West with its first significant exposure to Eastern religions, particularly Buddhism. She claimed to be receiving secret teachings through telepathic and written messages from spiritual masters living somewhere behind the Himalayas. A number of her followers believed that the highest of these masters, "The Lord of the World," resided in Shambhala, an invisible oasis hidden in the Gobi Desert. According to their belief, Shambhala was the spiritual center of the world and the original source of the secret doctrines of Theosophy.

Among a number of important figures influenced by Theosophical ideas was the Russian émigré Nicholas Roerich, a poet and artist who designed the costumes and sets for the celebrated premiere of Igor Stravinsky's ballet *The Rite of Spring* in 1913. Having delved into Tibetan mythology, Roerich developed a deep interest in Shambhala and led a scientific expedition through Central Asia to look for traces of the hidden kingdom. Shambhala became for him the ultimate symbol that bound together the quests and prophecies of all religious traditions. His many poetic writings on the subject, including a book entitled *Shambhala,* may have given Hilton his idea for Shangri-la.[18]

In any case, Roerich's interest in the Tibetan myth seems to have inspired him to create and promote the Roerich Pact and Banner of Peace, a treaty that bound nations to respect and preserve cultural and scientific treasures. A special symbol was supposed to be placed on museums, cathedrals, and other monuments and institutions so that in time of war they would not be bombed or otherwise destroyed. Representatives of twenty-one nations signed the pact in a ceremony at the White House in the presence of Franklin Delano Roosevelt; it was also endorsed by many other world leaders and prominent figures such as Albert Einstein. We can see the connection between Shambhala and the Roerich Pact in the following speech given at the Third International Roerich Peace Banner Convention in 1933: "The East has said that when the Banner of Shambhala would encircle the world, verily the New Dawn would follow. Borrowing this Legend of Asia, let us determine that the Banner of Peace shall encircle the world, carrying its word of Light, and presaging a New Morning of human brotherhood."[19]

The next speaker was Henry Wallace, the official protector of the convention and Secretary of Agriculture of the United States. Having met Roerich and become fascinated with his ideas, Wallace encouraged Roosevelt to endorse the pact. Letters he wrote to Roerich as his spiritual mentor show that Wallace had a deep interest in mysticism and knew about Shambhala. In 1934, with Roosevelt's blessing, Wallace sent Roerich on a government-sponsored expedition to Central Asia ostensibly in search of drought-resistant grasses, but according to *Newsweek* magazine, "around the Department of Agriculture the Secretary's assistants freely admitted that he also wanted Roerich to look for the signs of the Second Coming." Wallace could only have been thinking of the prophecy of Shambhala and associating the future King of the kingdom with the coming Messiah. Wallace's earlier mystical correspondence with Roerich nearly surfaced during the 1940 national election, when he won the vice presidency under Roosevelt. Later on, in 1948, Westbrook Pegler, a conservative columnist, published this correspondence as the so-called "Guru Letters," which discredited Wallace and ended his political career. If Roosevelt had died before the 1944 election instead of after it, a man deeply influenced by the Tibetan myth of Shambhala would have become President of the United States.[20]

The prophecy of Shambhala, which fascinated Roerich and Wallace, emerges from the history of the kingdom. Each of the Kings, starting with the first, will rule for a hundred years. There will be thirty-two of them in all, and as their reigns pass, conditions in the world outside will get worse and worse. Men will lose sight of truth and religion and will turn to warfare and the pursuit of power for its own sake. Dishonesty, greed, and cunning will prevail; an ideology of brutal materialism will spread over the earth. After crushing all opposition, the barbarians who follow this ideology will fight among themselves until an evil King rises to unify them all and take over the world.

Then, when this tyrant thinks there is no place left to conquer, the mists will lift to reveal the snow mountains of Shambhala. Outraged to find that he does not rule the entire world, he will attack the kingdom with a huge army armed with all kinds of terrible weapons. At that point the thirty-second King of Shambhala, Rudra Cakrin, "The Wrathful One with the Wheel," will rise from his throne and lead a mighty host out against the invaders. And there, in a last great battle, the evil King of the barbarians and his army will be destroyed (see Plate 4).

A popular Tibetan prayer composed by the third Panchen Lama reads:

You, the best of teachers, shall be born King of Shambhala
To vanquish the army of the barbarians,
To bring to pass the age of perfection.
At that time forget not your promise,
And hold me fast as the foremost of your disciples.

You, the best of holy teachers, shall ride a stone horse with the power
of wind;
Your hand will thrust a spear into the heart of Chipa, King of the
barbarians.

Thus shall the forces of evil be defeated.
At that time hold me fast as your disciple.

Your million warriors shall be of many colors—
Four hundred thousand elephants drunk with rage,
Golden chariots with weapons and young warriors,
All will enter the wrathful war.

. . .

By your elephants the other elephants shall be conquered,
By your stone horses the other horses shall be killed,
By your golden chariots the other chariots shall be smashed to dust,
By your princes the other princes shall be slain,
By all this the line of the barbarians shall be cut off forever.[21]

When the battle is over, the rule of Shambhala will extend over the rest of the world, and "the perfect age will dawn anew, better than anything that [has] happened before."[22] Food will grow without work, there will be no disease or poverty, and people will live to the age of a hundred years. Great saints and sages of the past will return to life to teach true wisdom, and many will attain enlightenment through the practice of the Kalacakra. Others will make great progress in their spiritual development. The world itself will become an extension of the Pure Land of Shambhala.

There is some controversy over whether the golden age will end, but all agree that it will last at least a thousand years. There is also disagreement over when it will begin: A few Tibetans believe the final battle is nearly upon us, but most think it will take place somewhere between two hundred and five hundred years from now. Lamas use the number of Kings of Shambhala and the length of their reigns to calculate the beginning of the golden age. They get different dates for it because the date they use for the starting point of their calculations, the Buddha's death, varies from a little before 2000 B.C. to around 500 B.C.—the usual historical date. In addition, a few lamas claim that the reigns of some of the Kings have been shorter or longer than a hundred years. According to the most prevalent opinion, however, we are now in the reign of the twenty-eighth King, and three hundred and some years remain until the thirty-second King will liberate the world from the tyranny of the barbarians.

Since the golden age has not yet come, the only way to experience it now is to take the journey to Shambhala—and find it waiting there. A number of Tibetan guidebooks have been written for this purpose, but their directions are puzzling and difficult to follow. The journey they describe runs through country filled with a curious blend of realistic and fantastic features: The traveler comes to mountains populated with gods and demons; he must cross vast deserts with the aid of magic powers and fly over a river whose touch would turn him to stone. Yet a number of features along the way seem to correspond to actual places such as Kashmir and the Tarim River of western China. In addition, the traveler must perform bizarre rituals, practice strange kinds of meditation, and endure superhuman hardships. All these leave one wondering whether the journey to Shambhala is pure fantasy—or whether it has some sort of reality.

The Eastern mystical view of the world can be quite different from the Western scientific view of it. A lama once remarked to me, "You know, it's a shame that the American astronauts wasted so much time and money going all the way to the moon only to see rocks just like the ones they could have seen right here. They never saw what was really there—the moon beings." A mountaineering expedition in the 1930s climbed a sacred peak in India that was supposed to have a golden temple on its summit. Afterward, when they mentioned to a high Hindu holy man that they had not seen the temple, he merely said with a smile, "No, you probably wouldn't have."[23]

It may be that the guidebooks to Shambhala are describing a landscape transformed by the visions of a yogi taking the journey there: Where we would see a mountaintop gleaming with snow, he would see a golden temple with a shining god. In that case, we might be able to travel the same path, but with a different vision of reality. To find out the nature of the journey and where it really leads, we need to go more deeply into the myth and its meaning.

An old Tibetan story tells of a young man who set off on the quest for Shambhala. After crossing many mountains, he came to the cave of an old hermit, who asked him, "Where are you going across these wastes of snow?"

"To find Shambhala," the youth replied.

"Ah, well then, you need not travel far," the hermit said. "The kingdom of Shambhala is in your own heart."[24]

2

The Existence
of Shambhala

With the entire surface of the earth apparently mapped and explored by modern science, the question naturally arises: How could such a place as Shambhala exist? How could a kingdom filled with rivers, mountains, temples, and towns remain hidden from the surveillance of aircraft and satellites? This is a question that troubles Tibetans today and has led some of them to dismiss the kingdom as the superstitious fantasy of an earlier, less sophisticated time. Yet many others still believe that Shambhala exists, and their reasons for doing so are worth considering: They tell us much about the nature of the myth itself and they suggest ways in which the kingdom might actually exist—even from a modern point of view.

The texts and teachings of the Kalacakra provide the basis for Tibetan belief in the existence of Shambhala. As the Dalai Lama pointed out, "If so many Kalacakra texts are supposed to have come from Shambhala, how could the country be just a fantasy?" He and other lamas find it inconceivable that an imaginary place could have been the source of a teaching that has produced so many literary works and has had such a profound influence on the culture and religion of Tibet. For over nine hundred years Tibetans have studied the Kalacakra, practiced its meditation, and used its system of astrology to determine the course of their lives. In 1976, eighteen thousand Tibetans, many of them laypeople with no special religious training, came to Ladakh in the Himalayas above Kashmir to receive an initiation into the secret teaching from the Dalai Lama himself—an initiation that was supposed to assure them of a future rebirth in the golden age of Shambhala.

The Kalacakra texts contain sermons delivered by the Buddha in which he describes Shambhala and the role it will play in history. Since he was supposed to know all, having attained supreme enlightenment, this in itself gives many Tibetans sufficient reason for believing that the kingdom exists. Although we might consider such a reason insufficient and unreliable, most of our knowledge of the world comes from a similar kind of reliance on the statements of authorities we respect and trust. We base our belief in atoms, for example, on the theories and observations of scientists who are supposed to know what they are talking about; very few of us actually perform the experiments and make the deductions needed to show that these particles exist. In a similar way, Tibetans base their belief in the hidden kingdom on the authority of the Buddha, who is supposed to have known what he was talking about. In neither case does the ordinary Westerner or Tibetan see either an atom or Shambhala for himself. In terms of their own experience, both possess the same kind of untested knowledge. As the Incarnate Lama of Tengboche once remarked to me, "How can you be sure that Mount Everest is the highest mountain in the world until you yourself have seen them all?"

The written history of Shambhala found in Tibetan texts gives Tibetans additional reason for believing that the kingdom exists. It provides what appear to be historical facts, such as the names and dates of the Kings, and records of what was happening in the outside world during their reigns. The texts specify, for example, who was King when Mohammed conquered Mecca in A.D. 630 and how many years the current ruler of Shambhala has been on the throne. All these tie the kingdom to events that have actually happened and give it a sense of concrete reality and historical continuity that lead up to the present and on into the future.[1]

By appealing to their deepest hopes and longings, the prophecy of Shambhala encourages many Tibetans to believe in the existence of the hidden country where the golden age of the future is even now ripening in secrecy. Just how much it has encouraged them to do so in the past becomes evident when we consider how successfully Dorjieff used the prophecy to convince the Dalai Lama that Russia was Shambhala and that he should therefore ally himself with the Czar. Recent events that seem to correspond to the predictions of the myth give added strength to Tibetan belief in the hidden kingdom. The destruction of Buddhism in Tibet and the obvious growth of materialism throughout the world, coupled with the wars and turmoil of the twentieth century, all fit what is supposed to happen before the final battle takes place. In addition, the advances of science and technology, which would seem to make the existence of Shambhala increasingly unlikely, seem to some Tibetans to make its discovery all the more imminent. Khetsun Zangpo, a noted scholar, remarked to me, "Your Western scientists have flown everywhere and explored almost all the face of the earth and are now looking for new and different places, so Shambhala may soon be found." According to the prophecy, the barbarians who take over the world will eventually develop the power and means of finding the hidden kingdom.

Widespread belief that important lamas have lived former lives in Shambhala and will be reborn there in the future gives Tibetans added faith in the existence of the kingdom. The Panchen Lama, a political rival of the Dalai Lama and his spiritual equal or superior, is supposed to have been Manjushrikirti, the King of Shambhala who simplified the teachings of the Kalacakra and founded the present line of twenty-five Kings. As we noted earlier, many Tibetans believe that the Panchen Lama will also be reborn as the last ruler of this line, the one who will liberate the world from the forces of evil. At that time, other high lamas are supposed to join him in the final battle as commanding officers of his army. Many of them already know the names and ranks they will have: The Dalai Lama's senior tutor, for example, will be a colonel in charge of the 5th Division, with the name of Senge Rinchen. Since these lamas are familiar and revered figures, they give Tibetans a feeling of having some sort of personal connection with Shambhala.

Various guidebooks to the kingdom locate it in the material world and make its existence seem plausible. The route descriptions they give start from well-known places in India and Tibet and gradually lead off into unknown regions of the Far North. In this way, they establish a physical link between the ordinary world and the magical realm of Shambhala. In reading the guidebooks, a Tibetan can imagine himself leaving his home and setting off for the kingdom. Although he may well be convinced that he himself lacks the capacity to go, he will feel that someone who has developed the necessary spiritual powers could follow the directions all the way to Shambhala.

Stories of lamas and yogis who have done so reinforce him in this belief. In addition to the Indian yogi-scholars who are supposed to have gone there for the Kalacakra teachings, numerous mystics from Tibet have supposedly made the journey and returned with tangible evidence of the kingdom's existence. One lama I met, Garje Khamtul Rimpoche, told me that he had seen and touched a strange piece of shriveled fruit that a former abbot of his monastery had brought back from a trip to Shambhala. Other lamas bring back reports of journeys they have made to the kingdom in dreams and visions—the most common way of going there. These mental journeys give Tibetans further evidence that Shambhala exists: They believe that what a high lama or advanced yogi sees in meditation or in sleep may have more reality than what others see when they are awake.

In the Tibetan view of reality, the world is not what it appears to be: Illusions cloud and distort our perceptions, creating the appearance of things that do not exist and masking those that do. When a lama claims to have seen Shambhala in a dream or a vision, he may have cleared his mind through meditation and seen something that was actually there. Just because he and others do not perceive it in their usual state of awareness does not mean that it was only a mental image or hallucination. A Tibetan might argue that just as we need a microscope to see microbes, so we need a clear and focused mind to see Shambhala.

This view of reality makes it fairly easy to believe in the existence of a place like Shambhala. The Tibetan language defines the world, in fact, as the realm of "possible existence," which means, according to Lama Kunga Rimpoche, that everything conceivable could, and probably does, exist somewhere, whether we see it or not.[2] This translates into a tendency to accept the miraculous and the supernatural as part of the natural order of things. As a result, Tibetans tend to be open to the real possibility of places even stranger than Shambhala.

Given their reasons for believing that Shambhala exists, where do Tibetans think it might actually be? Here they become vague and uncertain and express a number of different opinions. A few think it might be in Tibet, perhaps in the mysterious Kunlun Mountains; more point toward the region around Mongolia and Sinkiang Province of China; but most believe that Shambhala is in Siberia or some other part of Russia. Some Tibetans think that one must go still farther north to find the kingdom hidden in the icy wastes of the Arctic. A few lamas even guess that Shambhala exists outside the earth on another planet.

The texts that lamas use as their basic source for locating Shambhala present a problem that is responsible for much of this divergence of opinion: They describe the location of the kingdom in terms of a mystical geography that is difficult, if not impossible, to correlate with the world as we know it. This geography begins with a description of Mount Meru, a mythical mountain thousands of miles high with its roots in hell and its summit in heaven (see Fig. 3). Seven rings of golden mountains separated by seven seas surround this central world mountain. Outside the seventh ring lies an ocean with four continents floating at the four points of the compass. Each continent is flanked by two smaller continents and has its own distinctive shape—that of a square, a circle, an inverted triangle, and a half moon. A wall of iron mountains or blazing fire forms a great circle that surrounds and encloses the whole system.

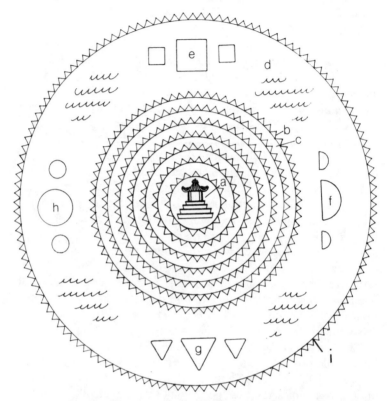

Fig. 3 *The Tibetan system of mystical geography.* a, *Mount Meru with Indra's palace on its summit, heavens and Pure Lands above, but not shown in the diagram;* b, *one of the seven rings of golden mountains surrounding Meru;* c, *one of the seven oceans surrounding Meru;* d, *the outer ocean;* e, *Uttarakuru, the northern continent, with its two satellite continents;* f, *the eastern continent, with its two satellite continents;* g, *Jambudvipa, the southern continent, with its two satellite continents;* h, *the western continent, with its two satellite continents;* i, *the outer ring of iron mountains.*

Within this system Shambhala is supposed to lie in the southern continent of Jambudvipa, somewhere north of Bodhgaya. Now, Bodhgaya is easy enough to find on a map—it lies near the Ganges River of northern India—but Jambudvipa is another matter. Tibetans today regard it as the entire earth and think of the other continents as planets in space, but in the past it seems to have also been identified with Asia and even with only the Indian subcontinent. The shape of Jambudvipa, an inverted triangle, corresponds to the shape of India, which strongly suggests that it originally referred to that country—in fact, some Tibetan and Indian texts use the term for India as well as for the world in general. If Jambudvipa refers to India, then the three other continents would correspond roughly to Western Asia to the west, Siberia to the north, and China and Indochina to the east. A closely related system of Hindu geography, which probably predated and inspired the Tibetan, seems to identify the central point, Mount Meru, with the Altai Mountains of Mongolia and makes a similar correlation.[3]

A number of Tibetan commentaries on the Kalacakra suggest another interpretation of the mystical geography that may mesh more easily with ours. They divide the southern continent of Jambudvipa into six zones that cover most of Asia and the Arctic. This suggests the possibility that Mount Meru corresponds to the earth's axis, and the seven rings of mountains surrounding it represent spherical shells, one within the other, that build up the planet from the inside like layers of an onion. According to this interpretation, the four continents would lie on the surface of the resulting globe, grouped around the North Pole, where Meru bursts out of the earth and soars invisibly into the heavens. Looking down from space, with the Pole at the center of the compass and Asia as the southern continent, Europe and Africa would be the western continent, the Americas the northern continent, and Australia the eastern continent. A relatively modern Tibetan geography of the world written by a nineteenth-century lama apparently adopts this view because it places Peru and the Caribbean in the northern continent of the Kalacakra system.[4]

Of course, the possibility also exists that the Kalacakra geography does not correlate with ours: The Kalacakra geography may symbolize a mystical reality that has little to do with the physical world. Although it mentions India and Bodhgaya, it may only be using them as points of departure for visualizing a mysterious realm of mythical mountains and seas that exist outside of space and time. In that case, as we follow the geography north, everything becomes more and more magical until we transcend the world altogether and behold in our minds the jeweled tower of Mount Meru shining at the center of the universe. This suggests the intriguing possibility that Shambhala is meant to lie on the edge of physical reality, as a bridge connecting this world to one beyond it.

All these make it difficult for anyone to locate Shambhala with any degree of precision. Depending on one's interpretation of the Kalacakra geography, it could lie anywhere from the northern part of the Indian subcontinent to somewhere beyond the North Pole. Sakya Pandita, one of the major figures of Tibetan history, combined the geography of the Kalacakra with another system found in the Abhidharma texts of Buddhist philosophy and concluded that Shambhala lay nine black mountains north of Bodhgaya, near a mountain that smelled of incense. But as Khetsun Zangpo pointed out, "There's no mileage given"—and the black mountains are almost impossible to identify. The guidebooks to Shambhala give more details, but as the traveler draws near the kingdom, their directions become increasingly mystical and difficult to correlate with the physical world. At least one lama has written that the vagueness of these books is deliberate and intended to keep Shambhala concealed from the barbarians who will take over the world.[5]

The guidebooks do, however, specify that Shambhala lies north of the River Sita. Although it might correspond to the Amu Darya or Syr Darya of the Russian steppes, the Sita is probably the Tarim River of Sinkiang Province in western China. An early guidebook written around the thirteenth century tells the traveler to cross this river and proceed north to a country of hermaphrodites on the southern slopes of the snow mountains bordering Shambhala. This suggests that the kingdom might be

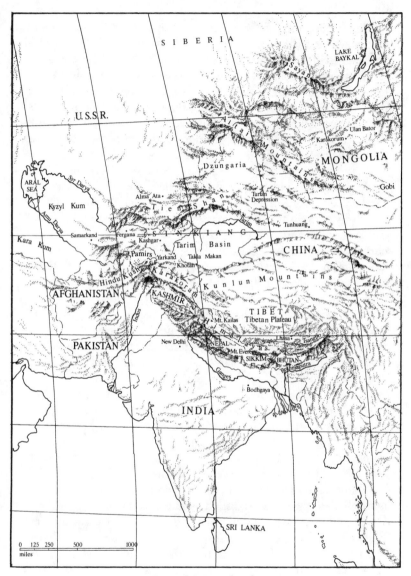

Central Asia and India

hidden in the basin of Dzungaria just beyond the Tien Shan, the first range of snow peaks north of the Tarim River. The prophecy heard by Abbé Huc about the future rebirth of the Panchen Lama in a country between the Tien Shan and the Altai Mountains seems to put Shambhala in precisely this area. However, most of the other guidebooks, including one that also mentions the country of the hermaphrodites, locate the kingdom many mountains and miles beyond the Sita, implying that it lies well to the north of Dzungaria.[6]

Most lamas who venture a guess as to the location of Shambhala turn for guidance to the commentaries that divide the southern continent of Jambudvipa into six zones. Going roughly from south to north, these texts list the six as India, Tibet, Li, China, Great China, and the Land of Snow. Depending on the particular commentary consulted, Shambhala lies in the western half of either Great China or the Land of Snow. Great China seems to include Manchuria, Mongolia, and parts of the Soviet Union. An eighteenth-century Tibetan text claims that Shambhala is in the neighborhood of Ayushi, King of the Torghut: The Torghut were a clan of nomadic people who wandered between the Altai Mountains of Mongolia and the Volga River of Russia. Ekai Kawaguchi, a Japanese priest and secret agent, visited Lhasa, the capital of Tibet, at the beginning of the twentieth century and reported hearing about another text, which located Shambhala three thousand miles northwest of Bodhgaya; if we measure this distance out on a map, we find ourselves in the vicinity of Moscow. Dorjieff probably used this book to back up his argument that Russia was Shambhala. With a Communist regime in power there now, few Tibetans believe this anymore, but many of them think that the kingdom may well be hidden somewhere in the vast and distant reaches of Siberia.[7]

A number of Tibetans opt for the Land of Snow—northern Siberia and the Arctic. According to Khetsun Zangpo, "Shambhala is not in Russia: it's north of the land under human use, somewhere up in the place of ice." Some lamas believe that the kingdom could only be hidden in the desolate, uninhabited wastes of the Arctic. As Lama Kunga Rimpoche put it, "Sham-

bhala is probably at the North Pole, since the North Pole is surrounded by ice, and Shambhala is surrounded by ice mountains."

In a conversation with Chopgye Trichen Rimpoche, a lama
who had expressed a similar view, I related a dream I had once
had of going with a guide to the North Pole. In the dream, as we
got closer, the air became warmer and the snow cover thinner
until there was only grassy tundra with flowers and a balmy
breeze. Finally we came to a round pond with a small island that
had a pole right at the center. I turned to my guide and
protested, "But this is impossible! This can't be the North Pole;
there's supposed to be ice and snow up here." The guide merely
pointed at the island and said with a smile, "There's the Pole."
And there was nothing more I could say. When I finished relating the dream, Chopgye Trichen remarked, "That may have
been the entrance to Shambhala."

Some Tibetans look even farther north for Shambhala. While
discussing where the kingdom might be, the Dalai Lama joked,
"If you go north in a straight line from India, you'll pass over the
North Pole and eventually come down in America, so perhaps
America is Shambhala." Another lama told me later, however,
that a few lamas take this idea seriously and point out that
America has the general size and shape of Shambhala, as well as
some of the material characteristics of an earthly paradise. The
Sakya Trizin, head of the Sakya sect of Tibetan Buddhism, re-
marked with a chuckle, "You Americans are looking for Sham-
bhala but nowadays Tibetans want to go to New York."

With so much of the earth explored and so little known of
outer space, Tibetans are also looking for Shambhala among the
stars. According to the Sakya Trizin, he and the Dalai Lama
have discussed the possibility that the kingdom exists on another
planet. Since some texts say that the future King of Shambhala
will come to Jambudvipa to destroy the barbarians, a few lamas
have taken this to mean that he will be coming to the earth from
an extraterrestrial world. During their meditations a number of
Tibetan mystics have reportedly seen the same vision of an iron
wheel that approaches a house and changes into the form of
Shambhala; according to Chugyal Rimpoche, "The house sym-

bolizes the earth, and the wheel the teachings of Shambhala coming from another planet." Mysticism aside, from a scientific point of view, many Tibetans feel that the kingdom could be most easily hidden in the infinite reaches of outer space.

If Shambhala exists on earth, which seems more likely according to the Kalacakra texts, how does it manage to stay hidden? Here again we find differences of opinion, primarily over whether or not the kingdom is visible to the ordinary eye. While some Tibetans believe that whoever succeeds in reaching Shambhala will see it as plainly as he sees Tibet, others argue that it will appear only to one who possesses the heightened awareness of a yogi. Lamas who hold the first view point out that the Kalacakra texts say nothing about the kingdom being invisible; they simply describe it as a distant country surrounded by snow mountains. According to these lamas, the remoteness of Shambhala, the uncertainty of its location, and the difficulty in going there are all sufficient to keep it hidden from the outside world. Even if someone should happen to go in the right direction and pass by the obstacles along the way, the snow mountains surrounding the kingdom would still block any view he might have of it. In any case, Shambhala lies far beyond the reach of most people, who lack the power and knowledge needed to find it.

Those who hold the second view, that Shambhala is invisible, believe that if an ordinary person should happen to stumble on the kingdom, he would see only an empty valley surrounded by desolate mountains. Instead of a country of golden pagodas and flowering trees, he would find a barren landscape swept by great clouds of dust and snow. A few lamas think that he might come across some of the towns and inhabitants of the kingdom but would fail to recognize them for what they were and would wander on, never knowing that he had been in Shambhala. Some argue that the same holds true of the features along the way: Only a yogi would be able to see the mountains, rivers, and other landmarks described by the guidebooks.

According to those who hold this view, Shambhala remains hidden from the outside world because most people do not possess the eye needed to see it. Tibetan mysticism distinguishes five different "eyes" or degrees of awareness that one can acquire through the practice of meditation. An ordinary person has only one, the "water eye," which sees the world as it appears to most people in their usual state of delusion. As a yogi purifies his mind through meditation, his vision becomes more acute and he gains in turn: the "flesh eye," which sees a distance of eighteen days' walk away; the "god eye," which reveals hidden things and places; the "wisdom eye," which can penetrate into other minds and know everything there is to know; and the "Buddha eye," which discerns the ultimate nature of reality. The third eye that commonly appears on the foreheads of images and paintings of Bodhisattvas indicates that they possess the wisdom eye of spiritual insight. Most of the lamas who believe Shambhala is invisible say that one needs at least the god eye or the wisdom eye to see it. Comparing the kingdom to a well-known place of pilgrimage in India, Oleshe (Gechung Ngawang Leshe), an old hermit who had been meditating for a number of years in the Himalayas, told me, "If you or I go to Rajgir, where the Buddha preached, we'll see only ruined temples covered with jungle. But," he added with a jab of the finger, "if we get the wisdom eye, we'll see all sorts of flashy things there."

Tibetans believe that the main thing responsible for keeping Shambhala hidden is karma—the effects of past thoughts and actions that have shaped one's present fate and character. Those who think the kingdom is visible say that without the right karma one will never get the opportunity to go there and see it. What one has thought and done in the past determine whether or not one will develop the inclination and power needed to make the difficult journey to Shambhala. Because of the destiny they have unwittingly created for themselves, most people will never even hear of the hidden kingdom, much less find it. Those who believe that Shambhala is invisible add that past thoughts and actions have created illusions that obscure people's vision and prevent them from recognizing or seeing the kingdom. The mind resembles a dirty window covered with the residues of karma; until it has been cleaned through meditation, it will not be clear enough to reveal a view of Shambhala.

Having examined Tibetan beliefs about the existence of Shambhala, we will now look into the question of how the kingdom might exist from a modern point of view. The answers to this question are of interest to Tibetans as well as to Westerners. Many of the younger generation have grown up under the influence of Western ideas and have abandoned their elders' mystical views of reality. As a result, the younger people tend to dismiss Shambhala as superstitious fantasy or to regard it as an immaterial paradise of the afterlife. Worried that this trend may undermine Tibetans' belief in more fundamental religious beliefs, some lamas, such as the Dalai Lama and the Sakya Trizin, are looking for scientific arguments to persuade the younger generation that Shambhala could indeed exist.

From a modern point of view, the size and shape of Shambhala would seem to make its existence extremely unlikely. The world as we know it today has no room for a hidden country of ninety-six principalities, nor does it contain mountain ranges neatly arranged in the configuration of an eight-petaled lotus blossom. The unlikely size and shape of Shambhala, however, suggest another possibility that would make its existence much more likely: The Kalacakra texts may well be using a symbolic representation of an actual place for the purpose of conveying mystical insights. In that case, their description of Shambhala could bear little resemblance to what it actually looks like, yet still give us some idea of its essential nature. Or, as another likely possibility, time and imagination may have simply exaggerated and transformed the size and shape of the kingdom beyond recognition. With this in mind we will examine various ways in which Shambhala might exist in different forms.

There is a very good chance that Shambhala lies hidden in time rather than space—as an ancient kingdom that passed long ago into myth. A number of Western scholars agree with the Dalai Lama's opinion that the Kalacakra teachings must have had an actual place of origin: They think that the teachings probably did come to India in the tenth century from a country somewhere in Central Asia. Helmut Hoffmann has written, "The land of Shambhala is undoubtedly outside of India, and originally it was in all probability a real area, whereas as time went on it faded into the idea of a purely mythical kingdom." Sir Charles Eliot, in his history of Hinduism and Buddhism, wrote, "This country is seen only through the haze of myth: It may have been in India or it may have been somewhere in Central Asia where Buddhism mingled with Turkish ideas."[8] The findings of archaeology strongly support this approach to the existence of Shambhala: They have shown that a number of apparently fantastic myths have had their origin in real places and events. The most famous example of this is the discovery of the ruins of Troy in modern Turkey: Until Heinrich Schliemann unearthed the city in the late nineteenth century, most scholars had assumed that Homer's *Iliad* was merely a poetic creation of the mythic imagination rather than the account of an actual war fought by the ancient Greeks.

Because of the great migrations that characterize the history of Central Asia, we know relatively little about the civilizations that have flourished there. For thousands of years, roving horsemen of the steppes, who had neither the script nor the inclination to record events, have disrupted other, more settled cultures and destroyed many of their written records. Those writings that have survived, along with scattered artifacts and the fragmentary reports of outsiders such as the Chinese, give us a vague and sketchy picture of Central Asian history. Although we know something about many of the civilizations that have come and gone, a number of them have simply vanished into unexplored tracts of time. No one knows how many ruined cities still lie buried in the vast deserts and mountains of Central Asia. Shambhala may well have been a kingdom there that we know under another name or an unknown country whose name survives only in legend.

If we look for Shambhala among the civilizations known to Central Asian history, we need to examine those that might have been the source of the Kalacakra. The most likely candidates would have existed around the tenth century, at the time the Kalacakra came to India, and would have incorporated the religious influences found in that teaching. In addition to Buddhism with its Hindu heritage, three other religions have left their mark on the Kalacakra—Christianity, Manicheism, and Islam. The main text of the teaching mentions the founders of all three, referring to Jesus as "Isha," Mani as "the man with the white garment," and Mohammed as "Madhumati." The monotheism of these religions may well have inspired the Kalacakra's conception of a supreme or primordial Buddha whose manifestation is the universe. The Christian prophecy of the second coming of Christ and the Manichean doctrine of warfare between the forces of light and those of darkness are probably reflected in the prophecy of Shambhala. The Muslims certainly figure in the texts as the prototypes of the barbarians who will take over the world and try to conquer the hidden kingdom. In addition, the Kalacakra seems to share with Manicheism the influence of Gnostic and Zoroastrian mysticism, along with certain features of numerical symbolism, such as a penchant for groups of five.[9]

By these criteria, the Uighur kingdom of Khocho in the Turfan Depression beneath the Tien Shan Mountains stands out as one of the most likely places to have been Shambhala. In accordance with Tibetan guidebooks to Shambhala, Turfan lies north of the Sita, which most Western scholars have identified as the Tarim River. Established by the Uighurs, a Turkish people, around A.D. 850, the kingdom of Khocho flourished for four hundred years as a remarkable oasis of culture and learning. A predominantly Buddhist country with numerous monasteries, it also had active centers of Manicheism and Nestorian Christianity—two of the three outside religions with the greatest influence on the Kalacakra. Although few Muslims lived in the kingdom itself, Islam was certainly familiar as the new and aggressive religion that was supplanting Buddhism elsewhere in Central Asia.

At the time the Kalacakra appeared in India, the kingdom of Khocho probably possessed the most advanced civilization and the highest standard of living of any country in Central Asia. Well-irrigated fields and orchards produced enough surplus food to allow the Uighurs to run welfare programs for the poor. Living together in peaceful harmony, people of different races, religions, and languages stimulated each other's thought and culture. Paintings found in the ruins of Turfan show houses built in the Chinese style, men and women dressed in embroidered silk, and a chamber ensemble complete with harps, guitar, and flutes. Even the Chinese, the most fastidious connoisseurs of culture, were impressed by the grace of Uighur society.[10]

Of all the regions of Central Asia, the Tarim Basin southwest of Turfan, however, comes closest in size and shape to Tibetan descriptions of Shambhala. A huge oval-shaped area enclosed by the Kunlun, Pamir, and Tien Shan ranges, it could be viewed as an enormous lotus blossom surrounded by a ring of snow mountains. The small kingdoms that have existed side by side in the numerous oases sprinkled around the fringes of the basin may well have provided the model for the ninety-six principalities of the outer region of Shambhala. Until shortly before the Kalacakra reached India and Tibet, Buddhism had been flourishing in the Tarim Basin for nearly eight hundred years. During part of that time, caravans following the silk route to China had brought the outside influences of Manicheism and Nestorian Christianity to bear on the development of Buddhist art and thought in the area.

Shambhala may have corresponded historically to the Tarim Basin as a whole or to one of the major oases such as Yarkand, Kashgar, or Khotan. Some scholars have singled out Khotan, the largest and most fertile oasis on the southern rim of the basin. Watered by melting snows of the Kunlun Mountains, it supported a thriving center of Buddhist learning, a people who loved music and culture, and a school of painting that impressed the Chinese and influenced Tibetan art. According to an old Khotanese tradition, an Indian prince of the third century B.C., who was blinded by rivals, fled his homeland to cross the intervening mountains and found a local dynasty in Khotan. Archaeological finds show that Indians did, in fact, colonize the oasis around that time. According to a Tibetan legend about the founding of Shambhala, a member of the Buddha's clan, called Shakya Shambha, was forced by enemies to flee north from India. After crossing many mountains, he came to a land that he conquered and that became known after him as "Shambhala."

Because of its similarity, the Tibetan legend may have come from the Khotanese tradition, suggesting a possible link between the hidden kingdom and Khotan.[11]

On the other hand, if the River Sita is the Tarim, then Khotan and much of the Tarim Basin lie south of this river, contrary to the directions given by the guidebooks to Shambhala. One guidebook, in fact, mentions Khotan and tells the traveler to go through it on his way north to the Sita. In addition, the Kalacakra commentaries that divide Asia into six zones all place Shambhala north of Li, the third zone, which corresponds to the region around Khotan. Another objection to identifying Shambhala with part or all of the Tarim Basin is that the area lies relatively close to India and was well-known to Tibetans at the time they received the Kalacakra. However, the teaching may still have come from this region but disguised its place of origin as a mysterious kingdom farther to the north.

West Turkestan, the area just west of the Tarim Basin in the Soviet Union, may have also held the historical kingdom of Shambhala. It too had a long history of Buddhism and was a major center of Manichean influence. Sogdian merchants from the region around Samarkand and the valley of Ferghana spread the teachings of Mani to China and could conceivably have taken the Kalacakra to India. Helmut Hoffmann claims to have traced the route described by the guidebooks to Shambhala into this region of the Pamirs, where he thinks the kingdom once existed. According to indications given by the older Tibetan religion of Bon, its version of Shambhala, Olmolungring, lies in the same general area, somewhere in the mountains between Samarkand and Alma Ata. In any case, as a crossroads of trade and conquest by Greeks, Indians, Persians, Turks, and numerous others, West Turkestan was certainly exposed to all the religious influences found in the Kalacakra.[12]

Two objections, however, make West Turkestan a little less promising than Turfan and the Tarim Basin. Well before the Kalacakra appeared in India, the Arabs had conquered the area, and their Muslim successors had converted the population to Islam, making it difficult for the Buddhist teaching to have come from there. Of course, the Kalacakra may have originated earlier and survived in an isolated mountain valley that became the model for the Tibetan version of Shambhala. And indeed archaeological finds have shown that Buddhism did survive until the twelfth century in the northern fringe of this area near Alma Ata.[13] The other objection has to do with the River Sita, the major landmark on the way to Shambhala. According to the most realistic guidebook to the hidden kingdom, this river flows to the east, but all the major rivers of West Turkestan, the Amu Darya and Syr Darya in particular, flow to the west. However, other guidebooks are confusing on this point and suggest that the Sita may be two rivers flowing in both directions.

There remain a number of other, less likely possibilities for the historical existence of Shambhala. The kingdom may have existed long before the Kalacakra came to India, having passed into myth centuries earlier. The Indian scholar Sarat Chandra Das thought that Shambhala was probably one of the Greek kingdoms of Bactria, left by the conquests of Alexander the Great, that flourished near the Amu Darya around the beginning of the Christian era. A more likely candidate of that period would be the Kushan Empire, which followed the Greeks and was responsible for the creation of Buddhist art and the spread of Buddhism through Central Asia. The guidebooks to Shambhala point to a location north of the areas we have considered, but because nomads dominated this territory, we know relatively little about its history—and the texts may well have exaggerated the distances involved. Uighur ruins found north of the Tien Shan Mountains around the basin of Dzungaria suggest the existence of some unknown kingdom that might have produced the Kalacakra and been the historical Shambhala. On the other hand, the pervasive influence of Hinduism on the Kalacakra has convinced some scholars that the teaching originated where it appeared—to the south in India, perhaps in Kashmir. All this suggests that Shambhala may turn out to have been a composite of many different countries and cultures. Whoever introduced the Kalacakra to India may well have blended together the sophisticated Uighur kingdom of Khocho, the size and shape of the

Tarim Basin, the various religions of Central Asia, and the Hindu influences of Kashmir. Perhaps the historical site of Shambhala lies hidden right on the map as the most obvious and overlooked spot of all—the entire region of Central Asia itself.[14]

Although the historical existence of Shambhala seems most likely—in fact, quite probable—there are other ways in which the kingdom might exist from a modern point of view. If Shambhala existed in the past as a small community rather than as an entire country, it could conceivably have survived right up to the present, hidden in some isolated valley of Central Asia. Around the turn of the century, Sir Aurel Stein, a British explorer and scholar who made many of the early archaeological finds in Turfan and the Tarim Basin, worked his way through nearly impassable gorges of the Pamirs to the valley of Roshan, where he found a people who had had virtually no contact with the outside world for centuries.[15] Other such communities, one of which could be Shambhala, may still exist in the remote mountain ranges of Central Asia. As we shall see in the next chapter, even the comparatively accessible Himalayas of Nepal contain valleys that few, if any, outsiders ever visit.

In Turfan we saw how a number of religions coexisted in an enlightened kingdom that survived for several hundred years; perhaps a group of dedicated mystics founded a similar, but smaller, community where they went on to extract the underlying wisdom of these religious traditions. Rumors of this place and a teaching derived from their insights may have then reached India in the form of Shambhala and the Kalacakra. If it deliberately kept itself secret, such a community could still exist as an isolated monastery or rustic village overlooked by the outside world. It would need none of the conspicuous signs of material progress that we normally associate with an advanced culture; the highest wisdom requires only the naked mind. The Indian sages who composed the *Upanishads*, some of the deepest expressions of Hindu philosophy, lived and taught in forest dwellings. The Taoist mysticism of China, which inspired many of the greatest works of Chinese art and literature, held forth the ideal of the simple, primitive life as the mark of an enlightened society. The royal trappings of Shambhala, with its Kings and palaces, may only be alluding to the nobility of spirit concealed in such a community; similarly, the great size of the kingdom may actually be symbolizing the depth and extent of the wisdom found there. The kind of place we are talking about does not even have to be hidden in some unexplored valley—it could be any one of thousands of inconspicuous villages that outsiders never bother to visit, or pass through on their way to somewhere else. What, after all, do most travelers really know of what goes on inside the houses they pass—or in the minds of the people they meet?

If Shambhala exists as a community of mystics, it need not be tied to a particular place: It could be a secret society with members scattered all over Asia—or even the world itself. A number of well-known secret societies such as the Rosicrucians and the Freemasons, who have worldwide memberships, claim to possess the kind of esoteric knowledge that is supposed to be kept in Shambhala. These societies are based in part on a widely held belief in the existence of a hidden brotherhood of enlightened people who have managed to preserve an ancient wisdom originating in Egypt or the Orient. Other present-day groups such as spy networks and subversive organizations keep not only their activities but also their very existence concealed. Two rather sinister secret societies of the past have given the English language the words *thug* and *assassin*. Until the British infiltrated and broke up their organization, the Thuggees or "Deceivers" of India formed a clandestine cult of religious zealots who roamed the roads and ritually murdered fellow travelers as offerings to the Hindu goddess Kali. In the eleventh century, from a mountain stronghold in Persia, Hasan ibn al-Sabbah, the leader of an Isma'ili sect of Islam, directed a secret network of agents whom he had implanted in the courts of Kings and princes throughout the Middle East. Having convinced them through visions induced by hashish that they had seen paradise and would surely go there if only they did his bidding, he was able to use his "hashashin," as they were called, to assassinate and terrorize all those who opposed the spread of his power.[16]

Shambhala itself may refer to a Tibetan society such as the Brotherhood of the Kelans mentioned by Abbé Huc. According to the Abbé's account of them, the members of this brotherhood were followers of the Panchen Lama, who believed they would join him in a future incarnation to fight in a war against the oppressors of Buddhism. From this description, it sounds as if the Kelans comprised those Tibetans who had been initiated into the Kalacakra—an initiation that is supposed to assure rebirth at the time of the final battle against the forces of evil. Since initiates into the teaching take vows of secrecy, they form a secret society that could be the actual Shambhala. If Shambhala does refer to these Kalacakra initiates—or to an inner circle of them—then the description of the kingdom may actually symbolize their organization; the King, for example, may represent their leader, and the ninety-six princes under him, subordinates responsible for various chapters of the society. Or, among other possibilities, the social rank of the inhabitants of Shambhala, from commoner to King, may stand for different degrees of initiation into the teaching.

As we saw earlier, some lamas have suggested another way in which Shambhala could exist from a modern, scientific point of view—as a civilization on another planet. On the basis of chance alone, it seems certain that somewhere in the universe there must be intelligent life that has developed a science and technology more advanced than ours. If Shambhala were such a civilization, it might even exist in the form described by the texts, and its inhabitants could actually possess the powers and riches attributed to them. In that case, the shape of the kingdom, round like a globe, might represent the planet on which they live. On the other hand, Shambhala might be an outpost that these aliens have established on earth and concealed through their advanced science and technology. In the summer of 1908, according to various documented reports, a bright object flashed into the sky, veered abruptly to the west, and exploded over a sparsely populated area of Siberia north of the Altai Mountains. Based on the discovery of high levels of radiation in tree rings, genetic changes in local plants, and the pattern of trees felled by the blast, some recent investigators have concluded that the object may have been a nuclear spacecraft carrying out a maneuver just before exploding over northern Central Asia—the region where many Tibetans think Shambhala might be.[17]

Finally, we come to a possibility that lies at the limits of scientific conceptualization, close to the Tibetans' mystical view of reality. Shambhala may be hidden in a fourth dimension that is as concrete and real as the three dimensions we normally see. Modern physics has revealed that space contains strange curves and warps that do not fit our usual picture of reality; perhaps physicists will someday discover the existence of other dimensions that lie outside the range of ordinary perception. The theory of relativity already speaks of a fourth dimension of time. Why not one of space? In any case, mathematicians and scientists commonly use the idea of multidimensional spaces as a tool to analyze the properties of what they investigate.

The fourth dimension is relatively easy to conceptualize but difficult to visualize. Our usual Euclidean model of space has three dimensions, each one perpendicular to the other two. We can represent them by three straight lines through a point—one going east to west, another north to south, and the third up and down. If we add a fourth line—call it "here to there"—that runs at right angles to each of the others, it will extend into the fourth dimension. Although we may not be able to do this visually, we can certainly do it mathematically.

If we should take a step into this fourth dimension, we would find ourselves in another world of three dimensions like ours. Just as two-dimensional planes lie parallel to each other in the third dimension, so three-dimensional spaces would lie parallel to each other in the fourth dimension. These spaces would be like paintings stacked against a wall; as long as we looked only at the first, or top, one, we would fail to see the others behind it —or even to suspect that they existed. Shambhala could conceivably be hidden right here, an inch away from us, in another world that we do not perceive because we focus all our attention on the familiar one we know.

Psychological experiments have shown that we unconsciously

filter and arrange our perceptions into meaningful patterns. If we did not, we would be overwhelmed and disoriented by a kaleidoscope of chaotic impressions. As we grow up, our culture, through its world view, helps us to make sense of what we see— to recognize an airplane, for example, as a machine rather than as a bird or a god. In the process it also trains us to ignore whatever it considers unimportant or unreal; as a consequence, we may have been conditioned to suppress whatever perceptions we might once have had of other dimensions. The fantasy world of a child may include things that belong to a real world of the fourth dimension, which he gradually loses sight of as adults convince him that it exists only in his imagination.

At times, in moments of mystical experience, some people become aware of a hidden, almost luminous depth in the most ordinary objects, such as flowers and stones. A fresh feeling of wonder, reminiscent of childhood, comes over them, and they sense what seems to be a deeper reality permeating their surrounding world. Some see visions of places like those described by the guidebooks to Shambhala—mysterious landscapes shimmering with jewels, endless deserts beneath strange skies, and awesome mountains floating above clouds of light. Rather than merely hallucinating, these people may, in fact, have dropped the mental conditioning that usually limits their vision and gazed for a timeless moment into the fourth dimension.

If this is so, it helps to explain why Tibetans insist on the necessity of purifying the mind in order to go to Shambhala. Most forms of meditation used for this purpose tend to cut off, or silence, the habitual thoughts and preconceptions that block the kind of mystic vision we have been discussing—the vision that may actually penetrate into other worlds as solid and as concrete as ours. By clarifying his mind in this way, ridding himself of the mental conditioning that limits his awareness, the traveler to Shambhala may be gaining the ability to see into the fourth dimension and take an actual journey through a strange, but real, landscape of fantastic deserts and mountains that lie parallel to the ones we find on maps of Central Asia.

Of course, all these possibilities, especially the last, are only conjecture; none of them prove that Shambhala exists, or ever existed. Even the most likely possibility—that it was a historical country of the past—is based on circumstantial evidence that makes it probable but not certain. On the other hand, the various possibilities we have considered, unlikely as some of them might be, make it difficult to dismiss Shambhala as mere fantasy: They show that the kingdom could always exist in a way that eludes our most sophisticated attempts to detect it. Even if we should scour the earth and turn up nothing, Shambhala could still lie hidden in the past, on some other planet, or in another dimension. Failing to find the kingdom tells us only that we have failed to find it—not that it fails to exist. Given the hidden nature of Shambhala, a conclusive proof of its nonexistence is impossible; only by actually finding the kingdom can we ever completely resolve the question of its existence.

But this question is really of secondary importance. Whether or not the kingdom exists or has existed as an actual place or community of people, it certainly does exist as a myth and symbol. As such, it has a power and reality of its own, independent of whatever material existence it might have. Even in an obviously fictional form, as in the story of Shangri-la, the myth has been able to move and deeply influence the minds of many people. The question that really matters is: What gives this myth its reality and power? What does the kingdom tell us about ourselves—about the secret yearnings and intuitions it awakens? A look at related myths, beginning with Tibetan legends of other hidden valleys, will help us to begin our search for the answers to these questions.

3

The Hidden Valleys

We were standing beside the monastery of Tengboche on a ridge beneath Mount Everest, gazing out over the blue-green valleys of Khumbu, set deep in ranges of shining snow peaks. Far off below us, where morning shadows still lingered, wisps of smoke from cooking fires floated like river mist over Sherpa villages scattered between terraced fields and forests of pine and rhododendron.

"Khumbu used to be sacred," Kalsang, the Head Lama's brother, remarked.

"Isn't it still?" I asked, continuing to gaze at the peaceful valleys below us.

"No, not anymore—not since people came to live here years ago. They built villages and fields and made it into an ordinary place like anywhere else. Now anyone can come here; it's no longer special.

"But somewhere up there, behind those mountains," he added, pointing at the snow peaks east of Everest, "there's a sacred valley called Khembalung. A long time ago, when Guru Rimpoche brought the teachings of Buddhism from India to Tibet, he set the gods to watch over it and keep it hidden from the world. It's supposed to be a peaceful place, with food and everything you need for meditation. Only the true followers of Guru Rimpoche, the ones who really practice his teachings, can find it. There's a guidebook to Khembalung, but if the wrong kind of people try to follow it, snow leopards will attack them at the mountain passes and drive them away."

Four years later, back in Nepal to do research on Shambhala, I decided to look into the legend of Khembalung as well. In a Sherpa village just south of the Himalayas, I ran into an old lama who mentioned that he knew someone who claimed to have actually gone to the hidden valley. "He told me he had to go through a cave in water for many hours," the old lama said. "It was very cold and dark inside, very bad. When he came out at the other end of the cave, he found a green valley with four or five houses and some people living with a lama."

"And that was Khembalung?"

"Yes."

"Where was the cave?"

The old lama began to unwind a long braid of matted hair from the top of his head and said with a shrug, "How should I know? I've never been there. Ask the man who went."

Unfortunately the man was away on a trip, but a monk running a teashop told me that Oleshe, a hermit who lived in a cliff house above the village, had tried once to go to Khembalung. According to the monk, Oleshe set out with a large group of Sherpas, including a little boy who was the reincarnation of the High Lama of the area. Partway there they stopped to sleep in an abandoned hut on a snowy ridge, but during the night the howling of a yeti, or abominable snowman, woke them up. Utterly terrified by the savage shrieks coming out of the darkness, they threw wood on the fire and clustered around the boy in a desperate effort to protect him from what seemed inevitable death. By the time dawn finally came to drive the yeti away, they were so exhausted and unnerved that they abandoned their attempt to go to Khembalung and went on a pilgrimage to India instead.

When I climbed the crags to his hut to check out the story with Oleshe himself, the spry old hermit chuckled and said,

"Yes, that's true, all right. The next morning we found yeti tracks in the snow as long as your forearm, and we went *psst* straight down to the lowlands!

"But we weren't trying to go all the way to Khembalung. That's only for great lamas, not for ignorant jungle monkeys like me. We were just going on a pilgrimage to a cave at the southern entrance to the hidden valley."

"The old lama down in the village told me that someone he knew went through a cave to Khembalung. Was that the same cave?" I asked.

"No, I know that person and where he went. He never got to the real Khembalung, just to the outer part where we were going. Some Sherpas live there and call it Khembalung, but the real place, the secret hidden valley, is deeper inside. You have to have the right karma to go there. Then you can follow the guidebook to it."

On the chance he might have it, I asked Tulshi Rimpoche, a Tibetan lama who lived nearby and who used to be abbot of Rongbuk Monastery on the Tibetan side of Mount Everest, if he had a copy of the guidebook to Khembalung. He scratched his shaven crown and said, "No, I think we left it behind when we had to leave Tibet."

A few minutes later a monk came in with a handful of tattered pages that Tulshi Rimpoche glanced through as we continued our conversation on another topic. Suddenly he stopped in the middle of a sentence and exclaimed, "Here it is—the guidebook! Why, it's been here all these years and I never knew it."

The book looked more like a wad of scrap paper covered with faded scribbling (see Plate 9). Its thirty or so pages dangled from a piece of old string that bound the hand-copied manuscript together along the top. A number of pages were missing from the end, and the last one of those that had survived was in shreds, but enough of it remained to piece together an enticing sentence: "If you meditate in this place, you will attain Nirvana in this life. . . ."[1]

I made a copy of the guidebook and took it back to Kathmandu, where a Tibetan friend, Chophel Namgyal, translated it with me. We found that the text described four ways into the hidden valley: one from the Sherpa region of Khumbu in the west, another from Tibet to the north, and two from Nepal in the south and east. The specific directions, however, baffled us: We could not even visualize many of the features, much less identify them. The instructions for the western route from Khumbu, for example, began with "the snow wall of Khumbu." That was easy enough. But then they told the traveler to proceed to "a valley that looks like a hanging ewe's stomach." How did one picture that and where was it supposed to be?

Fortunately the Incarnate Lama of Tengboche, abbot of the main monastery of the area, was in Kathmandu. He glanced at the passage and said, "Oh yes, there's a Sherpa village on that stomach." We went over the guidebook in detail, and he was able to show me how its puzzling descriptions fit actual places that he was familiar with in his native Khumbu. A huge bulge on the side of a valley below his monastery—an old alluvial fan suspended above the river—had the shape of a sheep's stomach hanging like a sack from a hook on the wall of a butcher's shop. The village he had referred to rested on the gently sloping bench formed by this bulge. The next feature, "the back of a hog's neck covered with upright bristles," was a ridge rising to Tengboche with pine trees bristling along its crest. The route went on over the site of the monastery itself, "a triangular piece of ground," past an obvious "horse-saddle snow mountain," and toward "the cooking pan of the Queen of the Five Sister Goddesses," which turned out to be Mount Everest under an unusual name. The route then turned right into a high valley the Tengboche Lama had never visited, and he could no longer identify the features mentioned in the text.

Intrigued by what we might find, my wife and I decided to go up that valley to see if we could follow the guidebook any farther. The way led up a glacier moraine between the enormous face of Lhotse—a twenty-seven-thousand-foot peak next to Everest—and the ice-streaked spire of Ama Dablam. Coming over a rise, we found ourselves on the edge of a remote basin with mountain walls glistening all around us. Katsering, our

Sherpa companion, pointed toward a distant dot in a snowfield by a frozen stream and said, "That's Takmaru, the Red Rock." He and other Sherpas had told us that the next landmark in the guidebook, "a red mountain," was actually this square boulder, which was supposed to contain the key to Khembalung. According to local legend, a crack that runs across one side of it is slowly opening, and one day, when the strife of the outside world finally reaches Khumbu, the rock will break in two and reveal the key, enabling a few fortunate Sherpas to flee to safety in the hidden valley (see Plate 11).

Beyond the boulder the mountains curved in from either side to meet in a ridge of rock and ice that barred the way. The only feasible route over it, a nineteen-thousand-foot pass called the Amphu Labtsa, looked like a wall of vertical snow mixed with overhanging cliffs. The guidebook said: "You should go between the glacier and the red mountain. That valley is the curtain of the outer door to Khembalung." Was this the curtain draped before us? Or was it some other wall around us that looked even less like a pass? The text did not help much: It gave a confusing description of a path of snow leading over something—perhaps the Amphu Labtsa—to a small mountain from which one could get a view of Khembalung. Since it was too early in the spring with too much snow to cross the pass safely, I decided to turn back to try another route into the hidden valley.

Most lamas and Sherpas who knew anything about it seemed to think that Khembalung lay hidden on the far side of the Amphu Labtsa in a wilderness of uninhabited valleys on the edge of the Himalayas. Snow peaks to the north and jungle-packed gorges to the south made this region difficult to reach from any direction. A Sherpa friend of mine named Urkien, however, had gone into the area with a British expedition in 1954. He told me that as they were climbing along a high ridge, they had seen a flat stretch of thick rhododendron jungle in the valley below them, and their guide, a lama from a local village, had remarked that the real center of Khembalung, the secret part, was down there, complete with the invisible palace of a King. According to the lama, people sometimes saw smoke coming from the trees and heard the sound of voices singing there. Occasionally herders and hunters in search of animals would wander into the jungle, never to return. Urkien added, "He warned us not to go down there either. He said that he didn't know what happened to the people who went—whether they died or got lost or just decided to stay—but he did know that nobody ever returned from that place."

"Did you go?" I asked.

"We tried but we couldn't get down: The rhododendrons were too thick."

After going up to the foot of the Amphu Labtsa, I joined some friends to attempt another, easier route into the region on the far side of the pass. Our destination was the valley that Urkien had seen. Two days out from the Sherpa country, at the last occupied hut, we met an old woman who told us about a shrine under an overhang ahead and added, "If you stand there and look across the valley, you'll see a snake high up on the mountain—that's the direction to Khembalung." When we reached the shrine, a wild and windy spot with three Buddha images in a cave guarded by lofty peaks, I looked where she had told us to look and saw, thousands of feet up a wall of granite dripping with glaciers, a band of metamorphic rock twisted into the shape of a cobra with its head drawn back ready to strike. I took a compass bearing and lined it up on our map: The arrow pointed right toward the valley we had identified as Urkien's. The Sherpas with us left juniper sprigs burning as offerings to the gods, and we moved on toward Khembalung.

Three passes, one of them over seventeen thousand feet high, still lay between us and our destination. As we were crossing a glacier on the first and highest pass, a Sherpa in our party suddenly dropped out of sight, leaving his load on the snow where he had just been walking. His companion shouted and we ran over: The Sherpa had broken through the deceptive surface and fallen into a hidden crevasse. We moved the load off a black hole in the snow and peered down, but all we could see were two gray walls of ice dropping away into empty darkness. A lama had told me, "It's difficult to go to Khembalung because of the danger of being killed on the way." And now, here it was. As we looked at each other in dismay, a voice came out of the depths, sounding muffled and remote. He was alive. After a few moments of confusion, we dropped a rope down and hauled him out. He came up gasping and covered with snow but miraculously uninjured: his sixty-foot fall had only bruised his cheek and knocked the smile off his face. We went on, thankful to luck —or the gods.

As we neared our destination, we entered a region that was poorly mapped and that few, if any, Westerners had ever visited. Our route took us high along the side of a mountain range toward the second-to-last of our passes. But partway there, clouds closed in around us and we could no longer distinguish the snow at our feet from the space around us; everything had become white and featureless. We tried to navigate by compass and altimeter but finally had to give up and camp for the night. I thought of a lama's warning: "In the guidebooks the directions look easy, but when you try to follow them, it's difficult: either you lose the way or you get covered by mist." A shining blue sky the next morning, however, allowed us to find the way across the mountain range.

The following day we reached the top of the final pass and looked across undulating snowfields to the rim of a green valley that sank away into mysterious depths hidden from sight. Somewhere down there was the place that Urkien had told me about —the stretch of jungle with an invisible palace at the center of Khembalung. A graceful ice peak soared directly over it, and all around, snow mountains gleamed in the early-morning sun. A line of cliffs around the head of the valley apparently cut it off from the snowfields where we were standing. There seemed to be no way into it.

We crossed over to the rim and peered down. There, far below us, lay a valley like none I had ever seen in the Himalayas. A slender river lined with white stones wound across a level floor cushioned with meadows and forest and sheltered by vertical walls of rock. Two pointed snow peaks hung in a blue haze over the far end. I had never expected to find a place that so perfectly fit my dream of a hidden valley, and my heart began wildly beating.

"Look, there's a way down!"

Filled with excitement, we plunged down a gentle snow ridge that seemed to give access into the head of the valley. But lower down it arched over into steep slopes of slick rhododendron that ended on top of the cliffs we had seen from above. A quick search to either side revealed no way down to the valley floor, which now seemed tantalizingly close. One slight chance remained—to the left, where one of the Sherpas had already gone and come back to say there was no passage. Leaving my pack behind, I hurriedly kicked steps across a steep snowbank and traversed around a rib of slippery grass. There, to my relief, at the last possible place, was a gulley that cut through the band of cliffs. We descended in mist to the valley floor and camped in a meadow beside a quiet stream.

The next morning, when we went exploring, we found an invisible palace in the beautiful forest of pine and rhododendron that filled the valley. We heard the clear voices of birds singing to one another and saw golden mist rising like smoke off the treetops. In the woods around us, drops of bluish water gleamed like diamonds on necklaces of hanging moss. Passing through corridors of trees, we came to sunlit clearings hung with tapestries of rich brown shadows and emerald leaves. And as we went deeper into the forest, through gaps in the foliage, we glimpsed and felt the presence of a majestic snow peak that seemed to rule over the valley, like the King of Khembalung.

The freshness of our surroundings brought back childhood fantasies of primeval jungles hidden in the imaginary wilds of my own backyard. This forest had the same remote and mysterious quality, but it also seemed close and oddly familiar, as if I had been here long ago. Although many miles and mountains separated us from the help we would need in case of an accident, I felt at home and secure. When we came to a glade with a spring welling out of the base of a mossy rock, I knelt to drink the water from my hands and felt the peace and beauty of the valley flow into my body. Something of it would remain, I sensed, something that I would carry back to my life outside. In coming to this place, I had touched a hidden source within myself. I had been trying to determine whether this valley was the Khembalung of the guidebook, but now that no longer mattered. I knew that this, whatever it was, was the hidden valley I had been seeking.

As we prepared to leave, the warning of Urkien's guide almost came true. During the night snow began to fall, threatening to trap us between avalanches on the cliffs above and impenetrable jungle in the gorges below. We were running out of food, and if we had to stay, we would probably starve. Lying in my sleeping bag with fear twisting at my insides, I remembered the stories of hunters and herdsmen who had wandered into Khembalung and never returned. Would we share their fate? Much to our relief, the snowfall stopped before morning and we were able to escape through the clouds.

On our return to Khumbu, the Tengboche Lama asked me to draw him a map of where we had gone. After looking it over and listening to my description of the valley, he said, "Yes, that must have been Khembalung. In fact, most of the valleys you went through on the way there were probably part of it too."

"But they didn't look like the way the guidebook describes Khembalung."

He shrugged. "That doesn't matter. The book was written for yogis who would see things you wouldn't be able to see. Where you saw snow and rock and empty forest, they would see something very different."

According to another guidebook to Khembalung, which I found later:

> If the time to go there has not come, everything, houses and all, will be covered by grass and trees, and all will be of the nature of forest and grassland. This description of the place will not match what you see and misunderstanding will arise. The foolish will get doubts, but the wise should carefully examine the country according to this book, and gradually they will find the mountains and valleys and towns.[2]

In the Tengboche Lama's opinion, our journey took us only to the surface of Khembalung. Many lamas believe that a bayul or "hidden country" such as Khembalung contains levels concealed within levels. Only the outer level appears to people in general. If an ordinary person has the fortune to reach it, he will find a peaceful valley filled with meadows and forest, but he will fail to appreciate the special nature of the place, and it will have no significant effect on him. The outer level may even have inhabitants who are unaware that they are living in a hidden valley. Some lamas think that whoever manages to reach the outer level will find whatever food and shelter he needs, but others feel that these necessities are only provided in the deeper levels.

Someone who has practiced meditation and attained a certain degree of awareness will find another level, which is invisible or inaccessible to ordinary people. This inner hidden valley, as it is called, may lie in the same place as the outer one, or deeper in the mountains. It will look like other valleys, with the same sort of trees, meadows, and streams, but a person with a heightened sensitivity will feel something in the atmosphere, a sense of greater space or freedom, which will affect him in a deep and powerful way. In addition to obtaining food and shelter there without effort, he will also find various spiritual treasures, such as sacred images and mystical texts.

An accomplished yogi can penetrate even deeper—to the secret hidden valley. There he will find more profound books and spiritual influences that will enable him to practice the highest stages of meditation and speedily attain enlightenment. The invisible palace of Khembalung is supposed to lie in either the inner or the secret level of the hidden valley. In order to see it, one must have obtained the special eye or awareness that some lamas say is needed to see Shambhala. At the deepest level the hidden valley no longer lies outside the yogi but within his heart and mind as well: He no longer knows any distinction between himself and the world around him. Sangye Tenzin, a lama scholar who lives near Khumbu, referred to this, the deepest level, as "the hidden valley of suchness"—the place of ultimate reality.

Rather than regard them as sanctuaries for meditation, lay Tibetans tend to view hidden valleys as paradises removed from the troubles of the outside world where those who have accumulated merit can lead lives free from toil and sorrow. They believe that if they should have the fortune to reach one of these havens, they would find lovely music, delicious foods, and whatever other sensual delights they might desire. Some think that like the gods of the heavens, people in the hidden valleys enjoy all kinds of pleasure, but when it comes time to die, they go to hell. Lamas agree that life in these sanctuaries is full of ease and contentment, but they add that the comforts found in them are there for the purpose of freeing one from distractions so that one can more easily practice meditation and proceed along the path to enlightenment. As with Shambhala, whoever truly reaches a hidden valley and stays there can never be reborn in a lower realm of existence, such as hell.

Lamas and laymen generally agree that hidden valleys provide the boons of health and long life. An old Sherpa in Khumbu told me, "If I could get to Khembalung, I would become young again, like you; and if you went, you would turn into a baby." One of the guidebooks to Khembalung gives instructions for digging out a buried spring and then describes the virtues of its water:

> By drinking this water, all women will become beautiful; they will bear beautiful children and have an unbroken line of descendants. In addition, the water will cure all their illnesses. If men drink it, they will become as strong as the warriors of Ling Gesar and as swift and skillful as birds.

The other guidebook mentions a couple of springs in Khembalung that give long life and "make women sexually passionate."[3]

In addition to healing fountains of youth and virility, the hidden valleys are supposed to contain a number of treasures sealed in rocks and caves. These include stockpiles of food, books of secret wisdom, ritual implements endowed with magic powers, and caches of gold, silver, and precious jewels. One guidebook to Khembalung gives this description:

> There is a blue cave that looks like a tigress, which has four corners and four sides, eight in all. Above it are three other caves. Inside them are old coins, four turquoise stones, two skull-cup containers filled with gold, a skin bag full of old "zi" stones, and written instructions for finding eighteen kinds of hidden treasures.[4]

But the real treasure concealed in a hidden valley is something intangible. Sangye Tenzin told me, "The guidebooks always talk about the gold and silver that hidden valleys are supposed to contain—and certain hidden valleys actually do. But gold and silver are just another kind of rock; what's really precious in a given place is the special blessing it gives." This blessing he referred to is a kind of spiritual power or radiation that is supposed to have a positive effect on whoever is open to it. He described how the subtlest contact with a hidden valley—even the thought of it—can dissolve poisonous thoughts and emotions that cause one to suffer. According to him, when this happens, "It's accompanied by clarity of mind and a warm, good feeling inside."

If one knows how to use this invisible power, it will make one's meditation extremely effective. For this reason a guidebook to Khembalung says:

> Just by being in Khembalung, compassion and benevolence will increase naturally, and greater wisdom and knowledge will come. It is much better to meditate one year in this place than a thousand years elsewhere, better to do one month's retreat here than a year's retreat outside.[5]

The spiritual influence of the place, something in the air or in the ground itself, will help to clear the mind and awaken the heart, the two basic prerequisites for attaining enlightenment. From this we can conclude, as lamas have, that the greatest treasure one can find in a hidden valley is Nirvana itself.

The legends of hidden valleys belong, in fact, to the Tibetan tradition of termas or "concealed treasures." According to the oldest sect of Tibetan Buddhism, the Nyingmapa or "Ancient Ones," when Padma Sambhava, the founder of their school, brought Buddhism from India to Tibet around the eighth century A.D., he hid a number of sacred treasures for his followers to find in future times (see Plate 7). These included various books and objects such as the ones described in Khembalung, as well as nonmaterial teachings implanted in the minds of certain disciples for them to remember in future lives. Texts supposedly hidden in this way by Padma Sambhava—or Guru Rimpoche, as he is also called—and discovered centuries later form the basis for many of the religious beliefs and practices of the Nyingmapa sect. Among these discovered texts we find the guidebooks to Khembalung and the Tibetan book most widely known in the West—the *Bardo Thodol,* translated as *The Tibetan Book of the Dead.* In addition to serving as repositories for such sacred objects, the hidden valleys themselves are regarded as concealed treasures.[6]

According to Tibetans, Padma Sambhava hid his texts and other treasures in rocks, streams, trees, and even in the sky. At the same time he also used his supernatural power to conceal numerous hidden valleys in the Himalayas and other mountain ranges bordering Tibet. Having subdued and converted local deities to Buddhism, he placed both valleys and treasures under their protection to keep the wrong people from finding them. According to lamas, the mist, snow leopards, and other natural obstacles blocking the way to Khembalung are actually the manifestations of such deities. Sangye Tenzin explained that the valleys and treasures are hidden in a way that lies beyond the comprehension of ordinary science and logic. In order to understand it, one must practice meditation and transcend one's limited conceptions of reality. A remark by another lama, Khempo Tsondu, illustrates the difficulty in trying to conceptualize how the valleys and treasures are supposed to be concealed: "The treasures hidden inside rocks aren't put in the way we put things in, but with power. The power hides them in such a way that we can't say they're inside the rock—or outside it either."

Sherpas tell the following story of how Padma Sambhava hid

the valleys of Khembalung. Over a thousand years ago, before it became hidden, Khembalung was ruled by an evil King with the face of a dog and the head of a goat—the result of his mother's having slept with the two animals. Actually a demon, he practiced cannibalism and backed the anti-Buddhist religion of Bon. Having decided to get rid of this threat to Buddhism and humanity, Padma Sambhava disguised himself as a servant and appeared at the King's palace in Khembalung. After winning the confidence of the King, he suggested that everyone go up to a high meadow to enjoy the view and make offerings to the local deities. When they got there, he persuaded them to go still higher for an even better view. As they climbed, he made mist and clouds come down between them and Khembalung so that they could no longer find the way back. Then he led the disoriented party over the mountains to Khumbu and out to the foothills of the Himalayas, where the King got sick and died. Having rid Khembalung of its evil inhabitants, Padma Sambhava sealed its borders and turned it into a hidden country, which it remains to this day.

According to prophecies made by Padma Sambhava himself, he set aside Khembalung and the other hidden valleys as sanctuaries for Tibetans to use in times of war and trouble. Each valley has a particular time when it is supposed to shelter people from turmoil outside; Khembalung's turn will come, for example, "when the warriors of Hor invade central Tibet." Although some valleys have already fulfilled their destinies, others await the future when wars will destroy all traces of religion and "houses will be made of human flesh." At that time demons will appear in the guise of teachers, women will kill their own babies, and life will become brief, like the passage of shooting stars. During periods of foreign invasion and internal strife, Tibetans have, in fact, fled to the safety of remote mountain valleys said to have been hidden for that purpose by Padma Sambhava.[7]

But before people can go to a hidden valley for refuge, a special person destined to open it must appear. The same holds true for the discovery of concealed treasures: Only prophesied tertons or "treasure revealers" can find them. Texts attributed to

Padma Sambhava contain prophecies with the names of those who will discover particular treasures and valleys and descriptions of the times and signs that will accompany their appearance. The prophecy of Padma Lingba, a fifteenth-century lama who discovered one of the guidebooks to Khembalung, reads:

> When forts stand over the village of Gokyiphagri, when poison is sold at Tagru in Lato, the time will have come: The treasure concealed in the Lake of Burning Fire shall no longer remain but shall be removed. A man by the name of Orgyen Padma Lingba will appear.[8]

The guidebook he discovered makes the following prediction about the opening of Khembalung:

> A person whose initial name is Gompo will come from the east, one whose initial name is Sonam will come from the north, and one whose initial name is Padma will come from the west.[9]

To help those he had prophesied to open hidden valleys, Padma Sambhava is supposed to have written or dictated guidebooks and to have hidden them as treasures to be found and used at a later date. In addition to describing the routes to be followed in great detail, the guidebooks also specify who should accompany the leader and what should be taken. According to Padma Lingba's guidebook to Khembalung, the party going should include a descendant of the evil King, seven youths and seven maidens, a doctor, an astrologer, yogis, monks, and even a Bon priest. These people are needed to perform the rituals required to subdue and propitiate various deities who guard the approaches to Khembalung. Besides the items to be offered in these rites, they must take provisions for the journey and tools for settling down and farming once they reach the hidden valley. The guidebook also sets forth the kind of laws and community that they should establish in Khembalung.

Lamas warn against trying to force a path into a hidden valley before the right time and person have come. Oleshe, the hermit who was driven away from Khembalung by an abominable snowman, compared it to planting potatoes and digging them up before they have had a chance to ripen. "If you try to go too soon," he said, "only hardship and suffering will come of it." This warning applies in particular to those who do not have the karma needed to go to a hidden valley. In 1975 a lama named Tulshok Lingba persuaded a number of people to leave everything behind and follow him to a sanctuary in Sikkim. Although he had a guidebook found by a discoverer of concealed treasures, he was not the person prophesied to open the hidden valley, and partway there he fell off a cliff and was killed. The people he had talked into following him had great difficulty returning, and some of them died along the way. Dudjom Khachopa Rimpoche, the Sikkimese lama who told me the story, added, "That was the punishment of the guardian deities."

Even those who have been prophesied to open a hidden valley may have problems. According to Oleshe, Padma Sambhava left a prediction that a Tibetan lama, Reting Rimpoche, and a wealthy patron, Urgyen Tinle, would go to Khembalung. A number of years ago, they set out for the hidden valley with a guidebook, scrupulously following its directions and building bridges along the way—an expensive undertaking. In midjourney, discovering that they had forgotten something, they returned to a village named Karte, where Urgyen Tinle lent the local people money at compound interest. When the villagers, who were unfamiliar with such interest rates, realized that they would not be able to pay back the huge amount they owed him, they beat him to death. Bereft of his source of financial support, Reting Rimpoche had to give up his attempt to open the way to Khembalung.

Once the right person succeeds in opening a hidden valley, it becomes visible to others, and those with good karma are able to go there. After it has served its allotted time as a refuge, it loses its special qualities and turns into an ordinary place accessible to anyone who wishes to visit it. According to Tibetans, the principality of Sikkim in the Himalayas between Nepal and Bhutan used to be such a hidden country, called Bayul Demojong or "The Hidden Valley of Rice." In those days a few natives lived there, but the region was basically empty and inaccessible from

Tibet. Around the beginning of the fifteenth century, Rigdzin Godem, a Tibetan lama who discovered many concealed treasures, managed to find a pass over snow mountains to the warm and sheltered valleys of Sikkim. Although he never returned to Tibet, he wrote a message describing where he had gone and sent it back to his monastery, tied to the neck of an eagle. Some two hundred years later, another lama, Namkha Jigme, completed the opening of the hidden country of Sikkim. Following the directions of Rigdzin Godem—or else those of a guidebook—he led a large number of Tibetans over the mountains to settle in Sikkim, where he appointed one of his party as the first Chogyal or ruler of the new principality. The line he established then in the seventeenth century continued unbroken to the last Chogyal, Palden Thondup Namgyal, who married an American named Hope Cooke in 1963 and lost his throne in 1974. A large stupa or relic mound outside the capital city of Gangtok contains the skull of Rigdzin Godem, the first person to open the hidden country of Sikkim.[10]

According to Khempo Tsondu, the outer and inner hidden valleys of Sikkim have been opened, but the secret part still remains closed. Gangtok is supposed to lie in the outer zone, while the inner includes a town named Tashiding and the well-known Indian hill resort and tea center of Darjeeling. The secret valley itself reportedly lurks in pockets concealed beneath the snows of Kangchenjunga, the third highest mountain in the world and one of the most lovely. Today Gangtok and other parts of the principality are filled with Indian soldiers on the alert to fend off possible attack by the Chinese from Tibet. As one lama who lives there remarked, "Sikkim doesn't feel like much of a sanctuary anymore."

Farther to the east, where the Tsangpo River of Tibet takes a great bend and, turning into the Brahmaputra, plunges toward the jungles of Assam, lies Pemako, which along with Sikkim is one of the two hidden countries best known to Tibetans. Around the beginning of this century, a lama named Sangye Thome set out with a guidebook to find it. Accompanied by monks of his monastery, he journeyed for five years, struggling across ice mountains and fighting through jungles of vine and bamboo. After undergoing innumerable hardships, they finally came to a valley like none they had ever seen—a beautiful haven veiled by foliage and flowers of all kinds. There they settled to build a monastery and were joined a few years later by a thousand families fleeing from fighting between Tibet and China. Many others who tried to reach Pemako at that time died along the way of snakebites and fever.[11]

According to Dudjom Rimpoche, who was born in the area, the outer and inner hidden valleys of Pemako, like those of Sikkim, have been opened. When he was still living there, the local people knew where the secret valley was supposed to be, but they had been unable to reach it. One hunter claimed to have found it and to have built a white pillar there to mark the spot, but no one else had seen it. According to Kunga Hochotsang, one of his uncles spent a year unsuccessfully searching for the secret valley, which was supposed to have rivers flowing with milk and home-cooked food hanging from the trees. When Tibetans were fleeing from the Chinese takeover of Tibet in the 1950s, another lama tried to lead a band of refugees to the safety of this valley, but an earthquake had changed the course of the Brahmaputra, making the directions of the guidebook impossible to follow and forcing them to escape to India instead.

A number of other hidden valleys are supposed to be scattered throughout the Himalayas of Nepal. The best known and most important of these is Khembalung, "The Valley of Incense Plants," which we have already looked at in detail. Other hidden valleys of importance include one near Helambu, a Sherpa region north of Kathmandu, and another concealed in an icy wilderness of peaks behind Dhaulagiri, one of the highest mountains in the world. A small hidden valley, apparently opened, lies between the mountains of Ganesh Himal and Manaslu in central Nepal. Known as Kyimolung, "The Valley of Happiness," it contains a three-tiered pagoda built on a promontory of pines flanked by glaciers and surrounded by peaks of sinuous rock and ice. A Western expedition that visited the place in 1973 found an old man and his sister living there, guarding the secluded temple with its sacred books and images. In addition to these valleys, the Himalayas of Nepal are said to contain hundreds of other sanctuaries so deeply hidden that no mention of them appears in either guidebooks or legends.[12]

According to Tibetans, hidden valleys lie not only in the Himalayas, but also in other mountain ranges bordering Tibet. Around 1956, an old lama riding a goat collected a following of more than a hundred people and started off toward Chang Demojong, a distant valley hidden somewhere around the Kunlun Mountains north of the Tibetan Plateau. After Tibetan Government officials ordered them to return to their homes, the lama lost most of his followers and went on with a small party of five retainers. As they journeyed across the bleak and windswept plateau, the goat died and the lama's companions dwindled away until only one remained. When the two of them finally came to hot springs that were supposed to be close to the hidden valley, the last retainer turned back, and the lama continued alone toward his destination, never to be heard of again. Gyalse Rimpoche, who told me the story, had seen the huge party leave his village and added that his father had once chased robbers for a month to the north and had glimpsed the mountains of Chang Demojong in the far distance.

At various times, especially during periods of turmoil, fake discoverers of guidebooks have persuaded large numbers of gullible Tibetans to give away all their possessions and follow them to the safety of legendary hidden valleys. Although these expeditions generally failed to find the particular sanctuaries they were seeking, they succeeded in settling many of the Himalayan areas bordering Tibet. The Sherpas, a Nepalese people of Tibetan origin and culture, probably migrated in this way to Solu Khumbu, the region south of Mount Everest in Nepal. The hermit Oleshe told me that one of his ancestors, in accordance with a prophecy of Padma Sambhava, led the first group of settlers over the mountains to colonize Solu Khumbu, which was a hidden valley at that time. Sangye Tenzin, a lama scholar and historian of the Sherpa people, pointed out, however, that Padma Sambhava's writings do not mention the Sherpa country as such a sanctuary.

"From the point of view of ordinary people, Solu Khumbu was a hidden valley," he said, "but strictly speaking, it was not. There's no indication that Padma Sambhava ever hid it or put any treasures there."

So far we have looked at accounts of those who have tried, successfully and unsuccessfully, to go to hidden valleys, but Tibetans also tell stories of people who have stumbled on these sanctuaries without even thinking of looking for them. In a typical story of this kind, a hunter from Dolpo, a remote region of western Nepal, was wandering in a rocky valley behind Mount Dhaulagiri when he heard the sound of lamas chanting and beating on their drums. Following the music toward its source, he came to a doorway in a cliff and passed through it into a beautiful valley complete with rice fields, villages, and a monastery. The people who lived there were all very peaceful and happy. They gave him a warm welcome and urged him to stay, but he wanted to go home and return with his family. Although they warned him that he would not be able to find the way back, he insisted on leaving and hung his shoes and gun on the cliff beside the entrance to mark it. Confident that he would have no trouble finding the spot again, he went off to get his wife and children. But when he returned with them, he found the shoes and gun hanging in the middle of a blank wall of rock.[13]

In another story of this nature, a hunter in Tibet spotted a deer and gave chase but was unable to catch it. The deer led him away to a distant snow mountain, where it vanished into a crevice. Since the opening in the rock was only large enough for his body, he left his bow and arrow behind and went through it unarmed. On the far side he found a place of great beauty and joy: Instead of water, milk flowed in the streams, and in the place of stones, there were delicious things to eat. Thinking of how happy his wife and children would be there, he marked the crevice and went home to get them. But when he came back with his family, the mark was gone, and he could not find the place again.[14]

Sherpas tell similar stories about Khembalung. A Sherpa on a mountaineering expedition east of Mount Everest was climbing

alone on a ridge when he came upon a vista of a beautiful valley
filled with villages and fields—a "new country." He rushed back
to tell the other Sherpas about it, but they scoffed at him and
said it was impossible for there to be such a place in that barren
region of rock and ice. He insisted, nevertheless, that he had
seen it and finally dragged them up to the top of the ridge to see
it too. When they got there, however, there was nothing visible
but dusty moraines and empty glaciers.

An interesting variation of this story comes from Sikkim. A
herder there was once grazing a herd of yaks near the foot of
Mount Kangchenjunga when one of the animals wandered off
and disappeared. Finding its tracks, he followed them to a pile
of dung at the entrance to a large opening in the side of a mountain. Realizing that the yak must have gone that way, he went
through the passageway and found himself in a beautiful valley
with a village of seven or eight happy families. When he asked
the people if they had seen his yak, they told him they had and
said, "Since you were lucky enough to get here, you must stay."

"No, I have to go back," he said, "or else my family will start
to worry about me."

Unable to dissuade him from leaving, the villagers gave him
seven grains of magic rice to take back with him. They tied them
in his belt so that he would not lose them and told him to cook
them only one grain at a time: No matter how many people he
invited to dinner, as long as he did not open the pot before the
rice was ready, it would feed everyone. They also warned him
not to tell anyone else about the magic rice or where he had
found it.

As soon as he got home, the herder called all his friends together to a feast, which he prepared from one of the grains. The
rice filled up the pot and provided more than enough for the entire company. Delighted with these results and anxious to
impress his neighbors, he invited even more people to an even
bigger feast, and this time he put two grains in the pot, figuring
in this way to make even more food. Having become very proud
of his luck, he boasted to his guests about the magic rice and the
hidden valley where he had got it. But when he then opened the

pot to show it to them, they found only two grains of ordinary rice and nothing more.[15]

As we can see, these stories all have the same basic theme: A lucky person doing something else happens to stumble on a hidden valley, but fails to appreciate his good fortune. Despite warnings or other indications of the difficulty of finding it again, he insists on leaving to tell others about the sanctuary and to bring them back to it. Although he thinks he can easily find the way back, he finds to his dismay that he cannot; the way and the place have vanished as if they had never existed at all. In the case of the last story, we can safely assume that the herder, having told others about the rice and where he got it, can never find the hidden valley again.

A famous poem of the T'ang Dynasty of China expresses the same theme in a particularly beautiful way. *A Song of Peach-Blossom River* was composed by Wang Wei in the eighth century A.D., but he took the story from Tao Ch'ien, a writer of the early fifth century (see Plate 13). It tells of a hidden valley somewhere in the cloud-covered mountains of China:

A fisherman is drifting, enjoying the spring mountains,
And the peach trees on both banks lead him to an ancient source.
Watching the fresh-colored trees, he never thinks of distance
Till he comes to the end of the blue stream and suddenly—strange
  men!
It's a cave—with a mouth so narrow that he has to crawl through;
But then it opens wide again on a broad and level path—
And far beyond he faces clouds crowning a reach of trees,
And thousands of houses shadowed round with flowers and bam-
  boos. . . .
Woodsmen tell him their names in the ancient speech of Han;
And clothes of the Ch'in Dynasty are worn by all these people
Living on the uplands, above Wu-ling River,
On farms and in gardens that are like a world apart,
Their dwellings at peace under pines in the clear moon,
Until sunrise fills the low sky with crowing and barking.
. . . At news of a stranger the people all assemble,
And each of them invites him home and asks him where he was born.
Alleys and paths are cleared for him of petals in the morning,

And fishermen and farmers bring him their loads at dusk. . . .
They had left the world long ago, they had come here seeking refuge;
They have lived like angels ever since, blessedly far away,
No one in the cave knowing anything outside,
Outsiders viewing only empty mountains and thick clouds.
. . . The fisherman, unaware of his great good fortune,
Begins to think of country, of home, of worldly ties,
Finds his way out of the cave again, past mountains and past rivers,
Intending sometime to return, when he has told his kin.
He studies every step he takes, fixes it well in mind,
And forgets that cliffs and peaks may vary their appearance.
. . . It is certain that to enter through the deepness of the mountain,
A green river leads you, into a misty wood.
But now, with spring floods everywhere and floating peach petals—
Which is the way to go, to find that hidden source?[16]

We find this theme presented a little more optimistically in the Western novel *Lost Horizon*. In that novel the hero, Hugh Conway, is hijacked to Shangri-la, never intending to go there or even suspecting of its existence. The High Lama reveals to him the purpose of the hidden valley and the magical property it has of giving long life, but when Conway tells his companion, Charles Mallinson, about it, the younger man scoffs and convinces him that it is only a fantasy and that they must leave. They do, and only Conway survives the terrible journey back to China, suffering amnesia along the way. When he suddenly recovers his memory, he realizes what he has lost and vanishes, heading back in an attempt to reach Shangri-la again.

When a theme keeps reappearing like this in different myths and cultures, we can be fairly sure that it carries some kind of deeper meaning concealed beneath its obvious surface appeal. Now, most of us have a yearning, in one form or another, for the sort of happiness found in the stories of hidden valleys. The theme of these stories seems to reflect the dilemma we experience in trying to capture this happiness: Whenever we seek it, we never seem to find it; it only comes upon us spontaneously, in unexpected moments. Like the characters in the stories, we must stumble on it, as if by accident. When we do, we seem for a brief time to enter a different world, a sanctuary of peace and happiness outside our usual harried state of existence. But then, like the herder or hunter, thinking that we know where to find it, we rush back to our old, familiar ways, perhaps to tell others about it, and when we return to the place or situation in which we originally experienced it, it is no longer there—it has vanished like a hidden valley behind a wall of rock. Where does this happiness really lie? How can it be found again? In this regard it seems significant that Tibetans have taken Shambhala to mean "The Source of Happiness": It suggests that the meaning of that kingdom may hold the resolution of the dilemma posed by the hidden-valley stories.

The myths of Shambhala and the hidden valleys share a number of interesting and potentially meaningful features. Although the kingdom belongs to a different tradition that has little to do with Padma Sambhava, some lamas consider it a hidden valley—in fact, the largest and most remote of all. Like the valleys, Shambhala contains various kinds of treasures, ranging from objects of material wealth to books of wisdom and the ideal conditions for attaining enlightenment. The way the two rings of snow mountains divide the kingdom into an inner region and an outer region invites comparison with the various levels of a hidden valley. In addition, the myths share prophecies about evil times to come when barbarians will make the practice of religion impossible in the world outside. When that happens in the period just before the golden age, many will flee to the refuge of hidden valleys to await the coming of the King of Shambhala.

Guidebooks describe similar kinds of journeys to both Shambhala and the hidden valleys. The instructions they give for rituals and meditation to be performed along the way suggest that these journeys have a spiritual as well as a physical dimension. The guidebooks to Shambhala, however, include many more supernatural obstacles and mystical practices and, as a consequence, have a much more allegorical nature. In addition, they give instructions for a single traveler to follow, whereas the guidebooks to the hidden valleys provide directions for large groups of seekers. Although both myths include numerous stories of journeys to their respective sanctuaries, we find hardly any tales of people who accidentally stumble on Shambhala. For the most part only those who set out for the hidden kingdom and know what they are doing manage to reach it. This suggests that reaching Shambhala represents a more advanced stage of spiritual development—and a more secure attainment of the happiness found in the hidden valleys.

Our examination of the myths of hidden valleys has brought out some of the features we need to examine more deeply in the myth of Shambhala. A look at various other related myths in the next chapter will bring out still more. In the meantime, however, a remark by a lama on the nature of hidden valleys points out the direction to take in our quest for the meaning of Shambhala: "Most people turn outside in search of hidden valleys, but the real and true hidden valley is your very own mind."

4

The Underlying Myth

All over the world, from Tibet to America, we find myths reminiscent of Shambhala. They range from obscure legends of hidden valleys to well-known prophecies about the end of the world. Some of them actually refer to Shambhala by name or speak of similar places hidden in the same general region as the kingdom itself; others have no direct connection with the country but include some motif or feature that brings it to mind, such as a savior King, a mystical quest, or an earthly paradise. In this chapter we will look into the ways these myths relate to Shambhala and see what particular insights each can contribute to our understanding of the Tibetan myth. In the course of examining these relationships, the most widespread and universal themes of the myth will emerge to show us where to focus our attention when we turn to uncovering the deeper meaning of the hidden kingdom itself.

We have already looked at one of the myths directly related to Shambhala: the Bon myth of the hidden country of Olmolungring. According to an inscription found on a diagram of the country, it has a number of names and is known in India as "Shambhala" (see Plate 14). Like the Buddhist kingdom, Olmolungring holds the highest of mystical teachings and has as its inhabitants people who are well on the way to enlightenment. It too lies hidden north of Tibet behind a great wall of snow mountains—laid out, however, in the form of a square rather than a circle. Within this barrier, as in Shambhala, rivers and other natural features divide the country into a central region surrounded by scores of small kingdoms filled with beautiful cities and parks. Around the inner sanctum itself are eight square-shaped principalities arranged like the eight petal-shaped regions around the central part of Shambhala. At the very center, instead of a palace, we find a mountain with the throne of the King of Olmolungring on its summit. The nine levels of this sacred peak, each dotted with the caves of meditating hermits, represent the nine ways of Bon that lead to enlightenment. This suggests that the palace of the King of Shambhala may have a similar kind of symbolic significance, having something to do with the teachings kept in the Buddhist kingdom.

Just as the Kalacakra was supposed to have come from Shambhala, so the teachings of Bon were supposed to have come from Olmolungring. According to Bonpos—the followers of Bon—their religion was first introduced into Tibet by Shenrab, a King of Olmolungring. Sometime later, like the Indian yogi-scholars who went to Shambhala for the Kalacakra, several Tibetan yogis journeyed to the homeland of Bon in search of additional teachings to bring back to Tibet. One of them left directions saying that Olmolungring lay northwest of Mount Kailas, twice as far from it as the peak is from Shigatse, a major town in central Tibet. Since then, however, no one has been able to follow his sketchy directions and make the difficult journey to Olmolungring. According to the Bonpo lama Tenzin Namdak, there are no real guidebooks for going to the mystical country, but many Bonpos pray to be reborn there as Buddhists pray to be reborn in Shambhala.

According to prophecy, some twelve thousand years from now, when religion has died out in the world outside, a great King and teacher of Bon will once again come forth from Olmolungring. Unlike the future King of Shambhala, however, he will not fight in a final battle against the forces of evil, nor will he establish a golden age; he will simply bring mankind a new and revi-

talized form of the old spiritual teachings. The Bon myth places
relatively little emphasis on the journey and prophecy that play
so great a part in the Buddhist myth. It mainly shares with
Shambhala the theme of an earthly paradise that is the reposi-
tory and source of the highest wisdom and enlightenment.[1]

The other major Tibetan myth that mentions Shambhala by
name directs its attention toward the prophecy of a savior who
will liberate the world from the forces of evil. The national epic
of Gesar tells the story of a hero who wins back his rightful kingdom in a horse race and goes on to destroy demons in Tibet and
defeat barbarians in countries as far away as Mongolia and Persia. Over the centuries up to the present day, bards and lamas
have added episodes to the original epic and transformed it into
a vehicle for expounding Buddhist doctrines. The Nyingmapas,
or "Ancient Ones," actually made Gesar into an incarnation of
their founder, Padma Sambhava, returned to clean up demons
that had sprung up in his absence. In the process of becoming a
defender and promulgator of the Buddhist faith, Gesar became
identified with the future King of Shambhala. Many Tibetans
came to believe that he, along with his warriors, would be reborn in the hidden kingdom and would once again come out of
the North, this time to free not only Tibet but also the entire
world from demonic powers. A number of important lamas became associated with the two myths, and the third Panchen
Lama, the author of the best-known guidebook to Shambhala
and himself a candidate to be the future King, took a deep interest in the Gesar epic.

The horse that Gesar rides to win back his kingdom and defeat his enemies provides another important link between the
two myths. We see it most clearly in the vision of a nineteenth-
century lama, in which this horse actually takes him to Shambhala. According to some versions of the epic, Gesar's steed has
the supernatural power of flight and is, in fact, the incarnation of
a well-known Bodhisattva. As such it appears in another lama's
dream—which we will examine in a later chapter—as the mount
of the future King of Shambhala. A number of Tibetan paintings
show him riding it into the final battle against the forces of evil

(see Plate 4). We can recognize here an extremely popular motif of folklore and mythology: the man on a white—or special—horse who comes to save the day.[2]

The myth most closely linked to Shambhala, however, comes not from Tibet but from India. It foretells the coming of Kalki, the redeemer of the world. According to Hindu mythology, the world passes through recurring cycles of declining virtue, each beginning with a golden age of perfection and ending in a dark age of discord, such as the one we live in today. From time to time as conditions get worse, Vishnu, the supreme deity of Hinduism, takes birth in a series of divine incarnations who fight the growing forces of evil and temporarily arrest the inevitable decline of religion and morality. Hindus generally believe that there will be ten of these incarnations in all, including Rama and Krishna, the divine heroes of the two great epic poems of India, the *Ramayana* and the *Mahabharata*. Nine have already completed their missions on earth, and only one remains yet to come —Kalki. Unlike his predecessors, he will put an end to this cycle and initiate the golden age of the next. The *Puranas*, old sources of Hindu mythology, describe, in terms that sound almost contemporary, the degenerate conditions of the world just before he comes:

> Wealth and piety will decrease day by day, until the world will be wholly depraved. Then property alone will confer rank; wealth will be the only source of devotion; passion will be the sole bond of union between the sexes; falsehood will be the only means of success in litigation; and women will be objects merely of sensual gratification. Earth will be venerated but for its mineral treasures. . . .[3]

When the situation becomes intolerable, Vishnu will finally heed the pleas of the gods and take birth as Kalki in a village named Shambhala. Having determined to end the age of discord, he will gather together a great army and ride forth on a great horse, a sword blazing in his hand, to destroy the same barbarians who tyrannize the world in the Tibetan prophecy. Following his victory over the forces of evil,

He will then re-establish righteousness upon earth; and the minds
of those who live at the end of the age of strife shall be awakened, and shall be pellucid as crystal. The men who are thus
changed by virtue of that peculiar time shall be as seeds of human beings, and shall give birth to a race who shall follow the
laws of the golden age of purity. As it is said, "When the sun
and moon, and the lunar asterism Tishya, and the planet Jupiter
are in one mansion, the golden age shall return."[4]

The relationship between the two myths is even more intimate
than it first appears. At least one Sanskrit version of the main
Kalacakra text refers to Rudra Cakrin, the future King of the
golden age, as "Kalki." In addition, some of the Kings who follow him actually bear the names of Rama and other incarnations
of Vishnu. There is also a close connection between Hanumanda,
the general who will assist Rudra Cakrin in the final battle
against the barbarians, and Hanuman, the monkey god of the
Ramayana who helps Rama defeat an army of demons on the island of Ceylon.[5]

Both Kalki and Rudra Cakrin are destined to be born in Shambhala. The Hindu prophecy, however, does not describe it as a
northern kingdom surrounded by snow mountains, but as a place
or village in some unspecified location. Since Kalki is supposed
to conquer a region between the Ganges and Yamuna rivers of
North India, scholars have tended to identify Shambhala with an
actual town there named "Sambhal." However, a close look at
the *Kalki Purana* reveals that after each of his conquests, Kalki
always returns to his birthplace, implying that it lies elsewhere,
perhaps in the direction of the Buddhist kingdom. In any case,
the Hindu texts do specify that Shambhala has a magnificent
palace comparable to the one described in the Tibetan texts.

Kalapa, the capital of the Buddhist kingdom, also appears in
the Hindu myth, but not as part of Shambhala. In the *Kalki
Purana*, a sage King named Maru, a descendant of an earlier incarnation of Vishnu, lives there in the Himalayas, awaiting the
end of the age of discord. When Kalki comes to liberate the
world, this sage will join him in the final battle against the barbarians. After their victory over the forces of evil, Maru will gain

a throne and assist Kalki in establishing the golden age. As seats of wisdom and power surrounded by snow mountains, the Hindu and Buddhist conceptions of Kalapa come closer to each other than do the corresponding versions of Shambhala.[6]

Like Gesar and the future King of Shambhala, Kalki rides a horse with the supernatural power of flight. In the Hindu myth it has special significance as the attribute or symbol that identifies and distinguishes Kalki from the other incarnations of Vishnu: Indian art invariably depicts him with either a winged steed or the head of a horse (see Plate 15). In the Buddhist myth, the King of Shambhala defeats the barbarians by entering into "the meditation of the best of horses." Through this meditation, he magically sends forth an army that includes stone horses with the power of flight. The role of the supernatural horse in both myths shows that it symbolizes the power that enables Kalki and the King of Shambhala to overcome the forces of evil.

Although the Buddhist myth probably came from the Hindu, the influence may have also gone the other way. The prophecy of Kalki represents a fairly late development of Hindu mythology that may have borrowed some of its features from Buddhism. From our point of view, however, which myth influenced which is less important than the fact that both came up with the same prophecy about a divine figure who will defeat the forces of evil and bring about a golden age. This shows the universality and power of the prophecy and indicates that it should be probed for deeper meaning. In this connection, the Hindu myth adds an interesting feature that may be useful to examine when we turn to interpreting the Buddhist myth. According to the *Puranas*, Kalki will come not once, but over and over, each time the world passes through another cycle of declining virtue. The prophecy of Shambhala may symbolize a process that recurs in a similar fashion.

Turning to China, the other great civilization bordering Tibet, we find a number of myths related to Shambhala. In the previous chapter we looked at one that appears in the T'ang Dynasty poem *A Song of Peach-Blossom River*. The hidden country accidentally discovered by the fisherman of the poem embodies the ideal society set forth in the *Tao Te Ching*, the basic text of the Taoist religion. In the course of time, as Taoism became increasingly concerned with the quest for immortality, it developed many legends about hidden places where the Immortals lived removed from the cares of the world. At first these earthly paradises were supposed to exist in remote mountains and islands beyond the borders of China, but as the empire expanded and the world became better known to the Chinese, the sanctuaries went underground in order to remain hidden. We can see this process beginning in *A Song of Peach-Blossom River*, where it is unclear whether the fisherman goes through a crevice in a mountain or down into a cave. In later legends, tunnels run down into subterranean worlds that have their own suns and skies; eventually the earth beneath China became honeycombed with mythical paradises. In order to reach them, a person had to attain a high level of spiritual development that corresponded to discovering the secret of immortality. Much of this calls to mind Shambhala and especially the Tibetan hidden valleys, some of which are supposed to lie underground and to possess the waters of longevity.[7]

While the Taoist caves bear a close resemblance to the hidden valleys of Tibetan legend, one of the older Chinese myths about an earthly paradise above the ground may refer to the same place as Shambhala. It speaks of the jeweled palace of the goddess Hsi Wang Mu, the Queen Mother of the West, situated on the heights of the Kunlun Mountains north of Tibet. There, on a jade mountain surrounded by a golden wall, live the Immortals in perfect ease and bliss. According to the *Shan Hai Ching*, the "Classic of Mountains and Seas,"

> . . . there is the Country of Satisfaction, which satisfies its people. In this place are the Fields of Satisfaction. Phoenix eggs are their food and sweet dew is their drink; everything that they desire is always ready for them.[8]

There beside the Lake of Gems grows a tree with the peaches of immortality. Every three thousand years it produces blossoms, which take another three thousand years to ripen into fruit. Then, once every six thousand years, on her birthday, the Queen

Mother of the West invites all the Immortals to a great feast held next to a magic fountain where they listen to beautiful music and partake of the peaches that enable them to live forever (see Plate 16). *Monkey*, a popular Chinese novel written in the sixteenth century, includes an episode in which the main character, a rambunctious monkey with supernatural powers, becomes custodian of the peach tree and gobbles up all the fruit, ruining the party.[9] The strange fruits that lamas bring back from Shambhala in stories of journeys to the Buddhist kingdom may have some connection with these peaches and the immortality they symbolize.

Just as Tibetans have tried to reach Shambhala, Chinese have attempted to go to the hidden palace of Hsi Wang Mu. Around 1000 B.C., King Mu of the Chou Dynasty, a historical figure wrapped in legend, took a journey to the north and west of China and reportedly visited the Queen Mother of the West. Chinese annals tell how he climbed the Kunluns and spoke and sang with her beside the Lake of Gems. Later on, sometime between the sixth and fourth centuries B.C., Lao Tzu, the founder of Taoism, became disgusted with corruption in China and left, heading west on a water buffalo. A guard at the frontier asked him to write down some of his wisdom, which he did in the sayings of the *Tao Te Ching*. According to legend, he then went on to the palace of Hsi Wang Mu, where he lives to this day as an Immortal. When the Chinese Empire spread into the Tarim Basin around 100 B.C., envoys sent to explore the new lands of Central Asia also went looking for the paradise of this goddess and the peach tree of long life. The Emperor of that period, Wu Ti, was especially interested in these matters, and his secret memoirs report that Hsi Wang Mu herself appeared in his room one night to give him seven of her peaches and the teachings needed to attain immortality.[10]

The palace of Hsi Wang Mu lies in the same general direction as Shambhala—north of India and Tibet. As we saw in Chapter 2, a few lamas think the kingdom may actually be hidden in the Kunlun Mountains, the usual location of the Chinese sanctuary. According to early accounts of Hsi Wang Mu, she lived even closer to where most Tibetans believe Shambhala might be—on a jade mountain north of the Kunluns and west of the Moving Sands, which could refer to the shifting dunes of the Takla Makan Desert. This would put her palace northwest of Bodhgaya, the place of the Buddha's enlightenment, in or beyond the Tarim Basin, the most likely location for the historical version of Shambhala. Since the myth of this goddess goes back to antiquity and was spread by the Chinese into the areas of Central Asia where the Kalacakra teachings probably originated, it seems likely that it had some sort of connection with the Tibetan myth—we know that the Chinese did identify the Kunluns with Mount Meru, the mythical mountain at the center of the Buddhist universe. A Western scholar, Wolfgang Bauer, has come to the conclusion that Hsi Wang Mu was originally the name of a small country west of China;[11] perhaps this country was the historical prototype of both the paradise of Hsi Wang Mu and the kingdom of Shambhala.

While the Chinese generally put the paradise of Hsi Wang Mu on the eastern end of the Kunlun Mountains, near the source of the Yellow River, the Kirghiz of Central Asia have legends about a similar place at the western end of the range. According to these legends, the prominent mountain of Muztagh Ata, an enormous dome of snow and ice over twenty-four thousand feet high, has a magical city on its summit named Janaidar. The people who dwell there enjoy perfect happiness and know neither cold, suffering, nor death. A Kirghiz story tells of a sage who climbed the mountain and found a white camel grazing beside a lake on the summit. Venerable old men, all dressed in white, were strolling about in a garden of plum trees. The sage plucked some of the fruit and ate it with relish. One of the old men came up to him and congratulated him on having eaten the plums: "If you had not," he said, "you would have had to stay here forever, like the rest of us." At that point a rider suddenly appeared on a white horse, lifted the sage onto the saddle, and carried him back down the mountain.[12]

The Kirghiz legends about Muztagh Ata display a number of motifs found in myths related to Shambhala: an inaccessible paradise, snow mountains, a sacred lake, magic fruit, sages, and a figure on horseback. Since these legends come from the area where the Kalacakra probably arose, they may well reflect traces of the older Buddhist myth of Shambhala. In any case, some sort of relationship clearly exists between the plum trees on the summit of Muztagh Ata and the peach tree on the jade mountain of Hsi Wang Mu. In an interesting twist of the fruit motif, eating the plums in the Kirghiz story frees the sage from immortality and allows him to return to the world of everyday life. This may reflect the Bodhisattva ideal of Shambhala in which the inhabitants of the kingdom vow to forego Nirvana and be reborn into the world in order to help others attain enlightenment. From the Buddhist point of view, the desire for the kind of physical immortality found in the Chinese myth of Hsi Wang Mu represents a spiritual trap that one must avoid.

North of the Kunluns, in the Altai Mountains between Mongolia and Siberia, a group of Old Believers, members of a Russian sect who had fled the persecution of the Orthodox Church, reportedly had a legend about a place that sounded like Shambhala. It spoke of a distant land of truth and justice called Belvodye, or "The White Waters," hidden among deserts and snow mountains. There wise men were supposed to have created an ideal society in which everyone followed the ways of wisdom. According to Nicholas Roerich, who visited the Old Believers in the Altai in the 1920s, secret texts, like the guidebooks to Shambhala, describe a long and arduous journey to the hidden country. They indicate that Belvodye lies in the direction of the eastern Tarim Basin and the mountains of northern Tibet. The name of the place, the White Waters, may refer to the white salt deposits left by landlocked lakes east of the Takla Makan Desert. A number of Old Believers reportedly tried to follow the texts, but most of them found the journey too difficult and either gave up or died along the way. A few claimed to have actually reached Belvodye and came back with tales of a peaceful valley surrounded by snow mountains.[13] As with the Kirghiz legends of Muztagh Ata, it is possible that this legend came from the same source as Shambhala.

If we look back into the distant past, we find a very old and widespread myth of a blissful land to the north that may have been the original source of Shambhala as well as related myths from both Europe and Asia. In ancient Indian texts this land appears under the name of Uttarakuru, Northern Kuru. The *Mahabharata* describes it in this way:

> On the south of the Nila mountain and the northern side of Meru are the sacred Northern Kurus, O King, which are the residence of the siddhas, the enlightened sages. The trees there bear sweet fruits and are always covered with fruits and flowers. All the flowers are fragrant, and the fruits, of excellent taste. Some of the trees, again, O King, yield fruits according to the will of the plucker. There are again some other trees, O King, that are called milk-yielding. These always yield milk and the six different kinds of food of the taste of Amrita itself [the nectar of immortality]. Those trees also yield cloths and in their fruits are ornaments for the use of man. The entire land abounds with fine golden sands. A portion of the region there, extremely delightful, is seen to be possessed of the radiance of ruby or diamonds, or of the lapis lazuli or other jewels and gems. All the seasons there are agreeable and nowhere does the land become miry, O King. The lakes are lovely, delicious, and full of crystal water. . . . The people of that country are free from illness and are always cheerful. Ten thousand and ten hundred years they live, O King, and never abandon one another.[14]

Once again we find the theme of an earthly paradise inhabited by sages and filled with magic fruit trees, some of which seem to confer the gift of long life.

Uttarakuru lies in the same direction as Shambhala, and, like the hidden kingdom, it too may once have been an actual country that passed into myth. According to the *Mahabharata*, it forms the northern of four regions that surround Mount Meru like four petals of a lotus. Hindu mythology places this mountain north of the Himalayas in Central Asia, and modern scholars have tentatively identified it with the Kunluns or with the Pamirs or Altai.[15] This would put Uttarakuru in the Tarim Basin or somewhere around Siberia—two of the more likely locations of

Shambhala. Since the *Mahabharata* deals with the early history of India and of other parts of Asia—as the *Iliad* does with that of Greece and Turkey—its description of Uttarakuru may well be referring, with mythical embellishment, to an actual country that once existed in the Tarim Basin. The detailed picture it gives of trees yielding fruit and cloth suggests the orchards and cotton fields that have flourished in the Tarim Basin for thousands of years. The "fine golden sands" that are supposed to abound in Uttarakuru could be a reference to the windblown dunes of the Takla Makan Desert, which would certainly fit the description of never becoming "miry." The epic also speaks of garlands of jade that come from Uttarakuru; in antiquity the region around Khotan was noted as the main source of this precious stone. During the time of the *Mahabharata*, the oases of the Tarim Basin were better watered and more lush than they are now and would have looked like paradises compared to the barren mountains and desert surrounding them.

A written itinerary reminiscent of the guidebooks to Shambhala describes a semimagical journey to Uttarakuru. The route leads to Mount Kailas, where the God of Wealth lives, and then on to another mountain inhabited by magicians. After going past a peak with women who have the heads of horses, the traveler passes through the region of Khotan and eventually comes to Uttarakuru. One of the main characters of the *Mahabharata*, a prince named Arjuna, journeys through the Himalayas to Lake Manasarovar at the foot of Kailas, crosses the mountainous region beyond it—evidently the Tibetan Plateau—and reaches the borders of the northern paradise. Like the Tibetan lamas who think that Shambhala is invisible, some sources say that Uttarakuru cannot be seen by human eyes nor reached by ordinary mortals.[16]

The myth of Uttarakuru dates back long before word of Shambhala reached Tibet, and probably well before the advent of Buddhism in India around 500 B.C. The Buddhists took it from older Hindu sources and moved the country, along with Mount Meru, northward and out of this world. For the Tibetans it became a pleasant paradise that satisfied all physical needs and

desires but lacked any religion or genuine spirituality. The Kalacakra texts put it north of Shambhala, but it seems likely that
the original Hindu version of Uttarakuru provided a model for
the hidden kingdom, which then replaced it as a northern sanctuary of enlightened sages.

In ancient times the myth of a blissful land to the north was
not confined to India. The Scythians, a nomadic people who
roamed the steppes of Asia during the first millennium B.C., had
legends about a place similar to Shambhala and Uttarakuru—
perhaps even the same as the latter. They believed that north of
their territory, beyond lands inhabited first by people they knew
of and then by mythical tribes of fantastic beings, rose the Ri-
pean Mountains, a desolate region of snow and darkness that no
mortal could cross. On the far side of this barrier, toward the
North Pole, lay a country graced by a warm climate, where the
sun rose and set once a year. There, sheltered from the icy winds
outside, a happy people lived in beautiful glades filled with fruit
trees. Since the Scythians were probably an offshoot of the
Aryan tribes who invaded India in the second millennium B.C.
and brought with them the Vedic mythology of Hinduism, the
myth of Uttarakuru—and Shambhala—may have originated
among the nomads of Central Asia and migrated along with
them to the Indian subcontinent—and to Europe as well.[17]

The ancient Greeks and Romans who recorded the Scythian
legends of a northern paradise seem to have identified them with
one of their own myths, which may have come from the same
source. This myth spoke of the land of the Hyperboreans, a mysterious people who lived far to the north, beyond the mountains
from which came the cold winds of winter. There, in a climate of
perpetual spring with the sun always shining, they enjoyed a
blissful existence free from the ravages of sickness and old age.
In constant harmony with one another, they passed their days at
feasts where beautiful maidens with hair bound in golden laurel
danced to the music of flute and lyre. Wise in their ways, the
Hyperboreans lived a thousand years, and when it came time to
die, their virtue enabled them to go to an even better world. The
Greeks made of their society a model of wisdom and equanimity.

According to the myth, none but the gods and great heroes could find the mysterious path that led to the land of the Hyperboreans. Perseus visited the inaccessible country in order to slay Medusa, the Gorgon with hair of snakes. Guided by the god Hermes, Perseus went first to the twilight dwelling of the Gray Women, who told him how to go to the land of the Hyperboreans. Then, following their directions, he proceeded to the northern paradise in order to obtain three things he needed to fulfill his quest: winged sandals to give him the power of flight, a cap to make him invisible, and a magic pouch in which to put Medusa's head so that the sight of it would not turn him to stone.[18]

In addition to speaking of sanctuaries hidden far to the north, the myths of Shambhala and the Hyperboreans share a number of interesting features. While Apollo, the Greek God of Light and Truth, resides in the northern paradise during the winter months, his Buddhist equivalent, Manjushri, the Bodhisattva of Wisdom, incarnates from time to time as King of Shambhala. Just as Hermes guides Perseus to the land of the Hyperboreans, so a tutelary deity guides the traveler to Shambhala. Along the way the traveler must also obtain the assistance of demonesses who resemble the Gray Women of the Greek myth. The journey to both places gives one magic powers, embodied either in objects such as winged sandals or else in the effects of mystical practices. These powers help one to overcome the forces of evil: They enable Perseus to slay Medusa, and the King of Shambhala to kill the tyrant who takes over the world. By turning people to stone, Medusa symbolizes the forces of bondage that work against liberation; we find a similar motif in the journey to Shambhala where the traveler must cross a river whose touch would turn him to stone. Finally, neither sanctuary is an end in itself, but rather a stage on the way to something higher: When it comes time to die, the Hyperboreans go on to a better world, and the inhabitants of Shambhala proceed toward Nirvana, which lies beyond any earthly paradise.

In Greek mythology the theme of a journey, which relates the myth of Perseus to Shambhala, finds its most complete expression in *The Odyssey*. As will become obvious when we examine them in a later chapter, the guidebooks to Shambhala have much in common with Homer's epic. The journey they describe leads past monsters as terrible as the Cyclops and temptations as deadly as the song of the Sirens. Just as Odysseus undergoes incredible trials and deprivations, so does the traveler to Shambhala. At critical junctures both of them need and get the help of female deities—Athena in *The Odyssey* and the Dakinis or "Sky Goers" in the guidebooks. There is one great difference, however, between the two journeys: One leads away to a mysterious kingdom; the other comes back to a familiar home. Although they seem to be opposites, the destinations of the journeys have a certain similarity: Both are sanctuaries and both are threatened by outside forces—Ithaca by Penelope's suitors and Shambhala by the barbarians. This suggests the possibility that the journey to Shambhala represents a kind of return—to the happiness and security of one who feels at home with himself and the world.

A much older epic from the Middle East, one of the oldest of all, comes even closer to the myth of Shambhala. The epic of Gilgamesh, dating from the third millennium B.C. and preserved on clay tablets from Mesopotamia, tells the story of a hero who journeys to the garden of the sun in search of the secret of immortality, held by Utnapishtim, the only immortal among men. As in the guidebooks to Shambhala, this journey leads across wilderness to a distant sanctuary hidden behind mountains that no ordinary mortal can cross. Scorpion beings, deadly hybrids of man and monster reminiscent of the guardian deities along the way to Shambhala, guard the gates of this barrier, whose "peaks are as high as the wall of heaven." Because the gods have made him two-thirds god, Gilgamesh manages to pass through the mountains and cross over the waters of death to reach the dwelling of Utnapishtim, who in some ways, as teacher and symbol, occupies the place of the Kings in the Tibetan myth.

The awareness and fear of death that prompted the Buddha to leave his palace in search of enlightenment—the same enlightenment sought by the traveler to Shambhala—also drive Gilgamesh forth on his quest for immortality. In a passage that could have been spoken by the Buddha when the sight of a corpse first made him aware of the existence of death, Gilgamesh expresses the anxiety that torments his soul:

> Enkidu my brother whom I loved, the end of mortality has overtaken him. . . . Because of my brother I am afraid of death, because of my brother I stray through the wilderness. His fate lies heavy upon me. How can I be silent, how can I rest? He is dust and I shall die also and be laid in the earth forever.[19]

Although he fails to free himself from death, Gilgamesh, like the traveler to Shambhala, finds wisdom at the end of his journey. Utnapishtim gives him a teaching similar to that of Buddhism on the impermanence of all things and the folly of striving for physical immortality. He sets him a test: If he can stay awake for seven days, he can get what he seeks. Gilgamesh, however, falls asleep and fails the test. As a second chance, Utnapishtim tells him where to find a plant that restores youth, but after Gilgamesh succeeds in fetching it from the bottom of the sea, he loses it to a snake and comes home at last with nothing— except the wisdom to accept his destiny as a man and thereby be freed from the anxiety of trying to escape his fate. Perhaps this too is an end of the journey to Shambhala—to return with the knowledge of how to live in the face of death; for all who go to the kingdom or dwell there, even the Kings, must die.

The journey to Shambhala brings to mind the legend that in Western literature epitomizes the theme of the quest: the quest for the Holy Grail. We find it bound up with legends about King Arthur and the knights of the Round Table. Although later stories focus on Sir Galahad, most of the medieval works dealing with the Holy Grail center on the life of Sir Perceval. They tell the tale of an ignorant youth who becomes a knight and chances on a mysterious castle hidden in a forest and guarded by strange knights. Allowed to enter, he sees the Holy Grail and a wounded King but fails to inquire about them. Had he done so, his questions would have cured the King and, in some versions, restored a surrounding wasteland to fertility. Shortly afterward the youth is told of his failing, but the castle has disappeared and he must spend years wandering through numerous adventures, trying to find it again. When he has finally gained the necessary wisdom and maturity, a maiden appears to lead him to the castle, and this time he asks the questions and restores the King to youth and health.[20]

The first part of the story reminds us of Tibetan stories about hunters and herdsmen who happen on hidden valleys. Neither they nor Perceval—as evidenced by his failure to ask the questions—perceive the nature of what they have found and the difficulty of finding it again. The Tibetan stories end with an unsuccessful attempt to return to the hidden valley, but the Western story goes on to begin the conscious quest that will eventually lead Perceval back to the castle and the fulfillment of his destiny. The second part of the story then resembles the journey to Shambhala, which is also a deliberate search for something already revealed. In the case of Shambhala, the traveler has read about it in texts and seen it in a dream or vision that comes as a sign that he is ready to go. Although both he and Perceval have been called, having glimpsed what they seek, they still need the hardships of their journeys to refine them and make them worthy of their goals.

There are a number of interesting parallels between the myth of Shambhala and the legend of the Holy Grail. In both, a female guide takes the seeker over the last stage of his journey to the King of a hidden place that holds something sacred—the Holy Grail on the one hand and the Kalacakra teachings and mandala on the other. Because the King is sick in the medieval myth or has not emerged in the Tibetan, the surrounding territory has become a wasteland, ravaged by drought or barbarians. In both myths we find a prophecy of renewal, of a golden time to come when the ruler is either healed or spurred into action to destroy the encroaching forces of evil. The object of the Western quest, the Holy Grail—sometimes described as a chalice, sometimes as a stone—is a source of physical and spiritual sustenance: It provides food, life, and divine grace. Yet by itself it can only keep the wounded King alive; to cure him it needs the help of

Perceval's questions. In Shambhala we find a number of objects with comparable powers, such as a jewel that grants the ruler's every wish, but the treasures closest in spirit to the Holy Grail are probably the mandalas, or mystic circles, of the Kalacakra that are kept in a park at the center of the kingdom. A Tibetan prayer says of them: "Just seeing them bestows the supreme attainment."[21] The power of divinity rests within the mandalas, but like the Holy Grail they will have no effect unless the traveler knows their nature and how to use them. Then they will cure him of the illusions that cause his suffering.

Another well-known quest of the Middle Ages, this one more obviously allegorical than that of the Holy Grail, appears in Dante's *Divine Comedy*. "The Purgatorio," the middle section of this work, describes the ascent of Mount Purgatory to the earthly paradise on its summit. Like the journey to Shambhala, this ascent leads to a hidden sanctuary that only the spiritually purified can reach. Each level of the mountain corresponds to a particular sin, such as envy or lust, that holds the seeker back and blocks his path. He must remain at each one until he has repented and purged himself of the failing it represents. This suggests that we may be able to read the guidebooks to Shambhala in a similar fashion: The features of the journey they describe, such as deserts and demons, may symbolize various passions and illusions that the traveler must find and overcome in himself.

The earthly paradise and the hidden kingdom are themselves only stages along the way to a higher destination. After reaching the summit of Mount Purgatory, Dante moves off into the heavens toward God; the traveler to Shambhala goes on to Nirvana. These ultimate goals, however, lie beyond the range of thought; we cannot really describe them nor say where they are in space and time. By belonging to this world, yet lying on the edge of it, Shambhala and the earthly paradise represent the last point of the journey that we can adequately picture. As such, they indicate the direction toward the ultimate goal—God or Nirvana—and serve as doorways into another realm beyond conception. In reaching them, the seeker attains the inner power and freedom needed to begin an even deeper and more mysterious journey. Virgil's last words to Dante reveal the stage that the earthly paradise—and Shambhala—symbolize:

> Here your will is upright, free, and whole,
> And you would be in error not to heed
>
> Whatever your own impulse prompts you to:
> Lord of yourself I crown and miter you.[22]

In *The Conference of the Birds*, a mystical poem of the Middle Ages by the Persian poet Farid ud-Din Attar, we find another allegorical journey, in which the birds of the world set out in search of a legendary King known as the Simurgh. Their leader, somewhat in the manner of the guidebooks to Shambhala, outlines the route they must follow and tells them what they will undergo along the way. According to him, they will have to cross seven valleys that in the Sufi tradition of Islamic mysticism represent seven stages of the spiritual path leading to union with God. The names of these valleys reveal what the birds will experience in each one of them: the Valley of the Quest, the Valley of Love, the Valley of Understanding, the Valley of Independence and Detachment, the Valley of Pure Unity, the Valley of Astonishment, and the Valley of Poverty and Nothingness. Our look at "The Purgatorio" brought up the possibility that the features of the journey to Shambhala might stand for the traveler's own passions and illusions. *The Conference of the Birds* suggests that they may also symbolize stages of mystical experience that he must pass through on the way to enlightenment.

Attar's poem stresses the theme of a King as the hidden goal of the journey. When after years of hardship, thirty worn-out birds finally stagger into the King's presence and look upon him for the first time, they discover that he and they are one and the same. His name, the Simurgh, means, in fact, "thirty birds." The one whom they sought beyond the farthest valley was hidden all the time in themselves, but they had to take the journey in order to be able to see him there and realize their identity with him. As we shall see, the King at the end of the journey to Shambhala also symbolizes what lies deep within the traveler, hidden from the beginning in the depths of his heart and mind.

The traveler to Shambhala, however, seeks not just a King but also a special place, a sacred country. Like the Children of Israel in the biblical story of the Exodus, he journeys across a wilderness to a promised land. In the Bible, this promised land is a land of freedom, the end of a journey out of slavery in Egypt. But before they are allowed to enter it, the Children of Israel must, through their years of wandering in the deserts of Sinai, become a free people; a new generation that trusts in God and obeys his laws must arise. In a similar way, the traveler to Shambhala must leave his old self behind and attain a certain degree of trust and inner freedom before he can reach his destination.

The most striking biblical parallel to the myth of Shambhala is, however, the prophecy of the Messiah. The prophets of the Old Testament, Isaiah in particular, speak of an anointed one who will deliver Israel from bondage and establish the Kingdom of God throughout the world. The New Testament identifies this Messiah with Christ, who will return to defeat the forces of evil at Armageddon and bring to pass "a new heaven and a new earth." According to the Christian prophecy, he will defeat the Antichrist, an evil figure who takes over the world much as the barbarian tyrant does in the Tibetan myth. In the Revelation of John, we see a vision of a divine King, like Kalki and the King of Shambhala, riding forth on a white horse to lead a heavenly host into battle against the forces of evil. A thousand years of peace under the reign of Christ will follow his victory and then, after a temporary return of Satan, the Last Judgment will take place and the world will be made new again. This corresponds to a belief held by many Tibetan lamas that the golden rule of Shambhala will also last a thousand years, to be followed by the return of degenerate times before Maitreya, the next Buddha, finally comes to restore the teachings of truth.

Islam has a similar prophecy about a redeemer called the Mahdi, who will also come to deliver the world from evil and establish a golden age. According to some accounts, he will slay al-Dajjal, the Deceiver, or else assist Christ in slaying him. Accord-

ing to others, he will be Christ himself, returned to teach Islam
and confound Jews and Christians alike. This idea of a divine
redeemer who appears at the end of the world probably originated in the ancient Persian religion of Zoroastrianism. According to that religion, which had a strong influence on later religions, a descendant of the prophet Zoroaster named Shaoshyans
will come at the end of history to fight on the side of Ahura
Mazda, the god of light, against Ahriman, the embodiment of
darkness. After finally defeating the forces of Ahriman once and
for all, Shaoshyans will transform the world into a paradise of
peace and truth. It seems very likely that this prophecy contributed to the development of the myth of Shambhala in Central
Asia.[23]

The themes we have found in myths related to Shambhala appear in modern literature as well. The most obvious example of
this occurs in *Lost Horizon,* but many other novels that have
nothing to do with Tibet or Asia show striking similarities to the
Tibetan myth. *Atlas Shrugged* by Ayn Rand comes remarkably
close to the prophecy of Shambhala in its story about the break-
down of the American economy and the emergence of a new
order from a sanctuary hidden in the mountains of Colorado.
The events of *The Magic Mountain* by Thomas Mann take place
in a sanatorium high in the Swiss Alps, isolated from the turmoil
of the outside world and even from the passage of time. *Mount
Analogue,* an allegorical novel by René Daumal, postulates the
existence of an invisible mountain whose ascent leads to a community of enlightened people such as those found in Shambhala.
Like the guidebooks to the hidden kingdom, *The Journey to the
East* by Hermann Hesse describes a journey through the physical world—in this case, Europe—that involves encounters with
magical places and mythical figures that ordinary people cannot
perceive. The goal of this journey is "the home and youth of the
soul," embodied in earthly paradises like Shambhala. In novels
such as *Island* by Aldous Huxley and *Walden Two* by B. F.
Skinner, the theme of the earthly paradise appears in its modern
form—that of the utopian society. Huxley's *Brave New World*
and George Orwell's *1984,* on the other hand, describe the kind

of world the Tibetan prophecy envisages under the materialistic rule of the barbarians. Many other works of science fiction deal with a version of the apocalyptic theme that concerns everyone today—nuclear war and its aftermath, the possibility of a new world emerging from an atomic holocaust.

In addition to influencing modern literature, myths related to Shambhala have had a profound influence on the course of history right up to the present day. Messianic prophecies gave Christianity much of its original appeal and the power it needed to take over the decadent Roman Empire. Since then, similar prophecies have inspired numerous movements and revolutions, both secular and religious. As Mircea Eliade and other scholars have shown, biblical myths of an earthly paradise and a golden age to come helped motivate the discovery and colonization of the New World and eventually gave rise to the American idea of progress that has spread around the globe. Christopher Columbus certainly had these myths in mind when he declared, "God made me the messenger of the new heaven and the new earth of which he spoke in the Apocalypse of St. John, after having spoken of it by the mouth of Isaiah; and He showed me the spot where to find it." Some of the Spanish conquistadors who followed Columbus went on to search for legendary places that promised the treasures of paradise—the Fountain of Youth and the golden realm of El Dorado. Many of the Protestants who colonized North America believed that Europe was dominated by the Antichrist and that their destination was to be the future garden of Eden; they and immigrants of later centuries came in search of an earthly paradise where they might find a new life —and a spiritual renewal.[24]

When the eastern part of the United States became crowded, the western pioneers set out on their epic journeys across deserts and mountains to find their equivalent of Shambhala in the fertile valleys of California and Oregon. The Mormons viewed the sanctuary they found in Utah in particularly spiritual terms. As the frontier dwindled away, the search for an earthly paradise and the expectation of a new world merged and changed into the conviction that material progress would transform the nation into a garden of Eden and bring in a golden age of freedom from want. The belief in this modern myth of progress lies behind much of the current push for greater economic development throughout the world.

Some movements have concentrated more on the social aspects of the earthly paradise and have tried to create various kinds of utopian societies. Throughout history, people have sought to establish communities apart from the outside world where they might live the kind of harmonious life found in Shambhala. In *The Republic,* Plato laid out a model for creating an ideal state based on the rule of philosopher Kings who possess integrity, wisdom, and a mystical vision of the ultimate good. According to the Tibetan myth, Shambhala is governed by just such a King—the incarnation of a Bodhisattva. Thomas More took many of Plato's ideas and incorporated them into his version of a utopian society hidden on an island far from Europe. More's name for that country gave the English language the word "utopia," which means "no place."[25]

The utopian movement of Communism is charged with a messianic prophecy that relates it to the myth of Shambhala. Communism too foresees first a period of decay and strife, as capitalist society falls apart, and then a final confrontation between the forces of good and evil, seen here as Communism and Capitalism. Following the inevitable victory of the proletariat, the communist doctrine will spread throughout the world and create a golden age in which all people will live in peace and harmony with no one lacking the necessities of life. This vision of the future has given Communism much of its power, as well as the need to wage a relentless struggle against the forces of Capitalism. The similarity between the communist and Tibetan prophecies carries some irony, since Tibetans today tend to regard Communism as the barbarian doctrine that will take over the world and threaten Shambhala. The way this theme can be and has been used by both sides, however, demonstrates its universality.

Looking over the myths and legends that we have examined, we find that they relate to Shambhala in one of three basic ways.

Some of them, such as the myths of Olmolungring and the palace of Hsi Wang Mu, focus on the theme of a hidden sanctuary or earthly paradise that holds something of great value that many people long to obtain. Olmolungring preserves teachings of wisdom while the palace of Hsi Wang Mu holds the peaches of immortality. Uttarakuru and the northern land of the Hyperboreans shelter peaceful communities of enlightened people who have everything they desire. The Holy Grail castle conceals a holy object that is the source of divine grace and sustenance. In most cases the sanctuary itself lies in this world, but hidden and nearly impossible to find or reach.

Other myths concentrate on the theme of the quest or journey to the distant sanctuary. Some, such as Dante's "The Purgatorio" or Attar's *The Conference of the Birds,* lay out a specific route with certain stages that one must go through in order to reach this sanctuary. In others, such as the quest for the Holy Grail or the biblical story of the Exodus, the hero or heroes must wander here and there until the hardships of their wanderings make them worthy of their goals. As in *The Odyssey,* the journey almost always involves the overcoming of supernatural obstacles through the assistance of divine powers; in the process it takes the traveler out of the ordinary world and into a magical realm of deeper meaning. In nearly all these myths the experience of the quest or journey transforms the traveler and opens him to greater wisdom.

The last group of related myths shares the prophecy of a golden age to come. Most of them predict a period of declining virtue followed by a final confrontation between the forces of good and evil, but at least one, the modern myth of progress, foresees a gradual improvement of conditions that will eventually transform the world into a garden of Eden. Many of these myths, such as the prophecies of Kalki and the Messiah, emphasize the role of a divine figure in bringing about the golden age. The theme of a golden age to come may appear at first to have little to do with the other two themes, but if we look more closely, we see that the kingdom of Shambhala preserves something of value during the period of decay before the final confrontation and is, in fact, the source of the power that will transform the outside world. In addition, a close relationship exists between the sanctuary at the end of the journey and the golden age at the end of the prophecy.

Most of the myths related to Shambhala concentrate on one, or two, of the three basic themes and leave the others out or pay little attention to them. The Chinese myth of the palace of Hsi Wang Mu makes no mention of a golden age to come; the prophecy of Kalki has little to say about Shambhala, his birthplace, or the way to it. Myths dealing with the journey, such as the epics of Gilgamesh and *The Odyssey*, speak of the sanctuary at the end of it but generally fail to talk much about any future transformation of the outside world. The myth of Shambhala, however, brings the three basic themes of these related myths together in one of the most complete and detailed expressions of a deeper myth, which seems to underly them all. If we strip away the particular features that ornament the individual expressions of this underlying myth, including the Tibetan one, we expose the myth in its simplest form: the journey to a hidden sanctuary that holds a source of liberation and renewal that will eventually transform not only the traveler himself, but the outside world as well.

If we examine this deeper myth, we find that the three basic themes that make it up each deal with some kind of liberation. This becomes clear when we look at each one through a representative of the myths that express it. In Dante's "The Purgatorio" the journey up Mount Purgatory releases the soul from its burden of sin so that it can rise toward the perfect freedom of heaven. The palace of Hsi Wang Mu holds the peaches of immortality that free the Immortals from death. Kalki and the Messiah come to liberate the world from the forces of evil. Without some kind of liberation, the traveler cannot complete his journey, the sanctuary loses its meaning, and the golden age cannot take place.

These various kinds of liberation have an inner dimension that gives the underlying myth its basic power and appeal. To a certain degree each one involves, or suggests, the attainment of a state of inner freedom from the concerns and worries that afflict the mind. In attaining immortality, the Immortals of the Chinese myth, for example, attain a state free from the fear of death and all the anxieties and inhibitions that fear entails. This kind of inner liberation lies at the heart of the universal appeal of the underlying myth. Whether or not we believe in the myths related to Shambhala, they have the power to resonate in our minds because at their deepest levels they remind us, if only subconsciously, of a journey that leads to a sanctuary hidden deep within ourselves where we can experience the freedom of the golden age. In the following chapters we will examine the symbolism of Shambhala to see what it can tell us about the kind of inner liberation embodied in the three basic themes of the underlying myth.

5

The Wheel of Time

The myth of Shambhala belongs to a mystical tradition that deals with precisely the kind of inner liberation suggested at the end of the previous chapter. The aim of the Kalacakra teachings kept in the hidden kingdom—and of Tibetan Buddhism in general—is to show people how to free their minds from the ignorance and illusion that cause their suffering. As incarnations of Bodhisattvas, the Kings of Shambhala represent those who have attained a state of inner liberation and are in a position to help others reach it. Many other features of the myth, such as the deities of the journey and the lotus shape of the kingdom, refer symbolically to the process of attaining this state of inner liberation. As a consequence, the symbolism of Shambhala offers a particularly clear and direct view into the deeper meaning of the underlying myth. In order to make use of this symbolism, however, we need to get some idea of the nature of Tibetan Buddhism and the Kalacakra in particular—both to see how they use symbols and what the features of Shambhala might symbolize. This will also give us a better idea of the kind of inner liberation envisioned by these teachings. With this preparation we can go on to interpret the myth of Shambhala in a way that has meaning and relevance today.

Before beginning, we should take note of the difficulties and limitations inherent in any explanation of this subject. Because of the paradoxical nature of its mystical view of reality, for almost anything we may say about Tibetan Buddhism, someone can come up with the opposite statement. In fact, the philosophical school on which much of its teachings are based strives to do just that—to destroy through contradiction whatever conceptions we might have of reality and how to perceive it.[1] The paradoxical nature of Tibetan Buddhism springs in part from the fact that what it deals with is ultimately inexpressible and therefore inexplicable: It lies beyond all thought and can only be apprehended through direct experience. Many lamas warn that without the practice and experience of certain kinds of meditation, we cannot really understand their teachings. Despite these difficulties, if we recognize the limitations of our explanation, we can still get a feel for the nature of Tibetan Buddhism that will help us interpret the symbolism of Shambhala.

Like other forms of Buddhism, Tibetan Buddhism has the overriding aim of liberating people from the bondage of suffering. More than most of the others, it tends, however, to focus on the actual means of doing so and makes extensive use of symbols in mystical practices designed to transform the practitioner into a Buddha or "Awakened One." Tibetans themselves distinguish three major kinds of Buddhism, which they equate with different levels or stages of the path to enlightenment. The first they call the Hinayana or "Lesser Way," and they identify it with the public teachings of the Buddha now practiced by the Buddhists of Southeast Asia. They say that it holds forth the selfish model of the man who strives only for his own enlightenment and pertains to the first stage of their path, which involves the preliminary purification of the mind. The second kind, the Mahayana or "Great Way," emphasizes the cultivation of compassion and has as its ideal the Bodhisattva who renounces Nirvana in order to help others along the path. Tibetans claim that the Buddha taught these more advanced teachings to selected disciples who could make use of the deeper wisdom and insight contained in them. The Mahayana, in turn, prepares the practitioner for the

Vajrayana or "Diamond Way," also known as Tantric Buddhism. By making use of the very passions and illusions that keep most people deluded, the Vajrayana enables one to attain enlightenment in this lifetime. Here, at the pinnacle of Tibetan Buddhism, we find the teachings of the Kalacakra Tantra.

Tibetans consider the Vajrayana a shortcut to enlightenment and compare it to the other kinds of Buddhism in various analogies. The Hinayana, for example, is like a path that leads to the foot of a mountain to be climbed. The Mahayana takes one up the mountain via a long, but gentle, road that winds around the peak and gradually reaches the summit after many lifetimes. The Vajrayana path simply goes straight up the cliffs, taking the shortest and most dangerous route to the top. If a person makes a wrong step and slips, he can fall all the way down the mountain and wind up in hell, worse off than when he started. To follow this route, one must have perfect co-ordination of one's faculties and a guide who knows the way. The person who takes the Mahayana, on the other hand, can afford to make mistakes and will find his path safer and less strenuous. Because of this, very few people actually attempt the Vajrayana, and even fewer succeed in following it to the end.

Lamas also compare the three kinds of Buddhism to three ways of dealing with poison—in this case, the poisons of hatred, lust, and delusion. Believing that poison can only produce sickness and death, the follower of the Hinayana shuns it: He tries to cut off his desires and to avoid anything that might stimulate them, such as women or wealth. The person on the Mahayana path, however, realizes that poison used the right way can act as bitter medicine: He therefore uses passions in small doses to cure his mind of its illusions. But the Vajrayana yogi knows that poison only appears to be poison: It is, in fact, the nectar of immortality, and knowing this, he drinks it and speedily attains enlightenment. By recognizing the pure energy deep within them, he can make use of precisely the passions and illusions that would drive an ordinary person mad. As we shall see, this analogy of poisons plays an important part in the symbolism of the journey to Shambhala.

The poison analogy reflects the tantric idea that whoever takes the shortcut to enlightenment needs to make use of all the means at his disposal. Rather than discard the passions and illusions that bind him, he must use their energy to break their grip and propel himself over the obstacles to attaining Nirvana. The more powerful the passion or illusion he uses, the more potential it has as a means of liberation—or as a source of bondage. Because sex, in particular, has such power over the mind, we find statues and paintings of Bodhisattvas in sexual union with female consorts, symbolizing the highest truths and the bliss that comes from their realization. Although lamas meditate on such symbols, hardly any of them actually use sex in their mystical practices. The tantric use of sexual imagery represents the attitude of making use of all sides of human nature, both worldly and spiritual, in the quest for enlightenment. According to Tibetan Buddhism, if we can reorient our perspective and see things as they really are, we will see that the world of illusion and bondage is actually Nirvana, the realm of reality and freedom.

The practitioner of the Vajrayana sees poison as nectar because both are empty and in essence the same; for him the nature of all things is emptiness. But lamas point out that this emptiness cannot be pictured or defined: It is not the image of blankness or dead space that may come to mind. It is reality itself, the indescribable source of everything, yet not itself a thing. We might call it the spiritual essence of the world that cannot be named, grasped, or otherwise limited. Beyond all substance it pervades all things. We cannot perceive emptiness as something separate from us; we can only experience it in the ultimate depths of ourselves and the world around us. It resembles the wind that can be felt but not seen, or the invisible space in which all things are immersed like pebbles in the pool of a mountain stream. The follower of the Vajrayana cuts through the opaque and solid appearance of the world to find at its core, gleaming like a diamond, the clear and indestructible emptiness that has nothing left in it to be seen or destroyed. But all this is merely metaphor to suggest an experience of reality that lies beyond words and thought. As a tantric poem says,

Though words are spoken to explain the Void,
The Void as such can never be expressed.[2]

According to Tibetan Buddhism, things have no reality of their own: They exist like images in a mirror, reflections of emptiness on emptiness. Since everything is subject to change and decay, even the stars, things have no abiding substance, only the illusory appearance of it. Moreover, nowhere in the universe or in ourselves do we find anything in perfect isolation; everything is made up of other things and exists in relation to something else. Even the most isolated island is composed of earth and surrounded by water. Remove either and it ceases to be an island. In a similar way, each thing—or person—depends on what makes it that particular thing and separates it from other things; by itself it is nothing, empty of any absolute nature of its own. As a result, the ultimate nature of reality, of things as they truly are, is emptiness.

Since emptiness, like a slippery pig, cannot be grasped and pinned down, we turn to substitutes that we can hang onto. This gives rise to illusory notions of self and things that bind us to suffering. Having created the illusion of possessing independent natures separate from everything else, we experience a painful feeling of deprivation and loneliness, a need to reach out and possess what we think we do not have. From this need spring innumerable frustrating desires that we can never adequately satisfy—for even when we get what we want, the fear of its loss eventually ruins our enjoyment of it. In the experience of emptiness, on the other hand, we realize the ungraspable nature of reality and let go of our illusions; our sense of separation from what we want vanishes—and with it our desires and the suffering they entail. At the same time, things themselves do not simply vanish; instead, like wax-paper lanterns that have been lit, they turn transluscent and begin to glow with the clear light of emptiness. The Vajrayana yogi uses the experience of emptiness to empty his mind of its illusions and open himself to reality.

Now, as Tibetan Buddhism points out, the mind is much deeper and richer than we imagine. On the surface it is composed of the conscious thoughts, feelings, and perceptions of everyday life, but it also contains deeper levels that normally remain hidden from our awareness. As we go beneath the surface, we encounter the subconscious levels that appear in dreams and sometimes burst into our waking consciousness in moments of intense passion, such as anger or love. Most theories of Western psychology stop here, but Buddhism probes deeper into other layers that we might call superconscious. These deeper levels of the mind normally lie dormant, but meditation or a shock, such as coming close to death, can momentarily activate them. When this happens, a person experiences new kinds of awareness and paranormal powers such as the ability to read others' thoughts and move objects at a distance. But more important, he gains, if only for a moment, a clearer perception of reality, with less illusion of separation between himself and what he sees.

Each level of mind embodies certain illusions that characterize it and its perception of reality. Since the surface consciousness consists of crude notions of things as fixed, distinct objects, it tends to have a rough and choppy nature. As we go deeper, the levels of mind and their illusions become more refined and subtle. The more refined the level of mind, the clearer it is and the closer it comes to revealing the nature of things as they really are. Only the most refined of all, the core or innermost mind, sometimes called the innate mind, can experience emptiness itself. This is because it alone embodies emptiness without any illusions. As long as we remain attached to more superficial levels of mind, however, the deeper ones remain dormant, hidden from us by our illusory conceptions of what the world is and who we are.[3]

According to Tibetan Buddhism, our minds create the world as it appears to us at each moment. Without realizing it, we project our illusions out onto the screen of emptiness, where they appear as concrete objects of our perceptions. Because of this, each object that we perceive outside ourselves corresponds to something hidden within our minds, either in the surface consciousness or at a deeper level. Everything that we meet in the external world has some kind of inner significance; even the most insignificant grain of sand can act as a symbol that tells us something profound about ourselves. This is an important key to the meaning of Shambhala and the various features of the journey to it.

Buddhist texts sometimes compare the appearance of the world to a dream created by the mind in sleep. According to this view, the universe as we see it is a kind of hallucination—but a collective one hallucinated by all of us together. A commentary on the Kalacakra uses the image of a white tent lit by the glow of a hundred butter lamps burning inside it.[4] If one lamp goes out or is removed, the light of the remaining ninety-nine keeps the tent glowing so that it continues to look the same. In a similar way, our minds together create the appearance of the things we see in the world, such as trees, rivers, and mountains. The contribution of each mind is so slight that when individuals die, nothing noticeably changes; the rest of us continue to see everything much as it was. In order to attain enlightenment, we must awaken from this collective hallucination and recognize the objects of our perceptions as products of our own minds.

If we observe the actual workings of our minds, we see that the thoughts and emotions of the surface consciousness each have a kind of energy of their own that gives them their particular character. Without a certain degree of turbulence, rage subsides into resentment; abstract thought about mathematical problems requires the calm intensity of concentration. This also holds true for the deeper levels of mind where awareness always goes together with energy as its vehicle or motive force. Without energy to sustain it, awareness fades, and without awareness to direct it, energy dissipates. Alter one and you alter the other. Lamas characterize this relationship by saying that the mind, as awareness, has eyes but no feet, and energy feet but no eyes; they go together as the eyes and feet of one body, two manifestations of a single entity.

The Vajrayana and the Kalacakra in particular go on to say that energy flows through our bodies in various forms, some deeper and more subtle than others. The form we can most easily observe is our breath. From the air we breathe, we get the energy we need to think and feel. At the same time the nature of our breath corresponds to the nature of our thoughts and emotions. When we get angry, our breathing becomes rough and heavy; when we feel calm, it becomes light and smooth. In the concentration of deep thought, our breath almost disappears. According to Tibetan Buddhism, our breathing reflects a subtle flow of energy that is inseparably linked with the deeper levels of our minds. Although we may not be able to show it to someone else or measure it with scientific instruments, we can experience this energy in meditation. When we do, we find that its rough or impure flow maintains the passions and illusions that cover up and conceal the innermost mind.

This observation gives rise to the two main paths of Tibetan meditation. One, the path of mind or formlessness, clears the mind of its illusions by developing the awareness of their empty nature; the other, the path of energy or form, purifies the flow of energy that maintains these illusions so that they dissolve away. According to the Vajrayana, if we purify our awareness, we automatically purify our energy, and if we purify our energy, we automatically purify our awareness. The practice of either kind of purification will clarify each level of mind so that it no longer conceals the levels beneath it. In this way, we can eventually reach the innermost mind, awaken it, and discover the true nature of reality, which liberates us from all suffering. Most forms of Buddhism concentrate on purifying awareness, but this takes a long time; the Vajrayana focuses instead on purifying energy as a much quicker, but more dangerous, path to liberation. In any case, at their higher stages the two paths come together and merge: Realizing that energy and awareness are really one, the yogi uses both to reach his goal.

Symbols can purify awareness by giving us insights into the nature of reality and the illusions that hide it from us. At the same time, they have the power to arouse and focus not only intense feelings, but also the deeper energy of the mind. While the path of formlessness makes some use of symbols, they play an especially important role in the path of form. They provide the means by which the tantric yogi brings the erratic flow of his energy under control, smooths it out, and redirects it toward washing away the illusions that obscure the awareness of the deeper levels of mind.

We can approach this use of symbols through the effects of sound. The explosion of a gun or firecracker sends a burst of adrenalin through us that momentarily heightens our awareness; a soft melody, on the other hand, drains off tensions and tends to put us to sleep. Tibetan Buddhism draws on these and other effects to make use of sound as symbol in the practice of mantra, the chanting of sacred formulas. Some mantras such as the popular *Om mani padme hum*—"Om, the jewel in the lotus, hum"—have apparent meanings, while others seem at first sight to be strings of unrelated syllables. Among the latter we find the main mantra of the Kalacakra—*Om ha sva ha ksha ma la va ra yam.* The repetition of even apparently meaningless mantras can smooth the breath and calm the mind. Done with alertness, it can also take our attention off distracting thoughts and help us develop our power of concentration. All of this would obviously contribute to the clarity and focus of our minds—one of the major objectives of meditation.

The path of form begins with these effects and goes on to use mantras as tools for mastering energy. When we speak or sing, we modulate our breath. According to the Vajrayana, if a yogi chants a mantra in the right way, he can control his breath and the flow of energy associated with it. Through the subtle use of sound, he can then release and direct the inner forces of the mind toward awakening deeper levels of awareness. Something similar happens when we hear or sing an inspiring piece of music and feel ourselves uplifted and carried away. The music of the mantra also lifts the yogi up, but rather than drop him back where he started, it carries him on toward enlightenment. Unlike a song or a symphony, it makes a directed use of the energy contained in the emotions it arouses. Even the meaning of a mantra works in this way, more through its poetic and evocative qualities than through its intellectual content. The content does convey insights, but primarily to the deeper levels of mind once the mantra has awakened them. Without the greater awareness of the deeper levels of mind, we cannot really understand the meaning of a mantra.

Although they may seem to do so, mantras do not bestow magical powers from the outside; instead, they draw forth and focus forces within the person chanting them. The sheer sound of a mantra has the power to resonate with the deeper levels of mind and awaken them. But for this to happen, it must be chanted correctly, and this must be learned from an experienced teacher. The written mantra is like a musical score that we must learn to read and play; otherwise, it remains so many dead markings on a page, a source of mumbo jumbo. The teacher not only shows his student or disciple how to intone the syllables and what feelings to bring to them, but he also initiates him into the experience of energy and awareness that they are supposed to arouse. In this way the mantra becomes associated with that energy and awareness, and the student can use it to call them back at will and deepen and control his experience of them. It works a little like a melody that brings back the memory of the beautiful evening when it was first heard.

The repetition of mantras goes along with the visualization of deities and other symbols. *Om mani padme hum,* for example, is the mantra of Avalokiteshvara, the Bodhisattva of Compassion (see Fig. 4); *Om ha sva ha ksha ma la va ra yam* embodies the

Fig. 4   *The Mantra* Om Mani Padme Hum *in Tibetan Script.*

power of the central Kalacakra deity. A yogi trains himself to visualize such deities in his mind as vividly as he sees them in paintings—even more so, in fact. We experience something similar when images appear to us in dreams. The practitioner of the Vajrayana develops the ability to "dream" or visualize symbols in the waking state. This strange practice has a number of useful effects. By forcing him to keep his attention solely on the image he is trying to visualize, it clears his mind of distracting thoughts and sharpens the focus of his concentration. But more importantly, the visualization of a symbol gives it an immediacy and power that it could not otherwise have: The yogi comes to feel it as a living part of himself.

The shape and color of visualized symbols act like the rhythm and tone of mantras to activate the deeper levels of mind. Rather than merely represent something else, they trigger actual experiences and channel their effects. Like a drop of sparkling dew or a beautiful golden sunset, they arouse powerful feelings that can awaken forces and insights deep within us. By visualizing their shapes in glowing colors, a yogi can transform even the abstract letters of a mantra into radiant symbols whose brilliant light burns away the illusions that cover up the innermost mind. The intensity of his visualization, combined with a feeling of reverence for them, brings these letters to life and gives them a power that far transcends whatever they might mean or describe.

We can see this more clearly in the visualization of deities. Each deity symbolizes a particular kind of energy and awareness found in the deeper levels of the mind. By visualizing Avalokiteshvara, for example, seated on a lotus blossom, radiating love to all sentient beings, the yogi can arouse and direct the forces of compassion latent within himself (see Plate 24). In doing so, he automatically activates the levels of mind that give rise to these forces: The deeper the compassion he arouses, the deeper the level of mind he awakens. At first he invokes a deity as an external source of power and wisdom, a source that seems to lie outside his surface consciousness. Then he moves the image into his heart and visualizes his body shrinking down and merging with it. By doing this, he experiences himself as the deity and gains access to the inner source of power and wisdom that it actually embodies. In a similar way, but to a much lesser degree, when we read a novel, we first visualize the hero as a separate character and then gradually identify ourselves with him, thereby taking on his thoughts and feelings as our own.

As he purifies each level of his mind and goes on to awaken the next, the yogi visualizes himself as another deity—or as the same one more clearly visualized. The resulting sequence of deities gives us a series of pictures of the yogi as he sees himself in the process of uncovering the innermost mind. In this way, the deities illustrate the course of his meditation and symbolize the stages and experiences he undergoes on the way to enlightenment. As a tantric text says:

> Let the practitioner remember that all these visualized deities are but symbols representing the various things that occur on the path, such as the helpful impulses and the stages attained by their means . . . the deities constitute the path.[5]

The details of each deity—ornaments, hand-held objects, bodily features, and so forth—tell us something about the stage or stages it represents. The thousand arms of one form of Avalokiteshvara, for example, can indicate either that the yogi has awakened the determination to rescue innumerable beings from the world of suffering or that he has gone on to develop the power to reach out and actually do so. The sword and diamond scepter held by one version of the main Kalacakra deity show that the practitioner is awakening the wisdom that cuts through illusions and reveals the diamondlike nature of emptiness. The way deities symbolize stages and experiences along the path to liberation will prove useful to us when we interpret the journey to Shambhala.

The sense of reverence that the deities inspire makes them appropriate symbols for arousing inner forces that seem to the surface consciousness divine. It also reminds the yogi that these forces are to be used for spiritual rather than selfish purposes: Although he finds them within himself, they come from a sacred source that does not belong to him alone. This counteracts the temptation to use them to build himself up as an isolated ego with godlike powers—a real danger of tantric practice that can easily lead to delusions of grandeur and eventual ruin. Maintaining a sense of reverence for the deities helps the yogi transcend such illusions and realize the divine emptiness of his true nature.

When visualized deities awaken the deeper levels of his mind, they reveal the liberating power and wisdom hidden in the deluded passions of his surface consciousness. Visualizing himself as a wrathful deity, for example, he uncovers a clean force in his anger that shatters illusions and converts that very anger into an open awareness capable of reflecting the real nature of reality. In a similar way, through meditation on other kinds of deities, he transmutes lust into compassion, pride into equanimity, ignorance into wisdom, and so forth. According to an analogy we used earlier, these symbols help him to recognize poison as the nectar of immortality.

The yogi's teacher will generally assign him a special tutelary, or guiding, deity designed to transform the major defects of his particular character. A person of angry temperament will get a wrathful Bodhisattva to visualize while someone with a romantic or lustful predisposition may get a seductive one of the opposite sex. By relinquishing himself to his tutelary deity and regarding it as his teacher, the yogi permits the deeper levels of his mind to take over and guide him along the path to liberation. The deity becomes the mouthpiece of an inner voice and ultimately the embodiment of the innermost mind. In visualizing himself as the tutelary deity in sexual union with its consort, the yogi draws together the male and female sides of his nature—regarded by the Vajrayana as active energy and passive awareness—and experiences the bliss of their basic unity in emptiness. In this way he transcends himself and gets a taste of enlightenment, which purifies his mind and orients him on the path to eventual liberation.

Once he has identified himself with a tutelary deity, the yogi goes on to visualize the energy system of his new and divine body: a network of nerves or channels radiating from five psychic centers shaped like wheels, or symbolized by lotus blossoms, and spaced along a central channel running from near the base of the spine to the top of the head (see Fig. 5). According to the Vajrayana, various knots or obstructions block the proper flow of energy through this system, thereby creating the passions and illusions of our usual state of consciousness. By visualizing tiny

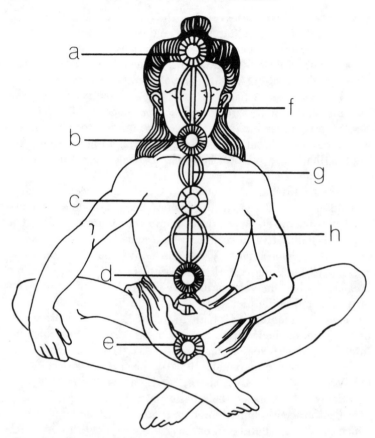

Fig. 5 *The psychic-energy system.* a, *crown center;* b, *throat center;* c, *heart center;* d, *navel center;* e, *secret, or sex, center;* f, *side channel;* g, *main, or central, channel;* h, *side channel.*

deities and mantras in these knots, the yogi can open them and shift his flow of energy into the central channel, where it becomes purified and activates the psychic centers and the deeper levels of mind they contain and control. The objective of the Kalacakra practice is to reach and release the innermost mind locked in the heart center. At that point the yogi will drop the visualization and slip into a state of blissful emptiness, to rise from it awakened and cleansed of illusions.

Whether or not this psychic energy system has any physiological existence, it does correspond to certain subjective experiences of the body. We tend to feel abstract thinking in our heads, sexual urges around our genitals, and the deepest love and anguish in our hearts—each where the center responsible for it is supposed to be. By visualizing these centers, the yogi focuses his attention on various sensitive parts of the body and stimulates the emotions or thoughts felt there in an especially intense way. Through the spiritualizing effects of deities and other symbols, he can then purify the energy of these thoughts and emotions and clarify his awareness of reality. Although this may suggest a physiological interpretation of the centers, the Vajrayana seems to imply that they actually belong to a subtle body that pervades the physical one and only reveals itself in meditation or mystical experiences. In any case, the yogi creates a mental image of this body so strong that it feels as real to him as anything made of flesh and blood.

Along with this kind of meditation, the yogi also visualizes the sacred realm of his tutelary deity: a mandala or mystic circle enclosing a jeweled palace with four gates that open to the north, south, east, and west. An outer ring of fire around a barrier of diamond scepters keeps out the profane and purifies those fit to enter. The tutelary deity himself dwells in royal splendor at the very center, surrounded by other deities who manifest various aspects of the power and wisdom he embodies. Some forms of the mandala leave out the palace and include only the circular arrangement of deities, which can also be represented by a lotus blossom with a center and four or more petals corresponding to the directions of the compass. Sometimes a letter or other sacred object symbolizing its essence replaces each deity. Whatever form they take and whatever they may include, all mandalas are characterized by perfect order and symmetry (see Fig. 6 and Plate 18).

When the yogi identifies himself with his tutelary deity, he identifies the world around himself with that deity's mandala.

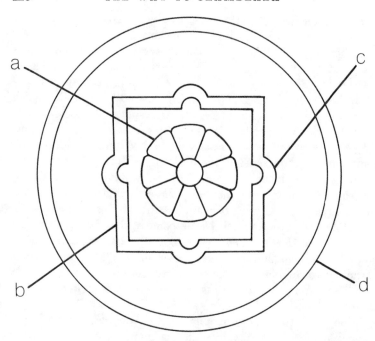

Fig. 6 *The structure of a mandala.* a, *central lotus blossom;* b, *palace;*
c, *an entrance to the palace;* d, *outer circle.*

His immediate surroundings become the palace, the people he
sees the other deities, and the horizon the outer ring of fire. This
visualization creates a mental atmosphere that he tries to maintain in daily life so that everything around him can begin to reveal its divine inner nature. Through the mandala he strives to
see this world as Nirvana, to hear all sounds as mantras, and to
regard all beings as Buddhas. Just as the deities of the mandala
manifest the nature of the central, tutelary deity, so he begins to
see that other people reflect various aspects of himself and that
through them he can discern hidden parts of his mind that he
needs to awaken. Everyone, each in his own way, can teach him
something of great value. As this awareness deepens, he gradually ceases to regard himself as an isolated entity set apart from

the rest of existence. Through the perfect composition of the mandala, in which no part is superfluous, he becomes aware of the hidden relationships that link and unify everything in the universe.

In Chapter 2 we saw the universe described by the Kalacakra texts as a mandala with Mount Meru at the center and our world as the southern continent. The yogi will sometimes visualize this mandala in his body, identifying Meru with his spine and the four surrounding continents with his four limbs. Among other things, this can lead to mystical experiences of unity with the universe. As a result of this practice, the yogi discovers that everything he wishes can be found within his own body. He no longer needs to grab and clutch at things outside himself, thereby perpetuating the attachments that bind him to suffering. Even the deities appear in the psychic centers, which he visualizes as lotus-shaped mandalas within the greater mandala of his body. Through these deities comes the divine power that opens the centers and brings the deeper levels of mind to life.

Mandalas also play an important part in initiations—ceremonies that are supposed to confer the power and wisdom, as well as the permission, needed to follow a particular practice or mystical teaching. In a typical initiation the teacher or meditation master consecrates an area of ground and prepares a mandala there, either by drawing it with paint or colored powder, or by constructing a three-dimensional model of it complete with pagoda palace. According to the Kalacakra texts, the first religious King of Shambhala built just such a three-dimensional model for the purpose of giving initiations into that teaching. The student or disciple to be initiated usually stands blindfolded outside the eastern gate and imagines himself reborn into the mandala as a baby entering a new world and a new life that will lead to liberation. The teacher than baptizes him with water from various vases, symbolically washing away the filth of his illusions and pouring the power and wisdom of the new teaching into him. The Kalacakra initiation includes a number of additional rituals for symbolically implanting the seeds of eventual enlightenment. The mystical atmosphere of the ceremony tends to awaken a heightened awareness through which the student can begin to understand the structure of the mandala, seeing how its features symbolize the teaching and reflect the nature of his own mind.

As this understanding deepens in subsequent meditation, he comes to realize and actually feel that no matter where he goes, like the central deity, he always stays in the same place—at the center of the world around him. It is as though, in visualizing the mandala, he climbs a mountain and sees from the top that he stands at the center of the encircling horizon—and manages to retain this awareness even after he has come back down to ordinary life and can no longer see where he is. This realization gives him a sense of inner balance and stability that enables him to withstand and make use of the forces of passion and circumstance that used to buffet him about. He discovers that the center of the mandala is a source of strength and power, like the axle that holds up and drives the wheels of a car.

In fact, everything in a mandala exists in relation to its center. In its visualization, the various features such as deities, palace, and the ring of fire usually issue from a central syllable and take their places around it. At the end of the meditation, they dissolve back into this syllable, which vanishes back into the void from which it came. The mandala therefore displays in vivid detail all that lies concealed and latent in its center. When the yogi identifies himself with the tutelary deity of the central syllable, the features that issue from it come to symbolize the hidden parts of his mind. The mandala spreads his inner world out before him, where he can recognize and become aware of it. In the process he sees how the different levels of his mind all have their source in the innermost mind at the center. By symbolically absorbing them back into the central syllable of the mandala, he assimilates them into his consciousness and thereby awakens them in himself. Then, at the end of the meditation, when he visualizes the center vanishing into the void, he finally experiences the emptiness of the innermost mind and everything that springs from it.

The tantras, or tantric teachings that make use of these practices, are generally divided into four classes, each more advanced than the preceding one. They begin with the preliminary purification of the mind and body and go on to develop and perfect the realization of emptiness that leads to final liberation. The Kalacakra Tantra belongs to the highest class, known as the Anuttara Yoga, and is probably the most involved and complex of all the tantric teachings. It has, for example, more initiations than the others—up to sixteen in all—and its mandala has a palace with not just one wall, but three walls, or levels, represented by three squares enclosed within each other (see Plate 18). Along with this mystic circle comes a vast and bewildering array of deities to organize in visualizations. The mandala itself includes 156, while the human body is supposed to contain 722. Few lamas can keep track of them all, much less know what they symbolize. In addition, the Kalacakra texts, like others from the highest class of tantras, are written in a secret "twilight language" that makes them extremely difficult, if not impossible, for the uninitiated to understand. Western scholars tend to regard the Kalacakra as the most abstruse of all Tibetan systems, the ultimate in ritualization and intricate symbolism. As a result, it remains perhaps the least known and most remote of all tantric teachings.[6]

A major reason for its complexity is that the Kalacakra attempts to embrace all phenomena, from the workings of the mind to the layout of the universe, in one all-inclusive system of knowledge and practice. It does so in three parts, called the "outer," the "inner," and the "other" Kalacakra. The first deals with the external world, beginning with the origins of the universe and going on to astronomy and geography. The description of Shambhala and its history and prophecy belong to this part of the Kalacakra. It also includes what we would call the physical sciences and engineering: It describes, for example, how to build catapults and other weapons that will be used in the final battle against the forces of evil. But its major emphasis is on time and astrology and the mathematics needed for their calculations. In the motion of the stars and the planets, the practitioner of the outer Kalacakra seeks to find the cyclical patterns of the forces that regulate our existence. He tries to read them as a scientist reads air pressure and cloud formations to forecast the weather. The Tibetan calendar and system of astrology come in large part from this section of the Kalacakra.

Unlike the outer Kalacakra, which Tibetan teachers will openly discuss, the other two parts are generally kept secret and revealed only to the initiated: Lamas feel that they contain ideas and practices that could harm those who might try to dabble in them without the necessary background and preparation. The first of these two parts, the inner Kalacakra, deals with the body and mind and how to use them in meditation. It goes into their internal structure, but with a mystical bent, and describes various fluids and secretions that are supposed to have special properties. According to the inner Kalacakra, male semen and a female counterpart, a kind of blood, carry the impulse to enlightenment and can spread bliss throughout the body, transforming it into a vehicle of liberation. To this end the yogi visualizes them as white and red drops, respectively, and by manipulating the flow of his energy, he moves them through the network of channels and psychic centers that we touched on earlier in the chapter.[7] The inner Kalacakra also explains the operation of the psychic nervous system in general and how it relates to the functioning of the various senses and kinds of consciousness. According to its explanation, the incorrect flow of energy through the body leads to imbalances that produce physical ailments and mental disturbances such as hallucinations. In a part that overlaps the fields of Western medicine and psychology, the inner Kalacakra prescribes ways to prevent and cure various kinds of illness, ranging from smallpox to schizophrenia.

The last of the three parts, the other Kalacakra, directs its attention to the spiritual realm and describes the deities and mandalas of the teaching and how to use them in the practice of visualization. The yogi becomes familiar with hundreds of these deities and develops an intuitive understanding of what they symbolize. In some of his visualizations, he places them throughout his body, from the central nerves of his psychic centers to the joints of his fingers and toes. The yogi also learns to chant

Fig. 7 *The Ten of Power, emblem of the Kalacakra. The flame, sun, and crescent moon on top represent the syllables* Om ha sva. *Intertwined below are the remaining seven syllables:* ha ksha ma la va ra yam.

and visualize the sacred syllables the deities embody, in particular a cluster of seven woven together to express the essence of
the entire Kalacakra teaching. This cluster, called "The Ten of
Power," is painted for good luck and protection on the outside of
most Tibetan monasteries (see Fig. 7). In the practice of the
other Kalacakra, it gives rise to the main tutelary deity, who can
appear in various forms, each suited for a particular purpose.
The most ornate form has a blue body, two legs, four faces of
different colors, and twenty-four arms holding various symbolic
objects. Other versions have twelve arms and four faces, or only
two arms and one face (see Fig. 8 and Plate 17). The yogi usu-

Fig. 8 *The main Kalacakra deity with consort.*

ally visualizes himself as the tutelary deity in passionate embrace with his naked yellow consort, experiencing the transcendent bliss of nonduality and emptiness. The union of these two deities, male and female, symbolizes the unity of compassion and wisdom that must be realized in order to attain enlightenment and help others liberate themselves from suffering.

All three parts of the Kalacakra Tantra come together in the principle of a Primordial Buddha, who underlies everything covered by their separate teachings—the external world, body and mind, and the realm of deities. Although he comes close to monotheistic conceptions of God, he does not create the universe as a creator distinct from his creation, but is, instead, the very essence of it. All things and beings, from stones to Buddhas, are his manifestations: Each in its true nature is the Primordial Buddha. Beyond form and emptiness, he lies somewhere in the unity of the two. According to the Kalacakra, he is the ultimate reality, empty even of emptiness. In meditation he appears in the form of the main tutelary deity, whose blue body, the color of the sky, symbolizes his vast and all-encompassing nature.

The Primordial Buddha gives rise to the Wheel of Time, the cycle of creation and destruction, of unceasing change, that defines our existence. Through the practice of the Kalacakra, the yogi comes to understand this wheel and to realize the emptiness of time as well as of space. He becomes aware that past and future exist only in his mind and that the present has no reality of its own. Yesterday survives in memories, tomorrow belongs to the imagination, and today will soon be gone. Under close scrutiny time, which seems so concrete and real, the very order and basis of existence, dissolves into emptiness, and along with it, everything the yogi seeks and hopes to find, all things and events that take place in it. Each thing or event, even if it materializes, lasts but a short while and then fades into memory. How can he possibly catch and hold what will inevitably turn to mist in his fingers?

Many people try to avoid this realization because it threatens to strip them of everything they treasure, including their lives and their very selves. They seek a moment in the future that will last forever or try to preserve the present in memories of the past. But they cannot avoid growing older, and as they age, they begin to feel trapped in time, condemned to dissolution. By facing the transitory and insubstantial nature of time, the yogi, however, discovers that instead of imprisoning him, it can actually liberate him from his present state of bondage. He sees that anything, even what he wants most, if it lasts long enough, will inevitably turn into a chain, whether of iron or gold. Since nothing, however, is permanent, he realizes that all the things that now bind him, the concerns and constraints of his present situation, will eventually pass away. For most people the fear of losing everything, even what causes their suffering, drives them to clutch at something old or new, which only perpetuates their bondage. Having understood this process, the yogi, on the other hand, stops adding links to his chains and lets time undo the ones he has already forged.

When, in doing so, he ceases to cling to the past or reach for the future, his sensation of time also passes away. He no longer worries about what will be nor yearns for what has been: He becomes fully aware of what he experiences now. This awareness transforms his perception of the present so that he no longer sees it as a brief instant rushing out of the future to hurtle by him into the past. Instead, he discovers a deep sense of timelessness in each passing moment. Moments continue to come and go— time is not frozen—but the awareness through which they pass remains. In the realm of actual experience, as opposed to thoughts about it, now is never then: Now is always now—and each moment reveals the eternal now. Rather than trying to follow moments into the past, the yogi stays with his awareness of the present, which, in fact, is all he can ever really do. To live in the past or in the future is impossible.

And yet, paradoxically, when he stops chasing after them elsewhere, he finds the past and future right here in the present. He sees that his entire experience of time can only take place now. When he remembers an event gone by, he experiences the actual memory of it in the present. And when he imagines the future, he does so now. Both past and future, and the present too, belong to the same timeless moment of pure awareness.

According to the Kalacakra, all of time—or the illusion of it—exists right now in the deeper levels of the mind. The memories and imagination of the surface consciousness reveal but a fraction of what lies hidden underneath. When the yogi awakens the deeper levels of his mind, he becomes aware of time as a simultaneous whole in which no moment comes before another because all exist together in the timeless present. He sees them like points on a spinning wheel, which pass but remain constantly in view. It makes little sense to say that one point precedes another; each one also follows the one that follows it. Spring comes after winter, but then winter comes after spring, and who can really say which is first and which is last? Although the Kalacakra, as the Wheel of Time, describes the various cycles that make up the Tibetan calendar and system of astrology, at a deeper and more important level, it really symbolizes the timeless nature of time seen as a whole.

All this is easy to talk about. Realizing it in actual experience is another matter, which requires the exercise of deep insight and meditation. In the practice of the inner Kalacakra, the yogi identifies the passage of time with the flow of energy through his body and learns to regard external events as reflections of his own internal processes. He visualizes the waxing of the moon, for example, as the movement and growth of a drop of white semen in his psychic nervous system. By regulating in this way the flow of energy that moves his mind from memories of the past to thoughts of the future, he gains control over his perception of time and comes to realize its empty nature—to know it as a succession of mental images that have no existence of their own apart from the timeless moment of actual experience.

The practice of the other Kalacakra uses deities to open a view into this sacred and timeless inner dimension of time. The yogi visualizes each month, for example, as a presiding deity surrounded by thirty or so attendants—one for every day of the month. This has the effect of radically transforming his perception of time: As a particular deity, each day takes on a divine quality that partakes of eternity. The deities of time lead him through the illusions of past and future to the reality of the timeless present. Along the way he comes to see them as different manifestations of the main tutelary deity of the Kalacakra, who embodies the timelessness of every passing moment. Through the visualization of these deities, he experiences the secret that past and future are but different phases of one time that happens now. By identifying himself with the tutelary deity who rules them all, he eventually becomes master of time itself.

Throughout daily life, even outside periods of formal meditation, the yogi tries to experience himself as the main tutelary deity and the world around himself as the mandala in which that deity dwells. In doing this, he gradually transforms his physical body into a spiritual one capable of embodying the innermost mind locked in his heart. In his visualizations he manufactures drops of special semen, imbued with the impulse to enlightenment, that slowly eat away and replace his flesh and blood. This process eventually produces an indestructible diamond body of enlightenment in which he can liberate the innermost mind and experience the emptiness of his real nature. After this happens, he may continue to look the same from the outside, as if he were still made of ordinary flesh and blood, but inside he feels entirely transformed. At the highest stages of the Kalacakra, he drops even this visualization, leaves deities and mandala behind, and realizes his identity with the Primordial Buddha beyond all form.

To attain this ultimate realization, the yogi must draw on everything he can. As a means to this end, he makes extensive use of correspondences among the outer, inner, and spiritual worlds of his experience. We saw an example of this in the visualization of the external universe as a mandala of deities within the yogi's body and mind. As a result of this kind of correspondence, any feature of geography, especially a place of pilgrimage, can become a symbol of both an inner and a spiritual reality. In some tantric teachings, Mount Kailas in Tibet, for example, comes to symbolize the spine or central psychic channel of the body as well as the seat of a tutelary deity called Cakrasamvara. The

Kalacakra develops this system of correspondences to its fullest extent; it even incorporates time into it by having deities and internal processes mirror external events such as the waxing and the waning of the moon.

At this point the symbolism of Shambhala becomes important. The kingdom lies within a mythical geography of the world that fits naturally into a system of mystical correspondences. The texts of the outer Kalacakra locate Shambhala in relation to Bodhgaya, the site of the Buddha's enlightenment, and Mount Meru, the center of the universe—both places of obvious inner and spiritual significance. In addition, they describe Shambhala as a sacred place of pilgrimage where the teachings of the Kalacakra exist in their purest form and can be most easily practiced. As a consequence, we can expect the kingdom to correspond to something of particular importance in the inner and other parts of the Kalacakra. With this in mind, we will turn to what Shambhala might symbolize in the worlds of psychological and spiritual experience.

6

The Inner Kingdom

A powerful symbol like Shambhala can do more than simply stand for some hidden truth or aspect of reality: It can also act as a window that opens up a view of something beyond itself. If we approach it in the right way, we may be able to look right through it and catch a glimpse of what it symbolizes. At such a moment, when a symbol yields a sudden insight or flash of intuition, it actually seems to turn transparent like a pane of glass and reveal a hidden vista full of unexpected depth and meaning. We suddenly see the implications of what it symbolizes stretching away before us, as if into a far distance. The symbol gives us a sense of an open and spacious panorama that extends beyond the limited horizon of what we know. In this panorama we may find the solution to a mundane problem or a mystical experience of the universe. We may get a sudden understanding of how an automobile works, or, like the English poet William Blake,

> . . . see a World in a Grain of Sand
> And a Heaven in a Wild Flower.[1]

Symbols act in this way by setting up mental images that awaken and direct the attention of the deeper levels of mind. Using the description or representation of a symbol as a guide, the intellect shapes and orients the frame of a mental window, so to speak, while the emotions fill it in with glass of the correct transparency and tint. If a physical window faces the right direction and is clear enough, it will give the view it was designed to give. In a similar way, if the intellect and emotions set up an image with the right orientation and clarity, it can awaken a deeper level of awareness that looks through it to see what the symbol is supposed to symbolize.

The intriguing aspect of a window is that it does not have to bear any resemblance to what it reveals. If it looks out onto a garden, the features of that garden, such as bushes and trees, can have an entirely different shape and color from the frame and glass through which we see them—unless the window has defects that twist the foliage into the patterns of its panes or give the leaves its own, say, purplish tint. The more perfectly made the window, the less it will impose itself on the view and look like what it discloses. Although it may help at first to direct our attention, a symbol that yields clear and undistorted insights does not have to resemble what it reveals, either. And, in fact, the deepest symbols cannot, since the reality they symbolize lies beyond all possibility of representation in words or images. All they can do is act as windows that open onto scenes too rich in subtle life and detail ever to capture in static pictures or descriptions. Although fixed and frozen, a window can give us a changing view of clouds passing by or tree limbs swaying in the wind—a landscape alive with motion. In a similar way, by acting as windows, symbols can give us varying insights into the dynamic and living nature of things as they actually are.

The design and transparency of a window tend to catch our attention first. If they have sufficient beauty or interest, they draw us to contemplate the window as a pattern on a wall. We admire the details of the frame, the way it is made, and the shiny, luminous quality of the glass. We speculate about their meaning: Are they representations or pictures of something? At first we pay little attention to the view they enclose, or else we regard it as part of the pattern, no different from the rest of the window. But after a while, we notice that the view moves relative to the frame and seems to have a separate and deeper character. Intrigued, we peer at it from various angles and see things that did not appear before—a new tree, a person, a cloud. As we realize the nature and function of the window, we cease to pay attention to it and focus our gaze instead on the far more interesting view it offers. At that point the frame and glass drop out of our awareness and we see only what lies beyond them. Vanishing into the view, the window becomes one with it.

We have here a beautiful analogy for the way we approach a symbol like Shambhala. At first we are attracted to it by its superficial beauty and intriguing appearance. As we examine it more closely, analyzing the details of its design, we come to regard it as a meaningful sign or as a picture of something else. After searching for what it might represent and trying to explain it in various ways, we recognize the symbol as a window and begin to look through it. In the process it turns transparent, loses its own features, and merges with what it reveals. At the end we cease even to see it as a window: It has become one with what it symbolizes. The view that it opened has transformed the symbol into an expression of reality itself.

For most of us such symbols are like windows of strange design covered with drapes and dust. Because of this, we fail to recognize them for what they are and treat them instead as signs or pictures—opaque patterns on a wall. In order to use these symbols as windows, we need to open the drapes and dust off the glass. A good interpretation can help us to do this: It can clarify a symbol so that we can look through it and see what it really symbolizes. Such an interpretation should aim at setting up the symbol as a window in our minds, not at simply analyzing the way it is constructed. If we focus too much attention on the frame and glass of a window, we run the risk of never looking at the view beyond them. In our interpretation, we should also avoid the trap of thinking that we can truly explain what a symbol like Shambhala means or symbolizes. Its real meaning lies in the experience of a direct insight beyond description—and therefore beyond all possible explanation, which must necessarily consist of words or other descriptive signs. Our interpretation can, however, make use of explanations to relate a murky symbol to others that we find more transparent. Then, with the help of what they reveal, we can look through it to the insights it can disclose. But if we take the symbols that our explanation refers us to as the meaning of the original one, then we simply replace one symbol with a combination of others, which we erroneously take for the experience of an actual insight. We wind up reducing a window with a view to a picture without any depth or substance.

What a symbol actually reveals ultimately depends, however, not on our interpretation, but on our level of awareness. No matter how thoroughly we interpret symbols, our usual surface consciousness will always treat them as mere signs or pictures. Only the deeper levels of mind can use them as windows that give direct insights into what they symbolize. The deeper the level of mind we have awakened, the more we will actually see. Since our awareness changes from moment to moment, depending on how alert we are, the meaning of a symbol will fluctuate in our minds: Sometimes it will seem to be no more than a meaningless design; at other times it will seem to reveal a profound truth. A good interpretation can make it more likely—but not certain— that a powerful symbol will momentarily arouse a deeper level of mind that permits a glimpse into the depths of what it symbolizes. A moment of this kind of transparency can leave us with the memory of an insight that gradually undermines our deluded beliefs about the nature of reality. Over time, a number of such insights may open permanent windows through the walls of illusion that surround us and block our view of things as they really are.

In a sense we live walled in by symbols that we have misinterpreted and taken the wrong way. Many of these symbols come from actual insights that we once had but have since frozen into pictures or preconceptions that now dictate the way we perceive and experience the world. As a result, whenever we see something new, a preconceived image of how it should look leaps forward to push it aside and take its place in our minds. Instead of a direct perception of the thing as it is, we see a faded picture of it that has the features of other, similar things that we saw long ago. The process happens so quickly and automatically that we are not even aware of it; we notice only that our perception no longer seems as vivid as it did. By taking pictures for actual perceptions of things, we create walls that cut us off from the experience of reality. But many of these pictures were once symbols that gave us insights into what they symbolized—and they can do it again. We need to turn them back into windows that can give us a fresh view of the world and of ourselves.

The most important picture each of us forms is his image of himself—what we will call the ego and what Buddhism refers to as the notion of self. More than a mere idea, this image is a symbol charged with emotions and rich with all the features of how we see ourselves. It can include everything from our philosophy of life to the way we think our toenails curl. Without realizing it, we visualize our egos with such intensity that they seem as real and concrete as any block of cement we might bump into. As we do this, we identify ourselves so completely with these images that we experience them as ourselves. In our minds we become these symbols of ourselves and feel them as the essence of our real nature. In this we do unconsciously what a Tibetan yogi does deliberately when he visualizes himself as a deity—except that the deities we use are our own egos.

When we identify ourselves with our egos, we cease to experience ourselves as we actually are. We replace the direct awareness of our real nature with pictures that lack the fullness of life. Since they can never duplicate the depth and complexity of a living person, we wind up limiting our consciousness of ourselves to the superficial features these pictures depict. Everything else that our egos do not or cannot portray, such as the deeper levels of mind, becomes unconscious and slips out of reach. As a result, we lose access to the kind of awareness we need to see through the illusions that envelop us; we end up trapped in mental pictures that block our view of ourselves and the world around us.

But the ego does not have to create illusions: Being a symbol, it can also yield insights into our real nature. Taken as a picture, it will mislead us, but approached as a window, it can give us a view into ourselves. Since the ego has no nature of its own, being an empty image of the mind, it is, in a sense, transparent. If we can recognize this in actual experience by acknowledging and seeing it for what it is, we will be able to look through it to what it really symbolizes. In the process, we will discover that much of the ego, especially its idealized parts, consists of images that have come from past insights into the deeper levels of mind. For example, a person who regards himself as kind and considerate but treats others badly may have developed this false image of himself from an actual glimpse he once had of a deeper level of mind endowed with compassionate qualities. Having identified himself with the attractive picture derived from that experience, he believes that he has become what he has only glimpsed but not yet awakened within himself. By recognizing that he is not a kind and considerate person and ceasing to identify with that image, he can begin to use it to actually awaken the deeper level of mind it symbolizes. The picture that covered up his inner nature will then become a window that reveals it.

Since we have identified ourselves so strongly with them, however, we have great difficulty at first in disengaging ourselves from our egos and using them as windows to see into our real nature. Any attempt on our part to let go of them or to question their apparent reality would seem to threaten the basis of our existence. In addition, whatever insights they might reveal we would probably convert into images to embrace or reject, depending on whether or not we found them attractive. As a consequence, symbols of distant, external places, such as Shambhala and the hidden valleys, can more easily give us our first glimpses into the depths of our inner nature. Having no real attachments to them, no stake in their existence, we can afford to let them turn transparent and reveal the hidden regions of our minds.

This becomes clearer when we see how naturally the hidden valleys can symbolize the deeper levels of the mind. As we saw in Chapter 3, these valleys are supposed to have different levels of accessibility. An ordinary person, if he has the right karma, may happen on the outer level, but to see the inner one concealed within it, he needs to have developed a certain degree of spiritual power and insight. Only an accomplished yogi can go on to find the secret valley and perhaps another, even deeper one that we might call the ultimate. All this makes it evident that the level of hidden valley a person sees depends on the level of awareness he possesses. Moreover, what he finds there—treasures and such—must also reflect the nature of this awareness. The waters of youth found in Khembalung, for example, go along with a fresh and energetic view of life.

In other words, we can read the hidden valleys as maps of the mind that show us the various levels concealed within it. From this point of view, the outer valley corresponds to a level of awareness just beneath the surface consciousness—or else to an overlooked part of the surface consciousness characterized by a sense of peace and security. In a like manner, the inner valley symbolizes the deeper levels of mind that we can only arouse and sustain through the practice of meditation. With their help we can discover hidden aspects of ourselves and the world of which we have not been aware. The secret valley, in turn, symbolizes the innermost mind, which sees, or rather experiences, the true nature of reality, embodied in the ultimate hidden valley of suchness.

One example, that of books, illustrates how the treasures found in the various levels of a hidden valley can give us insights into the nature of the different levels of the mind. According to Sangye Tenzin, Hinayana texts are concealed in the outer valley, Mahayana in the inner, Vajrayana in the secret, and the highest tantric in the ultimate. As we noted in the previous chapter, lamas regard these divisions of Buddhism as graded teachings meant for different stages along the path to enlightenment; they characterize each by the way it deals with the passions and illusions that block this path—whether it shuns them as poisons, treats them as medicine, or recognizes them as the nectar of immortality. The placement of the different kinds of texts in different levels of a hidden valley suggests that they are meant for corresponding levels of mind. It implies that the surface consciousness, for example, cannot make use of the Mahayana teachings: It lacks the power and wisdom needed to handle passions and illusions, which it must avoid as deadly poisons. The deeper levels of the mind, on the other hand, can make use of the Mahayana texts but lack the awareness needed to understand the Vajrayana. Only the innermost mind has the absolute clarity needed to see passions and illusions for what they are—manifestations of the compassion and wisdom of enlightenment itself.

Now we can better understand the meaning of the hidden-valley stories. Just as the herder or hunter of one of these tales accidentally stumbles on a hidden valley, so at chance moments we unwittingly awaken a deeper level of mind. As a side effect, this produces the sudden and inexplicable feeling of happiness that we associate with the sanctuaries of Tibetan legend. For a moment the walls of illusion that limit our awareness—in particular, the illusion of the ego—open like the entrance to a hidden valley and reveal a fresh view into the depths of ourselves and the world around us. But then our old attachments and habitual ways of thinking, symbolized by the family the hunter goes home to get, bring us back to our usual surface consciousness. The deeper awareness that momentarily awakened vanishes, and the happiness that it sustained fades away.

Like the hunter we mark the place or situation in which we experienced this moment of happiness. Thinking that it lies there, outside ourselves, we try to return to that place or re-create that situation, but when we do, we find only the dead memory of a past experience. A faded picture of what happened has covered up and replaced the vivid glimpse we had into the depths of our minds. Having gone back to the illusions of the surface consciousness, we no longer have the awareness needed to find the happiness we seek—the door to the hidden valley has disappeared. Instead of trying in vain to return to the place of happiness, we need to turn our attention toward its source in the deeper levels of the mind. As a hidden sanctuary whose name has been taken to mean "The Source of Happiness," Shambhala may be able to give us the insights we need to recover and hold what we all, at one time or another, have glimpsed and lost.

Before delving into the meaning of Shambhala, however, we should have a clear idea of what we are doing and what we can and cannot expect from it. In the following pages we will attempt to clarify the symbolism of Shambhala so that the kingdom can act as a window to reveal insights into the deeper nature of the mind. The interpretation we will use for this purpose can make it more likely that this will happen—or help us to recognize and make use of it when it does—but it cannot give us the actual insights themselves. What we see through a symbol like Shambhala we cannot put down on paper; it involves an act of seeing, an experience that each of us must have for himself. When we say that Shambhala, like the hidden valleys, symbolizes the deeper levels of mind, we actually mean that it symbolizes not them, but the reality that they in turn symbolize. The deeper levels of mind themselves exist only as symbols of an experience beyond conceptualization. Seeing them through the symbolism of Shambhala really means experiencing the energy and awareness symbolized by them—awakening that energy and awareness in ourselves. Now, we cannot expect this to happen in the course of our interpretation—that will depend on whether or not we are ready for it—but we can hope to get some understanding that will help us eventually, sometime in the future, to see and experience the inexpressible reality symbolized by Shambhala.

According to Khempo Noryang, we can talk about three Shambhalas corresponding to the three divisions of the Kalacakra teachings. The outer Shambhala exists as a kingdom in the external world, the inner lies hidden in the body and mind, and the other is the Kalacakra mandala with all its deities. In other words, there are three versions to consider: physical, mental or psychosomatic, and spiritual. In order to uncover the hidden meaning of Shambhala, we need to see how the physical version described in the texts reflects the nature of the other two. The inner kingdom is thought to be the most important of the three: If a yogi can find it through the practice of the Kalacakra, then he will possess the awareness needed to see the physical and the spiritual kingdoms. For this reason our interpretation will focus on the inner version of Shambhala.

As we noted in the first chapter, Tibetans often describe Shambhala as the only Pure Land that exists on earth. But some lamas, such as the Sakya Trizin, say that because of this its inhabitants do not have quite the purity of mind possessed by those who live in the other Pure Lands, which lie outside the defilements of this world. This suggests that the inner Shambhala includes deeper levels of mind that are clear, but not completely so. Moreover, it implies that we can find this version of the kingdom hidden right here in the body, imbedded in the passions and illusions of the surface consciousness. On a spiritual level the description of Shambhala as a Pure Land existing on earth suggests that the other kingdom, the sacred realm of the Kalacakra deity, lies concealed in the profane world of everyday life: If we could but see things as they really are, we would find divinity in everything.

All this becomes more apparent when we consider the symbolism of the most striking feature of Shambhala—its lotus-blossom shape. In Buddhism the lotus has a special significance as a symbol of purity and enlightenment, even in the midst of delusion and ignorance. In Tibetan art, for example, we usually find Buddhas and Bodhisattvas depicted standing or sitting on lotus blossoms to show that they have attained a pure and enlightened state that cannot be defiled by the world around them. A look at the way the flowers grow reveals the origins of this symbolism. Beginning in darkness as seeds hidden in the bottom of a river or pond, they send shoots up through mud and murky water to form blossoms that open in the sunlight above. Although the blossoms rest on the water's surface and draw sustenance from the muck below, they remain clean and dry, untainted by their surroundings. In a similar way, a Bodhisattva overcomes the darkness of ignorance and emerges into the light of wisdom; and although he continues to live in the world, he remains untouched by its delusions.

The shape of Shambhala therefore suggests that the inner kingdom lies buried like a lotus seed in the depths of our minds, hidden beneath the mud and murky waters of our passions and illusions. By drawing energy from these very passions and illusions, it can, however, begin to grow and eventually emerge from the darkness of the unconscious to open like a flower and reveal the enlightened awareness of the deeper levels of mind.

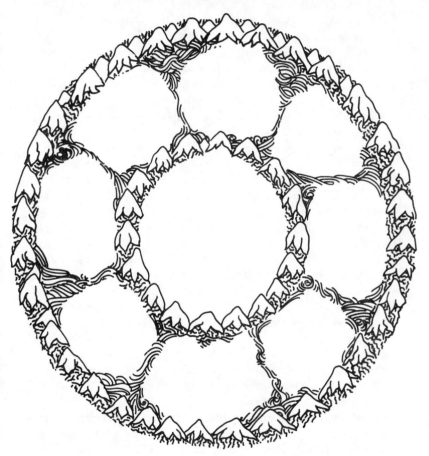

Fig. 9   *The lotus shape of Shambhala. The kingdom as an eight-petaled lotus blossom.*

The imagery of the most popular Tibetan mantra, *Om mani padme hum*—"Om, the jewel in the lotus, hum"—suggests, in addition, that the lotus of the inner Shambhala conceals in its center the jewel of the innermost mind, gleaming with the diamond-like clarity of the deepest awareness of all—the awareness of the absolute nature of reality itself. Only after the deeper levels of mind have emerged, unfolding like petals around it, will it awaken to dispel the last of our illusions.

The shape of Shambhala also shows us where a yogi expects to find and experience the inner kingdom within his body. As we saw in Chapter 1, rivers and mountains divide the outer kingdom into eight regions surrounding a central region, giving the country the form of an eight-petaled lotus (see Fig. 9). Most Tibetan tantras, and the Kalacakra Tantra in particular, use a lotus with this number of petals to symbolize the most important center of the psychic nervous system—the heart center, called the Dharma Cakra or Wheel of Truth.[2] Certain lamas, such as Samdong Rimpoche and Chopgye Trichen Rimpoche, therefore identify the inner Shambhala with this center and point out that the highest or innermost mind, the only one capable of knowing the true nature of reality, is supposed to be hidden there.

The reason for putting the innermost mind—or the experience of it—in this part of the body is easy to understand. Since our lives depend on it, we instinctively feel that the heart holds the essence of our being, the core of who we really are. Words, thoughts, and feelings that seem to come from there have a truth and power, a kind of sincerity that no others can match. Numerous folk sayings throughout the world attest to a widespread belief that the wisdom of the heart is somehow deeper and truer than the knowledge of the head. We experience the most profound love in the heart, a love that enables us to know its object more deeply than we ever could through intellectual observation and analysis. At its most sublime, this love leads us to a sense of the sacred in everything, to an awareness of the ultimate reality, be it God or the Void. Because of this, many religions regard the heart as the seat of the soul. The *Upanishads*, sacred texts that contain the basic mystical teachings of Hinduism, even use lotus imagery reminiscent of Shambhala to refer to the experience of the divine Self in precisely this part of the body:

> This Self, who understands all, who knows all, and whose glory is manifest in the universe, lives within the lotus of the heart.[3]

According to Khempo Noryang, the eight petal-shaped regions of Shambhala stand for eight psychic nerves or channels that are supposed to radiate out like spokes of a wheel from the center of the heart. These nerves then divide and subdivide into thousands of threadlike branches that fan out, in turn, to the various sense organs and mental faculties of the body (see Fig. 10).[4] Each of

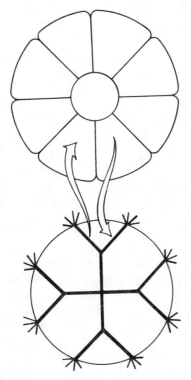

Fig. 10 *Correspondence between the lotus shape of Shambhala and the nerves of the heart center.*

the original eight channels serves one of eight kinds of consciousness through which we experience ourselves and the world. They include: the consciousness of each of the five senses, the consciousness of thoughts, the consciousness of self or ego, and the store consciousness of past impressions. From this we can conclude that the eight petal-like regions of Shambhala symbolize these eight kinds of consciousness and their relation to the innermost mind at the center of the heart.

This conclusion gets further support and amplification from the obvious mandala symbolism of the kingdom itself. In the lotus shape of the country, we can clearly discern the basic pattern of a mandala or mystic circle. In addition, like Shambhala, most mandalas contain at their center a magnificent palace lavishly ornamented with gold and jewels. As the incarnation of a Bodhisattva, the King of Shambhala obviously plays the role of the central deity found in such a mandala palace. Some lamas even maintain that the King is, in fact, the Kalacakra deity himself and the kingdom that deity's mystic circle. According to Dardo Rimpoche, the texts describe Shambhala in the form of an eight-petaled lotus so that yogis can visualize it as a mandala in their hearts.

As we saw in the previous chapter, the contents of a mandala emanate from the center and display whatever lies latent or concealed there. Now, as we have seen in this chapter, the center of Shambhala, like the center of most mandalas, symbolizes the innermost mind—or the point within ourselves where we can experience it. This implies that the eight kinds of consciousness symbolized by the petal-like regions of the kingdom issue from the innermost mind and manifest its awareness in various specialized forms. According to Tibetan Buddhism, these eight kinds of consciousness normally give rise to illusion and ignorance, but as we advance toward enlightenment, they reveal themselves as different manifestations of the enlightened wisdom or awareness of a Buddha. The egotistic consciousness of self, for example, turns into the compassionate awareness that recognizes the equality of all beings.

In other words, we can distinguish in each kind of consciousness various levels of manifestation of the innermost mind.

Depending on how far removed these levels are from their source, the more or less deluded a view of reality they give. If we take the least deluded ones and extend each one through all eight kinds of consciousness, we get the deeper levels of mind with their purer and more accurate awareness of things as they really are. We can see them symbolized in Shambhala by visualizing them as concentric rings running around through the eight petal-shaped regions of the kingdom (see Fig. 11). The closer a

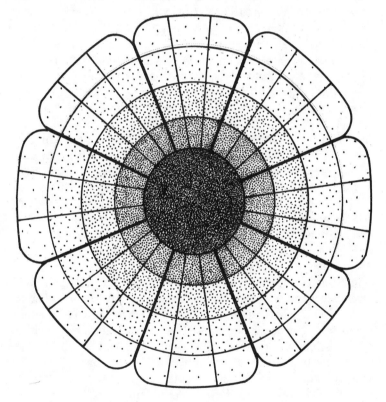

Fig. 11   *The shape of Shambhala as a representation of the deeper levels of mind. Rings of increasing darkness represent progressively deeper levels of mind, with the deepest level, the innermost mind, as the dark circle at the center.*

ring comes to the central region, the deeper the level of mind it symbolizes. This suggests that in the deeper levels the eight kinds of consciousness are closer together and more concentrated than they are in the outer or shallower levels; as a result, they function there with greater co-ordination and precision—our inner consciousness of ourselves, for example, tends to clash less with our outer perceptions of the world around us. According to this scheme, at the deepest level of all, in the innermost mind of the center, the eight kinds of consciousness merge into one awareness that experiences the true nature of reality without any distinctions of thought or perception.

Shambhala can reveal the deeper structure of the mind in another, perhaps clearer way. As we saw in the description of the kingdom, the King at the center rules over the lesser Kings of the ninety-six principalities in the surrounding petal-shaped regions. These, in turn, rule over governors, who rule over lower officials, and so on down to the lowest householders or servants of Shambhala. Like the tutelary deity of a typical mandala, the King obviously embodies the innermost mind: As the incarnation of a Bodhisattva, he has, at the very least, awakened it within himself. In the chain of command that runs down from the King to his subjects in the eight petal-like regions of Shambhala, we can see the emanation of the innermost mind into the eight kinds of consciousness to form the various deeper levels of mind. Viewed in this manner, the lesser Kings symbolize the deepest of these levels, their governors the next deepest, and so on down to the simple householders or servants, who symbolize the shallowest level associated with Shambhala. Depending on which region he inhabits and what rank he holds, each citizen of the kingdom embodies a particular kind and level of consciousness, such as the consciousness of sight or the consciousness of self. Unlike those who live outside the country, such as the barbarians who will try to conquer it, all the inhabitants of Shambhala acknowledge the King as their ruler and act according to his command. This points out a major feature that distinguishes the levels of mind associated with Shambhala: Only they possess an awareness deep enough and clear enough to recognize and heed the promptings of the innermost mind. When they awaken within us, they automatically shift our allegiance away from the ego of the surface consciousness with all its capricious desires and demands; as a result, we become open to a deeper and more reliable source of guidance in our lives.

Like other mandalas, Shambhala can symbolize the body as well as the mind. According to Khempo Noryang, if we identify the eight petal-shaped regions of Shambhala with the eight psychic nerve channels emerging from the heart center, then we can regard the ninety-six principalities with their millions of towns as the network of subsidiary nerves that spread throughout the body to the various organs of thought and perception. From this point of view, the inhabitants of the kingdom would embody the energy and consciousness carried in these nerves and channels. Khempo Noryang added that the outer ring of snow mountains represents the skin covering the body, while the inner ring, or else the central palace, symbolizes the main channel of the psychic nervous system as it passes through the heart center on its way from the bottom of the spine to the top of the head. As we saw in the previous chapter, two side channels are supposed to twist around the main channel and form knots that cut off its flow of energy (see Fig. 5). The two lakes near the central palace of Shambhala can be regarded as symbolizing these two side channels. A yogi might use this kind of visualization to undo the knots they form so that energy can flow through the main channel and awaken the innermost mind at the center of his heart.

As we have seen with other mandalas, a yogi can also visualize the world as Shambhala. He can identify himself with the King at the center, the people he meets with the inhabitants of the kingdom, and the eight directions of his surroundings with the eight petal-like regions of the country. In visualizing the world as the Pure Land of Shambhala, he strives to purify his perception of it and eventually to experience it as the innermost mind does. If he succeeds, he sees into the deeper nature of things and loses sight of the superficial appearances that used to provoke feelings of annoyance and anger; in their place he finds a growing sense of respect and compassion for others. The peace and harmony that prevail among the inhabitants of Shambhala spread into his relations with people in ordinary life. He discovers that what he finds in the depths of his heart lies outside too—in everything and everyone he meets. Through the visualization of the world as Shambhala, he attains the state of mind that Tibetans say is symbolized by the hidden kingdom.

Having looked at what the kingdom as a whole might symbolize, we can now turn to the symbolism of some of its features. The most important single feature of Shambhala is probably its King. As we have seen, he embodies the innermost mind with its pure energy and awareness. On the spiritual level he corresponds to the central deity of the Kalacakra mandala. According to a Tibetan prayer for rebirth in Shambhala:

> Each year at the new moon of the black month, the great King, who has the power of accomplishment, manifests the body of the all-pervading lord, the glorious teacher, the Kalacakra himself; and with initiations he ripens the minds of his disciples.[5]

As this passage suggests, the King of Shambhala also symbolizes the human teacher of the ordinary, external world—the guru whom the meditator visualizes as the Kalacakra deity himself. At the deepest level of symbolism, the King reveals the underlying unity of all three realms of experience—physical, mental, and spiritual.

For most lamas the next most important features would be the teachings kept in the kingdom and the mandalas built near the center. From an inner point of view, the teachings symbolize the wisdom or awareness of the deeper levels of mind. According to the Sakya Trizin, the Kalacakra Tantra exists in Shambhala in its purest form. This suggests that all other forms, such as the written ones found in texts, have their real source deep in the mind, in someone's experience of the inner Shambhala. Since the King uses the Kalacakra mandalas to initiate his subjects into the knowledge of the Primordial Buddha, the essence of everything, these mystic circles apparently symbolize the ultimate nature of reality revealed by the pure awareness of the innermost mind. In this sense they correspond to the highest tantric treasures found in the hidden valley of suchness. Experiencing what the mandalas symbolize leads to final liberation: According to another prayer for rebirth in Shambhala, "just seeing them bestows the supreme attainment."[6] Lying within the central region of Shambhala as they do, the Kalacakra mandalas symbolize the emptiness of the innermost mind and everything that emanates from it.

The various features of the palace of the King reflect different aspects of the power and wisdom of the innermost mind. The light that radiates from the magnificent building, turning night into day, symbolizes the bright, clear awareness that dispels the darkness of ignorance and illusion. Through it one gets a direct experience of reality that makes all other forms of knowledge seem pale by comparison; as a Tibetan text says, "Through that light the moon becomes no more than a dim spot." The skylights fitted with lenses that give a view of life on distant stars and planets suggest the great range and extent of this awareness. In the magic screen that permits the King to observe whatever is happening closer by, we can recognize a reference to the clairvoyant powers of the innermost mind. The golden throne supported by eight lions symbolizes the underlying power and steadiness of the innermost mind, which can achieve its aims effortlessly, without having to make the slightest movement. The description of another treasure makes this quite clear: "The serpent deities have given the King a jewel that fulfills all the wishes of his heart, so long as he sits on his throne." According to Khempo Noryang, the jewels of the palace in general represent the mind as the wish-fulfilling gem, a very common metaphor in Tibetan Buddhism. As such they symbolize the power of the innermost mind to fulfill the deepest wish of all—the wish for liberation itself.[7]

The ninety-six lesser Kings of Shambhala have magic rods called "Possessors of the Power of Mind," which enable them to send messengers to wherever they wish in an instant. These rods symbolize the efficient communication and control the deepest levels of mind can have over the body and its different kinds of consciousness. In our usual state, with these levels dormant, we cannot direct our actions as we would like nor very effectively co-ordinate our perceptions of what we experience. For example, when we try to do something, we often stumble over ourselves and succeed in accomplishing our objective only with a great deal of effort. Similarly, from what we see and what we hear, we often get two conflicting impressions of a person and have difficulty distinguishing what he really thinks and intends. As soon as the deeper levels of mind awaken, however, these difficulties vanish, to be replaced by a sense of ease and precision.

Since a yogi goes to Shambhala to free himself from attachments to worldly things, the lavish riches he finds there might seem somewhat paradoxical. According to one text, "even those with only a little wealth each have nearly one hundred bins full of jewels," while just one of the many residences belonging to the King "is worth a large ship filled with gold."[8] From an inner point of view, however, the presence of these riches in Shambhala makes perfect sense: They symbolize the true wealth, the unimaginable treasures of the spirit, to be found in the depths of the mind. We tend to value precious objects such as gold and jewels precisely because they have an indestructible and transcendent quality, a divine gleam that makes them seem to belong to another, more spiritual realm of existence. The incredible amount of wealth possessed by the inhabitants of Shambhala—countless times more than they could ever use—suggests the inexhaustible nature of the riches hidden in the deeper levels of the mind. Once we have found them and made them our own, we will no longer feel a need or a desire for anything else; we will have lost whatever sense of impoverishment we might have had.

According to Chopgye Trichen Rimpoche, the lakes near the center of Shambhala symbolize the fruits of spiritual practice—the results of meditation. We can see one of these results in a poetic description of the kingdom that says, "It is as if the lake naturally clears the mind." The name of this lake, Padma Karpo or "White Lotus," implies that it reflects the pure awareness of the innermost mind. Another passage from the same work alludes to an even more important fruit of spiritual practice:

. . . there is a park called Malaya where sandalwood trees grow with intertwined leaves and branches. Beautiful clouds floating in the air above make cool rain fall with the scent of camphor, which seems, so one feels, to remove all the sufferings of existence.[9]

Drawing on Buddhist metaphors for the attainment of liberation, the author uses Malaya, meaning "The Cool Grove," to symbolize the cool and refreshing awareness of reality that extinguishes the painful fires of desire and illusion.

At certain moments, just as the herder or hunter of Tibetan stories stumbles on a hidden valley, so we catch fleeting glimpses of this kind of awareness and the overwhelming sense of relief and happiness it brings. If we pursue these glimpses, looking for their source, they may begin to come and go with greater frequency. If we persevere long enough in the right way, we may eventually reach a point at which they cease to fade away. From this point of view, Shambhala represents the stages along the path to enlightenment in which we no longer merely glimpse but actually live in the deeper levels of mind symbolized by the kingdom. The first stage, in which we permanently awaken the shallowest of these levels, corresponds to that of the least advanced inhabitants of Shambhala. According to one text, "Even the lay attendants who do not practice meditation can, at the time of death, transfer their consciousness to the Pure Lands and avoid rebirth in the lower realms." In other words, they represent a point far enough along the path to enlightenment so that once having attained it, a person can never fall back to a lower level again. The highest stage symbolized by Shambhala corresponds to that of the King, who has awakened the innermost mind, and who experiences the true nature of reality. The remaining inhabitants represent the stages in between. According to the text just quoted, "Most of the inhabitants become enlightened in that lifetime." As this passage indicates, Shambhala as a whole does not symbolize the ultimate goal of Nirvana, but it does represent an important stepping-stone toward reaching it.[10]

The conditions of life in Shambhala can tell us a great deal about the stages the kingdom symbolizes. The peace and harmony that prevail throughout the country indicate that whoever reaches even the least of these stages is no longer subject to the inner conflicts and turmoil that afflict so many people. Having submitted his desires to the will of the innermost mind, just as the inhabitants of Shambhala have willingly acceded to the rule of their King, he has attained an abiding state of inner calm and unity. No longer confused and distracted by contradictory impulses, he can see things as they are and relate to others with openness and compassion. Secure in himself, like the inhabitants of Shambhala, he has overcome the fears and anxieties that lead to feelings of distrust and hostility.

According to one description of Shambhala, "The inhabitants are bound and live by gentle laws, and there is never any harsh punishment."[11] Whoever sets out on the path to liberation has to make great efforts at first to overcome the habitual desires and inertia that bind him to his usual state of delusion. He needs to adopt some kind of external discipline and force himself to follow its rules; otherwise he will never be able to free himself from his old habits and inclinations. The difficulty in living up to these rules will give him painful insights into himself that will feel like harsh punishments for his apparent failings and transgressions. The gentle laws of Shambhala indicate that one who has reached the stages symbolized by the kingdom has gone beyond the need for such a discipline. He has sufficiently mastered himself so that he now does spontaneously whatever he needs to do to continue along the path to liberation; his discipline has become something natural that originates within him. Just as the inhabitants of Shambhala have subdued demons and made them their servants, so he has tamed his wilder impulses and now uses their energy to help him reach his goal. The sight of his failings—still there but considerably diminished—no longer sets off reactions of dismay and self-recrimination; he sees his failings for what they are and deals with them accordingly. He has overcome the most serious of his inner obstacles and can now proceed smoothly toward the ultimate goal of complete liberation.

Having reached the stages symbolized by Shambhala, a person can, like the inhabitants of the kingdom, enjoy wealth and comfort "without loss of virtue." He no longer has the tendency to form attachments to material objects that would hold him back in his progress toward liberation. Having transcended his sense of separation from the world around him, he has no need to amass possessions: He already possesses everything as part of himself. At the same time, the deeper levels of mind he has awakened enable him to find beauty and richness in all that he sees, even in the most worthless clod of dirt. Since these levels of mind also enable him to endure discomfort and to make himself comfortable wherever he is, he can enjoy luxuries without the risk of becoming attached to them either. The extraordinary wealth and comfort of Shambhala show that the kingdom symbolizes the stages in which our perceptions of the world are radically transformed. The distinction between the wonders of Shambhala and what we see around us has begun to blur and fade away.

Whoever reaches the stage symbolized by the King of Shambhala gains complete mastery over himself: He becomes the undisputed ruler of his body and mind. As Chopgye Trichen Rimpoche remarked, "If you can use your body properly, then the body becomes Shambhala, the ninety-six principalities concur in all their actions, and you conquer the kingdom itself." Having mastered oneself, one awakens the innermost mind and experiences the true nature of reality, which lies beyond all words and symbols. In the process, one transcends the limitations of space and time and finds the essence of the hidden kingdom and the golden age to come right here in the present moment. In the light of pure awareness, the entire world becomes the Pure Land of Shambhala, the sacred realm of the innermost mind. Jamspal Lama put it this way: "Shambhala is here too, for there is nowhere where Rigden Dragpo [Rudra Cakrin, the King of Shambhala in the future battle with evil] is not, and where he is is Shambhala."

For most of us, however, such a vision of the world as Shambhala must seem remote and unreal. Caught up as we are in the concerns and illusions of the surface consciousness, we find ourselves far from the clear awareness of the inner levels of mind.

As in the guidebooks to Shambhala, a great distance separates us from the inner kingdom hidden deep in our minds. Although our interpretation of Shambhala may have given us a glimpse of these deeper levels of mind—or at least some idea of them—it tells us almost nothing about the mysterious reaches of the unconscious that we must cross to awaken them. For that we must turn to stories and guidebooks that describe the way to Shambhala. Through their symbolism we may be able to get some valuable insights into the nature of the inner journey that leads from the surface consciousness to the hidden sanctuary of the innermost mind.

7

The Journey

Tibetans believe that there are various ways of going to Shambhala. Many of them think that the only way open today, however, is through death and rebirth. They feel that it is no longer possible to develop the superhuman powers needed to follow the guidebooks to Shambhala: All a person can do in these degenerate times is pray and hope to be reborn there in some future reincarnation. Despite the prevalence of this belief, a number of Tibetans still believe in the possibility of reaching the kingdom in this very lifetime. In support of their position, they cite stories of people who are supposed to have actually taken the journey to Shambhala. Some of these stories tell of yogis or lamas with exceptional powers who claim to have traveled to the kingdom in their physical bodies. Others speak of spiritual or mental journeys taken without the body in meditation. We also find a number of accounts of people who are supposed to have visited the kingdom in their dreams. In this chapter we will examine stories of all three kinds of journey to Shambhala: physical, mental or spiritual, and dream.

Before proceeding, we should note, however, that Tibetans tend to regard death and rebirth as a fourth kind of journey, which can also lead to Shambhala. According to Tibetan Buddhism, when a person dies, his consciousness leaves the body and begins to wander through a visionary landscape of the after-death state. If he can realize the empty nature of everything he meets, recognize the lights, deities, and demons he sees as products of his own mind, he will attain enlightenment. If, on the other hand, he takes these visions to be real and flees from them in terror, he will eventually seek refuge in the safety of a comforting womb and wind up born in a miserable state of existence. Lamas read the *Bardo Thodol* or *Tibetan Book of the Dead* over a dead person's body to guide his consciousness away from these pitfalls, toward enlightenment—or at least to a good rebirth in a Pure Land such as Shambhala.[1]

In the following story, told by Dudjom Rimpoche, we can see death and rebirth clearly treated as a means of taking the journey to the mystical kingdom. A man in Lhasa, who was very loyal and devoted to his guru, once asked him, "Is it possible for me to go to Shambhala?" In answer the holy man gave him his blessings and told him to meditate in a certain way for several weeks. "If you do this," he said, "you will certainly reach Shambhala." So the disciple went off and conscientiously did the meditation exactly as he was told. And at the end of the week in which he was supposed to attain his aim, he died and was reborn in Shambhala.

On first hearing, the story may sound a bit cruel or capricious, as if the guru had played a dirty trick on his unsuspecting disciple. Most Tibetans, however, would not view it this way; after all, the disciple gets his wish to go to Shambhala and a new life that assures him an excellent opportunity to attain the highest good of all—enlightenment. In addition, the story itself suggests that the guru may have given his disciple an advanced kind of Tibetan meditation that is supposed to enable a dying yogi to transfer his consciousness to a Pure Land such as Shambhala. According to tantric texts, if practiced too much beforehand, this meditation can weaken the body and cause premature death.[2] It sounds as if the disciple may have used such a practice as a means of deliberately inducing his own death in order to go to Shambhala.

The story offers an important insight into the nature of the other kinds of journey to Shambhala. It suggests that whichever way one tries to go, one can only reach the kingdom by undergoing some kind of death and rebirth. The ordinary self or ego that one feels oneself to be simply does not have the power or purity needed to make the journey; it must die and give way to something deeper and more powerful. Although the story speaks of a physical death, it also hints of another kind, which can take place in this very life. For it to happen, one must relinquish the cherished beliefs and attachments that maintain the ego and give it a sense of concrete existence—a painful experience that can feel like death itself, as if one's guts were being ripped out of one's body. When one undergoes this experience and dies to one's old self, the deeper levels of mind come to life: A new person capable of making the journey to Shambhala is born.

Among the ways of going to Shambhala in this lifetime, Tibetans consider the physical journey the least likely. The few who believe it possible insist that the guidebooks were written for it; otherwise, they would have no meaning. Others agree that the texts speak of a physical journey but argue that they are meant for use in the future when yogis with the power to follow their directions will appear. According to the Dalai Lama, most people cannot even read the guidebooks properly, much less recognize the features they describe. Too many illusions muddle their thinking and cloud their vision. In any case, the physical journey to Shambhala requires more than a clear eye and a fit body; one must also possess the spiritual powers needed to carry one over the supernatural obstacles that block the way. As Kunga Hochotsang put it when questioned about the necessity of these powers, "It's like going to the moon: Suppose you try to go without your launching system?"

A yogi must meditate to develop the spiritual powers needed to take the physical journey to Shambhala. But he can also use the same means to go directly there without his body. In the secret autobiographies of yogis of the past, we can find records of mental journeys that some of them were supposed to have taken to Shambhala and other Pure Lands. Many Tibetans believe that

certain present-day lamas go there too when they withdraw into
their chambers to meditate in solitude: Who can tell from the
outside where their minds roam while their bodies sit in motionless silence? A lama might go to Shambhala by using paintings
and descriptions of the kingdom to visualize it until it seems as
real as the world around him. Then he could enter his visualization and experience himself in Shambhala. Depending on his degree of proficiency, he might see the kingdom fixed and solid or
wavering and changing like a mirage. Since this kind of practice
tends to awaken the deeper levels of mind, it could involve more
than mere imagination: The lama might conceivably gain the
clairvoyant power to see the kingdom itself, rather than just an
image of it.

Another, more difficult, way of going through meditation
would involve a practice of consciousness transference similar to
the one we noted in relation to the death journey. A yogi would
use this technique to separate his consciousness from his body
and send it instantaneously to Shambhala. In such a journey, his
mind would travel by itself or in a refined mental body capable
of passing through obstacles, as light passes through glass. On
reaching the kingdom, the yogi would see everything as it is,
without any wavering or distortion. Since ordinary people can
only separate their minds from their bodies when they die, the
method of consciousness transference involves an experience of
death—and a high degree of risk. If the yogi has not mastered
the practice, he may leave his body only to find that he cannot
return. Then, according to lamas, he will actually die and become a disembodied spirit condemned to wander in a hell of his
own devising.[8]

Although many lamas agree that yogis can go to Shambhala
mentally, they disagree over whether this kind of journey is easier or more difficult than the physical. Some believe that the
mind, being light and insubstantial, needs little energy to reach
the kingdom, but to travel there in a heavy body requires much
more power, which can only come from a higher level of spiritual development. Others maintain, however, that only a yogi
who has reached a very advanced stage can take the elegant way

of meditation, while more ordinary people have to go physically, dragging their cumbersome bodies with them. According to Samdong Rimpoche, reaching Shambhala mentally means that one has released the innermost mind locked in the heart center. From this point of view, the mental journey is much more significant than the physical. If one has awakened the innermost mind, then one can go to Shambhala in the body at any time. But if one reaches the kingdom physically without opening the heart center, then one will still have to go there mentally—for the ultimate object of the journey to Shambhala is to release the innermost mind and attain enlightenment.

Tibetans also speak of dream journeys, which are sometimes difficult to distinguish from the visionary journeys of meditation. Most of the stories they tell about this kind of journey describe dreams that happen spontaneously: Without trying to go or even thinking of it, a person has a dream in which he finds himself traveling to Shambhala, where he receives something of great value, usually a teaching or a prophecy. In some cases he may have the same dream on a number of different nights, suggesting that a deeper level of mind is trying to communicate with the surface consciousness. As we shall see, some lamas believe that certain dreamers actually travel to Shambhala in a refined body similar to the one used by yogis in meditation.

Although most of these journeys are supposed to happen spontaneously, a yogi might also try to go deliberately by practicing a special dream yoga. In this kind of meditation, the practitioner trains himself to recognize his dreams and stay in them, remaining aware that he is dreaming. Then, while in this state, he makes various things appear and transforms his body into different forms—animals, objects, people, deities. A text dealing with this yoga suggests how a yogi might use it to travel to Shambhala in his dreams:

> Visualize oneself as becoming the tutelary deity, and instantaneously, like a shooting star, arrive in the Heaven of Indra, or some other heaven; observe the place before returning. When this is stabilized, one should then journey to one of the Buddha's Pure Lands, such as the Pure Land of Vairocana, of Amitabha, or the

like. This, too, is done in a split second. Reaching the Pure Land, he should make obeisance and offerings to the Buddha and listen to his teaching. . . .[4]

Of the three ways of going to Shambhala in this lifetime, the dream journey has the best chance of happening first. While dreaming, a person can experience and accept as real what his waking consciousness rejects as fantasy. When he falls asleep, the fixed ideas he holds of what is possible and impossible loosen and slip away, permitting the deeper levels of mind to emerge and carry him off to Shambhala. In some of the guidebooks to Shambhala, the traveler has to have a dream of going there before he can actually set out for the hidden kingdom. The dream journey establishes the initial contact with the deeper levels of mind symbolized by Shambhala, but it lacks the precision and reliability of the physical and mental journeys. According to Samdong Rimpoche, such dreams come from the subconscious and are contaminated and colored by its preconceptions.

Turning to the stories themselves, we find that the earliest— and for Tibetans the most important—describe the journeys of Indian yogi-scholars in search of the Kalacakra. In Chapter 1 we looked at the story of Tsilupa, the first to bring the teaching back from Shambhala. As we saw in that story, Tsilupa did not go all the way to the hidden kingdom. Partway there, on top of a mountain, he met a monk who turned out to be the King of Shambhala in disguise. After warning him about the difficulty of going on, the monk gave him the basic Kalacakra teachings and sent him back to India.

Some Tibetans use this story to prove that one can go to Shambhala only by dying and being reborn there. If a great yogi like Tsilupa could not reach the kingdom, they argue, how can anyone else? At a deeper level, however, the story suggests that with the proper dedication one can find what one seeks even if one does not go all the way to Shambhala. The essence of the kingdom, what it contains and symbolizes, lies hidden right in the journey itself. This reading of the story would go well with the Tibetan view that the path and the goal, enlightenment and the way to it, are in reality one.

Those who wish to refute the contention that one cannot go to Shambhala in the body can point to stories about Dushepa, the other Indian yogi-scholar to bring Kalacakra teachings back from the kingdom. According to these stories, after studying with one of Tsilupa's disciples, Dushepa realized that Tsilupa had failed to get a number of important texts. Anxious to study them, he prayed to an image of Tara, the Savioress, and she magically

Fig. 12 *Dushepa, the second Indian yogi-scholar to seek the Kalacakra from Shambhala.*

spoke to him, telling him how to take the journey and predicting that he would reach Shambhala. Following Tsilupa's route, he came to a mountain and met a stranger dressed in white, who asked him where he was going. When Dushepa told him of his quest, the man—who was the King of Shambhala and an incarnation of Avalokiteshvara, the Bodhisattva of Compassion—said, "Even if you travel this way for a whole lifetime, you will never get to Shambhala. Let me give you some of the teachings here." Practicing the meditation that the stranger taught him, Dushepa gained the magic power of flight and was able to fly over the snow mountains to Shambhala. When he arrived there at the great mandala in the grove of Malaya, the King met him again and gave him the rest of the Kalacakra teachings, including the commentaries composed by the first ruler, Sucandra. Then Dushepa flew back to India and recited all the texts to a vast assembly of yogis and scholars.[5]

In later stories travelers often return from Shambhala with souvenirs such as fruit or flowers. According to one story of this kind, about four hundred years ago there was an abbot of Litang Monastery in eastern Tibet who had two disciples who looked after him with great care and devotion. One of them, a cook, noticed that every night the abbot would quietly saddle up his horse and ride off to a mysterious destination. Aha, he thought, the lama must be sneaking off to see some woman. In order to find out where the old man was going, he hid one night in the stable. After a while, the abbot appeared with a saddle and put it on the horse. Thinking that he could simply trot along after it, the cook took hold of the horse's tail, but suddenly the horse leaped up and soared into the air, pulling him along with it. Frightened to death but having no choice, he hung on and flew through the sky with the wind blowing against his face. After a long flight the horse finally landed in front of a palace that the abbot entered, leaving his astonished disciple, whom he had not noticed, outside. At that moment a tall, fierce-looking man spotted the cook and demanded to know where he had come from and how he had gotten there. When the cook told him what had happened, the stranger said, "Ah, you are extremely lucky!"

After telling him that he was a guardian deity of the country, he gave him a fruit shaped like a mango. The cook put it in his pocket and waited for the abbot to return. Then, once again, the cook hung onto the horse's tail, and they flew back to the monastery, where the abbot took off the saddle and retired to his quarters, still not having seen his disciple. The next day the cook put the mango-shaped fruit on a plate and served it to his master. "How did you get this?" the abbot asked in surprise. After the cook told him, he nodded and said, "You are indeed lucky; the country we went to was Shambhala."[6]

The story presents us with two important symbolic motifs: the horse that magically takes the traveler to Shambhala, and the special fruit that he brings back from the kingdom. In the rituals and stories of Central Asian shamanism, which has a number of links with Tibetan Buddhism, shamans commonly use horses to take their mystical flights from this world to the supernatural realm of the heavens. The flight on horseback clearly symbolizes the leap of transcendence that a shaman or mystic makes to other, heightened states of awareness.[7] The horse itself embodies the inner power that enables him to transcend his usual state of consciousness and awaken the deeper levels of mind, if only for an instant. As for the other motif of our story, Buddhist texts often use the word "fruit" as a technical term for the fruits or results of spiritual practice. These may include magic powers, wisdom, bliss, or even enlightenment itself. The mango-shaped fruit brought back by the cook symbolizes the insights and other attainments that a mystic can bring back to the world of everyday life from his forays into the deeper levels of the mind.

The fruit brought back from journeys to Shambhala can take on various forms, ranging from food for the stomach to food for thought. One of the more interesting forms appears in the following story about Samden Lodu, a former abbot of Derge Gomchen Monastery in eastern Tibet. According to accounts of his autobiography, he had seven recurring dreams in which he went to Shambhala and received directions for a physical journey that he was supposed to have taken later. During one of his dream journeys, he heard the inhabitants of the kingdom singing a melody, which he managed to remember after he woke up. Taking an offering prayer, he set it to this melody and taught it to the monks of his monastery. They in turn made it into a tradition and passed it down through the years. A Tibetan lama in Sikkim, Kunga Hochotsang, recorded some old refugee monks from Derge Gomchen singing the prayer and played the tape for me. The melody rises and falls in long wavering notes that sound as if they were drawn out of the very depths of the body and mind.

In Tibet, stories about the journey to Shambhala had a popular as well as an esoteric appeal. Large crowds used to gather around lama manis, wandering minstrels of art, to watch them trace the way to the hidden kingdom on paintings they would unroll and display at festivals. According to Kalsang Namgyal's account of one such performance that he witnessed as a child in Lhasa, the storyteller started at the bottom of the painting and worked a pointer stick up through a landscape of mountains and valleys dotted with villages and temples. After describing the various obstacles along the way, he pointed to a snow mountain with a staircase rising into the clouds. That, according to the lama mani, was the doorway to Shambhala: As soon as a traveler passed over it, his body would become light as an insect. Cleansed of his sins, he would be able to walk on clouds, as if on cotton wool, and continue on toward the idyllic kingdom, hidden somewhere above the painting. As we can see, both he and the crowd evidently regarded Shambhala as some kind of heaven beyond the clouds.

The journey to Shambhala also provided a popular theme for parables with obvious morals. In a typical example of this kind of story, two Tibetans who wished to go to the kingdom asked the Panchen Lama for his permission and help. Raising his arm, he showed them a vision of Shambhala under his armpit and gave them directions and blessings for the journey. Somewhere along the way, after many days of difficult travel, they ran into a group of nomads who offered them gifts of money and gold. One of the travelers declined, saying, "No, these are worldly goods; we can't take them with us." But the other saw no harm in the offer and said, "Why not? We may need them." He took the gifts, but the gold became such a heavy burden that he got bogged down and could not go on. His friend, who had turned down the offer, however, went all the way to Shambhala and attained enlightenment.[8]

We have here a classic example of one of the basic choices confronting a person on the spiritual quest: whether or not to renounce worldly possessions for the sake of attaining the ultimate goal. At a deeper level the treasures offered by the nomads symbolize the desires and attachments that the seeker must abandon. Having built up over the past, they weigh him down like a load of gold, keeping him bound in his present state of illusion. A similar choice confronts the traveler in the guidebooks to Shambhala when he comes to lands of wealth and comfort such as Kashmir. Until he reaches an advanced enough level of spiritual development, he must leave such temptations behind and travel lightly on. In a similar way, the herder or hunter of the hidden-valley stories can only enter one of the valleys alone, without the burden of family or possessions.

Another story of this sort highlights the need for faith and dedication, even in the face of death. Two friends wanted to go to Shambhala and went to see the Dalai Lama, who sent them on to the Panchen Lama. "You seem to be ready," said the Panchen Lama, and gave them a sealed note to take to a butcher in Lhasa. On receiving the letter, the butcher opened it and read its contents. "All right, if you're ready to go, lie down there," he said, pointing to a wooden board used for cutting meat. One of the two friends lay down and the butcher chopped off his head. Then he turned to the other and said, "Okay, you're next." But the second friend cringed against a wall and refused to come forward. At that point the butcher said, "Look!" and showed him a vision under his armpit of the first friend on his way to Shambhala, looking back for a glimpse of his companion. Shaking his head, the butcher added, "Because you lack sufficient faith, you cannot go to Shambhala."[9]

Since we see the first friend going to the kingdom, the story raises an interesting question as to whether he goes alive or in the after-death state. Does the butcher really chop off his head, or does he only create the illusion of having done so to test the other friend's faith? Or does he actually kill the first one but then bring him back to life? Tibetan stories of teachers using such means to test their disciples make all these alternatives possible. Our story does not resolve the question, but the ambiguity it leaves in place of an answer serves an important function: It reminds the listener that life and death are both illusory and that ultimately there is no distinction between the two. According to the Buddhist doctrine of impermanence, since we are constantly changing, at every moment we are dying and being reborn. In addition to this idea, the story points to the death and rebirth experience we looked at earlier and the need for some kind of faith or trust to undergo it.

So far we have looked at secondhand stories of people, both historical and fictional, who were supposed to have taken the journey to Shambhala. I was, however, fortunate enough to meet a lama who had himself had a dream of going to the hidden kingdom. At the time of our meeting, in the fall of 1975, Garje Khamtul Rimpoche was working at the Council of Religious and Cultural Affairs of the Dalai Lama in Dharamsala, India. Although an incarnate lama of the Nyingmapa sect, he no longer wore robes and drew little attention to himself. I was immediately impressed by his friendly, open manner. I had already met with him several times and had planned to leave the previous day when I decided to see him once more on the chance he might have another journey story to tell. When I made my request, he thought for a moment, jotted down some notes, and asked me to turn on the tape recorder. This is the dream he told:

> In the year of the earth mouse (1948), at the age of twenty-one, I was told by Jamyang Kenze Wangpo to go to Potang Ngatse and recite the Guru Rimpoche mantra four hundred thousand times. So I went there and stayed about five months in retreat. Then I started back. Two days' journey from there I stopped at a sacred mountain.
>
> That night, sometime after midnight, my thoughts became unusual. Slowly they became purified, and then there appeared before me a land I had never seen before. A girl appeared too

and now, if I think about it, she looked almost like a girl from the Punjab here in India. She wore narrow pants of many colors and a narrow shirt; a long piece of brocade was draped around her shoulders. She said, "Don't sleep. Wake up and come: Your lama is calling you."

I was very surprised since I had never seen the girl before and she was wearing Chinese or Indian clothes. So I told her, "You look half Indian, half Tibetan. I don't know who you are, and I don't want to go with you."

She said, "Don't doubt me."

Then she spoke many beautiful words, but I can't remember them now. So I will tell you the gist of what she told me. She said, "You must discriminate between good and bad. If you don't, then you will always think that everything is bad. When the Buddha was in this world, his cousin Devadatta saw him as evil, but the Buddha himself possessed only good qualities. If Devadatta had seen his good qualities, he would have gotten faith. If someone has faith, then even a dog's skull turns into a holy relic. That's why you shouldn't doubt me and should come with me right away. Your lama sent me to you because you are the person with the right karma."

I replied, "You're an ordinary lady wearing only cotton clothing, nothing special. You don't impress me."

Then she showed me her hands and said, "Look." And there were two eyes in her hands, three eyes on her face, and two eyes on her feet. She asked, "What are these?"

I said, "That's not unusual. In the realm of desire there's a goddess with nine eyes and three heads."

She said, "Don't have bad faith. I am Phagma Chendunma, The Noble One with Seven Eyes."

Then my thoughts changed: Maybe this is Phagma Chendunma and my impressions are all wrong. I said something to her, but just then she snapped her fingers, and at the same instant I felt my flesh body melt away, as if I had no body left but could still think. Then she took me in her hand and swallowed me.

Inside there was nothing but three nerve channels, one in the center of her body and the other two on either side. The two on the sides rose like pillars and came together in a point at her nose. I took a zigzag path into a nerve channel, and inside it was a lady exactly like the first one. She took me through the central channel up to the top of the head, where there was the crown center, the wheel of great bliss. It had many different nerve branches but I can't say exactly how many. In this center were the Primordial Buddha and many other Buddhas, some of whom I recognized and others I didn't. Also many lamas.

After that she took me down to the throat center, the place of the body of enjoyment. All the nerves there were square [in cross section] and there were many deities. Each one was half wrathful, half peaceful, and ornamented with jewels and bones.

Then we went to the heart center, where all the nerves were half-moon-shaped and interconnected. I could recognize three groups of deities, but there were many others I couldn't identify. Of course, this was a dream so I couldn't understand everything in it.

After that she took me to the navel center, where the nerves were triangular in shape. There were three deities I could recognize and many other, female ones.

Then we went down to the secret [sex] center, where there were four nerves of four different shapes, symbolizing the four activities. The outside ones were round. Inside them were half-moon nerves and inside the half-moon nerves, triangular nerves. And inside these were the male and female guardian deities who perform the four activities.

After that she went out through the sexual organ and I followed. When I came out, I felt very unusual, as if I had no body at all. My mind was comfortable, clear, and without thoughts. At the time it seemed as if I could go anywhere I wanted without walking, and the girl said, "We should go now."

I went with her through the sky. I saw many places, but not like this world. At that time I had no idea of maps, but afterward I wrote my dream down in a book that I lost, and in this book I drew a sort of map of what I saw very carefully and clearly. As we were flying, the girl pointed down and said, "That's India."

It didn't seem like India, but the shape of the land was pointed in the southern direction. She also showed me a land that she said was China. From the sky I couldn't see very clearly, but the countries seemed to have slightly different colors. China wasn't completely triangular but shaped more like a shoulder blade with the narrow, pointed end next to Tibet. Then I saw many smaller lands—Nepal, Japan, and others. I also saw Ceylon and she said, "That's Ceylon, which symbolizes the kingdom of Ravana. The mountain you see there is Ribo Malaya Namche Barwa."

We continued flying through the sky and saw many lands of a deep hue. Then we came to a country that was green with bits of white. Since she seemed to be my guide, I asked the girl, "Which land is this?"

She replied, "This is the land of Kangden, the place of snow, and the mountain there is called Ribo Kangden."

The white that I saw there was snow mountains. We continued on beyond this land to another that was completely yellow. "This is Dzambu Chu Ser," she said. "All the land and its mountains are made of gold."

After that we came to another land that was entirely red, and she told me, "All this land is made of rubies." I saw here and there blue mountains, and she added, "Those are made of emeralds and sapphires. All these lands are full of jewels."

Then I saw another land surrounded by snow mountains and filled with many towns. I cannot tell you their shapes, but there were many and in between them were lakes and rivers. From the sky each town looked almost like India in size. The girl said, "In the center of this land is your lama. I must take you there."

We went to the center, where there was a great lake, and I asked her how we should cross it. She replied, "There are three bridges—upper, middle, and lower. We have to go by the lower bridge. We can't go by the middle one or the upper one."

We continued in the direction of the lower bridge—I didn't know where the other two bridges were, only that she said they were there. There were many rocks, generally like rocks of Tibet, but there were also white and red ones, of many colors and shiny. They seemed to be made of jewels, gold, silver, coral, and other precious things. Then we came to a bridge shaped like bridges in Tibet, but it wasn't made of iron, wood, or woven grass, and I couldn't tell what it was made of. As we crossed over, I looked under it and saw water with waves. At the far end of the bridge was another girl with a vase in her hand, and she anointed me with the water that was in it.

Then my guide said, "We should go to the east side," and we went. There were many rocks and among them was a huge rock shaped like a door and I asked her, "What is this?"

She said, "This is for the future when barbarians take over the world and everyone is suffering. Then Rigden Dragpo [Rudra Cakrin], the great King of Shambhala, will come and open this door with his spear, and out of it will come many treasures, weapons, and soldiers. You should make a wishing prayer to this rock."

And I looked at it very carefully, and it was just a rock, but its nature was like the crystal that comes from very old mountains. On top of it the mantra *Om mani padme hum* was written several times in raised letters of white stone. The girl said, "This is an image of the voice of Avalokiteshvara, the Compassionate One."

In another place there were hand- and footprints, and she said, "Pray here, for these represent the liberation of sentient beings through the powers of sight, hearing, memory, and touch."

After I had prayed, we continued. Everywhere there were flowers of all kinds. One kind I haven't seen in Tibet but I have seen in India: It was a rose like a rose of our world—the same shape, petals, and color—but bigger than ours. Some of the flowers were still buds, some were beginning to open, and some were completely open. Most of them I had never seen before, and the biggest ones were big enough to wrap my arm around while some of the smaller ones were the size of a teacup.

We went on into a smooth meadow, and when we reached the south side of it, I saw a building that looked like a palace with a golden roof. Near the door was a gatekeeper; my guide asked him to open it and he did. From the outside the palace hadn't seemed very big, but now, as we went inside, it looked huge. Everywhere it was like turquoise. In some places there were springs and in other places sand. Deep inside and far away from us, I could see a blue horse not like an ordinary horse. It was very big and I asked the girl, "What horse is that?"

And she replied, "That is Tamchog Mahabala, the great strong one, most excellent of horses, and he is an emanation of Avalokiteshvara. Rigden Dragpo, the King of Shambhala, will be an incarnation of Manjushri, the Bodhisattva of Wisdom. In the future the barbarians will take over the world, and he, Rigden Dragpo, will destroy them. This horse is for him to ride at that time. The horse is an emanation of Buddhahood, and there are many stories of his past activities. Pray to him."

Plate 1 The kingdom of Shambhala. Rudra Cakrin, the future King of Shambhala, sits in his palace, surrounded by the eight petal-shaped regions with their towns and principalities. The figures along the top are, left to right: Amitabha Buddha, the Kalacakra deity and consort, the Medicine Buddha, and the Third Panchen Lama, author of the most popular guidebook to Shambhala.

Plate 2 The hidden valley of Khembalung. A view from the snowfields above the valley where Khembalung is supposed to be hidden.

Plate 3 Tengboche Monastery. The main temple of the monastery with Macherma Ri, about 20,000 feet high, in the background.

Plate 4 Rudra Cakrin, the future King of Shambhala, in the final battle against the barbarians. He rides a blue horse and thrusts a spear into the leader of the barbarians.

Plate 5 Sucandra, the first religious King of Shambhala. The Tibetan-style book to his right represents the Kalacakra teachings that he received from the Buddha in India and wrote down in Shambhala.

Plate 6 (*left*)
The Hermit Oleshe
in his hermitage in the
Himalayas.

Plate 7 (*right*)
Padma Sambhava.
This Indian yogi brought
Buddhism to Tibet and concealed
the hidden valley of Khembalung.

Plate 8 Tulshi Rimpoche reading from his guidebook to Khembalung.

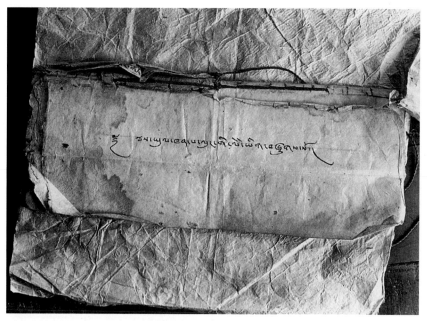

Plate 9 The title page of Tulshi Rimpoche's guidebook to Khembalung. It reads: "Here is the description of the way to the hidden country of Khembalung."

Plate 10 Kangtega, the horse-saddle snow mountain on the way to Khembalung. The peak is 22,240 feet high.

Plate 11 Takmaru, the red rock with the key to Khembalung. The crack slanting across the rock is supposed to be slowly opening. Mount Taweche, 21,463 feet, is in the background.

Plate 12 (*above*)
Snow mountains above Khembalung.
View from the second-to-last pass
on the way to the hidden valley.
The mountains rise to over 22,000 feet.

Plate 13 (*right*)
Peach Blossom River.
At the bottom of the painting, the fisherman
of the Chinese poem is entering the
hidden country of Peach Blossom River.

Plate 14 Olmolungring, the Bon equivalent of Shambhala. A square of snow peaks surrounds the kingdom. At the center rises the nine-stage mountain symbolizing the nine ways of the Bon religion. The inscription at the bottom gives various names for Olmolungring, including that of Shambhala.

Plate 15 Kalki, the future incarnation of Vishnu. The Hindu equivalent of the future King of Shambhala stands beside his winged horse, ready to put an end to the age of discord.

Plate 16 The palace of the Immortals. Chinese Immortals gather in the Kunlun Mountains beneath the palace of Hsi Wang Mu, which appears in the clouds of the upper left corner.

Plate 17 The Kalacakra deity with consort. The tutelary deity stands in the center, surrounded by Buddhas, Bodhisattvas, and guardian deities.

Plate 18 The Kalacakra mandala. The three squares within each other represent three walls or levels of the Kalacakra deity's palace.

Plate 19 Garje Khamtul Rimpoche. This is the lama who had the dream of going to Shambhala.

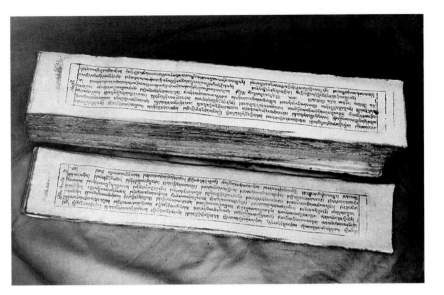

Plate 20 (above)
A guidebook to Shambhala.
The *Tengyur* text translated
into Tibetan by Tarantha. The
guidebook begins on the upper
page and continues through the
lower stack of pages.

Plate 21 (left)
White Tara, the Savioress.
The form of the female
Bodhisattva who guided
Khamtul Rimpoche in his
dream of going to Shambhala.
Note the eyes in her palms
and soles of her feet, making
seven in all.

Plate 22 Vajrabhairava, a form of Yamantaka, Conqueror of the Lord of Death. He embraces his consort and tramples down demons who symbolize the illusions of the ego. Around him appear a number of lamas and a sage, a Mongolian king, and various guardian and tutelary deities, lower left, Yama, the Lord of Death.

Plate 23 (left)
Manjushri, the Bodhisattva of Wisdom. The sword in his right hand symbolizes the transcendent wisdom that cuts through the illusions of ignorance.

Plate 24 (right)
Avalokiteshvara, the Bodhisattva of Compassion. His right and left hands hold a rosary and a lotus, his middle hands a jewel.

Plate 25 The Buddha preaching the Kalacakra. Above him appears the spire of the stupa of Dhanyakataka in India. In the lower left corner King Sucandra of Shambhala requests the teaching with hands folded above his head.

After I had prayed, we went on to the west side, and she said, "Now here is your lama."

I saw a palace there and this is how it appeared to me, although I can't say exactly what shape and color it had. It looked more or less like a monastery of our country with a big courtyard like the ones we use for religious debates. There were steps made of black and white marble, which I climbed. When I reached the top, I could see all kinds of ornaments. I went inside the palace, and there was a great hall exactly like the main hall of one of our monasteries. At the far end was a shrine room, and in the middle was a golden throne resting on eight lions, as is usual in our country. On this throne sat a lama I had never seen before. The color of his skin was brown and he looked somewhat old. He held a rosary in his hand and was reciting, *Om mani padme hum.*

The girl said, "This is your lama."

But I thought, What is this? My real lamas are three others, and he is not any one of them. Who could he be?

The girl said, "Don't hold a wrong view. This is your true lama, the one linked to you by karma."

But because I didn't know him, I didn't do prostrations to him. Then the lama melted and turned into Avalokiteshvara with four hands. The two middle hands were folded in prayer with a jewel between them. Of the other two hands, the right one was holding a crystal rosary and the left a lotus. He had the form of the usual Avalokiteshvara that we visualize with the ornaments of the complete body of enjoyment. Then faith came over me, and I prostrated myself and prayed to him.

This Avalokiteshvara said to me, "Stay there." And then, with great care, he gave me many teachings and much advice.

When he was through, I said to him, "I'm very lucky to be here in what must be a holy land. May I stay here and continue to get teachings from you? Don't send me back to the world."

Avalokiteshvara replied, "The time for you to stay has not yet come: You must return. I have given you all this counsel so that you can go back to the world and tell it to others. Also, you need to look after your monastery. This is almost the time of the end, but even so, you must go back."

He gave me many other reasons for returning. Then I said to

him, "Since I have to go back, please give me more advice and tell me what I should do in the future."

Then he told me in a kind of poetry what will happen in the three regions of Tibet. What he said took me thirty or forty pages to write down later, after I woke up. At the end he blessed me with his hands on top of my head and said, "Now go around and see this land—and then you must return. After you get back, recite *Om mani padme hum* one hundred million times. If you do this, your life and practice will be fulfilled. Then, when you are sixty or seventy, you will be reborn here. Pray for that, and I will pray for it too."

Then I asked him, "Where is this land?"

And he said, "This is Shambhala. All that I have told you here, you must remember. Do not forget any of it."

Then the girl led me back to this world by the way we had come. At the end I felt as if I were absorbed back into my flesh body, and at that instant I woke up.

The next day I could remember all of the dream very clearly. I stayed in that place for one or two days and wrote it all down in a book without leaving anything out. In this book there is a prophecy that says, "When you are thirty years old, you will no longer be able to stay in your monastery and you will have to leave. At that time you must do a special kind of religious practice." So the reason I didn't stay when the Chinese came and was able to escape from Tibet was because of this prophecy. I came from my country, which is very far from here, past the weapons of many soldiers. That was simply because I believed in this that I only dreamed but never experienced in my body of flesh.

There are many people in Rajapur and at the refugee camp at Kato who saw my book—which I had to leave behind in Tibet. If you ask them, they will remember what it said. In Kato there is a man called Tsenor: He definitely saw the book and knows.

This book tells completely what will happen in our country and how the Chinese will come and how, in the future, the Shambhala war will happen.

What I have told you is only how I dreamed and how I got my connection with Rigden Dragpo by dream. . . .[10]

As Khamtul Rimpoche's account makes vividly clear, this was no ordinary dream. According to Chophel Namgyal, who translated it with me, it belongs to a very rare class of "pure visions" that sometimes appear to yogis who have practiced a great deal of meditation. Unlike most dreams, which tend to be murky and confused, it displays an incredible degree of clarity and cohesion. For the most part it lacks the usual idiosyncratic features that pertain only to the dreamer's own life and have meaning for him alone. As we shall see, everything in Khamtul's dream, no matter how bizarre it might first appear, fits together and makes sense to those who are familiar with the symbols and practices of Tibetan Buddhism.

Khamtul himself identified the first feature of his dream, the girl who comes to lead him to Shambhala, as Tara, the Savioress. Her name, Phagma Chendunma or "The Noble One with Seven Eyes," gives away her identity: Tibetan art commonly depicts this female Bodhisattva with a third eye on her forehead and one eye on each of her hands and feet, making seven in all (see Plate 21). They symbolize the all-seeing compassion that prompts her to take pity on sentient beings and help them over the ocean of suffering to the far shore of Nirvana. Since according to legend she sprang from a tear shed by Avalokiteshvara, it is appropriate that she should be the one to take Khamtul to this Bodhisattva. As we saw in an earlier story, Tara was also supposed to have guided the Indian yogi-scholar Dushepa on his journey to Shambhala in search of the Kalacakra teachings.

The girl's remark about a dog's skull refers to a popular Tibetan story about an old woman who asked her son to bring her a sacred relic from India. When he was nearly home from his trip, he suddenly remembered her request, and not wishing to disappoint her, he broke a tooth off a dog's skull lying on the road and gave it to her, saying it had come from one of the Buddha's closest disciples. Overjoyed, the old woman reverently put it on her shrine and worshiped it with such devotion that it began to shine with a divine light and turned into an actual relic venerated by the entire community. Devadatta, the person mentioned by the girl as one who lacked such faith, hated his cousin, the Buddha, so much that he tried to kill him with a mad elephant.

The next episode of the dream, in which she swallows Kham-tul, may sound bizarre, but it makes use of well-established tan-tric symbolism. In being swallowed and then emerging from her sexual organ, Khamtul goes through an obvious death and re-birth experience connected with the initiations he evidently re-ceives in her psychic centers. He feels his body melt away and comes out like a new person with his mind "comfortable, clear, and without thoughts." We can recognize a precedent for this episode in the following passage from a text describing the life of Padma Sambhava, the Indian sage who brought Buddhism to Tibet:

> "Behold," said the goddess, "the deities. Now take the initia-tion." . . . Then she absorbed all the deities into her body. She transformed Padma into the syllable *hum.* . . . Then she swal-lowed the *hum,* and inside her stomach Padma received the secret Avalokiteshvara initiation. When the *hum* reached the lowest psychic center, she conferred upon him initiation of body, speech, and mind; and he was cleansed of all defilements and obscura-tions.[11]

As we can infer from this passage, Khamtul's guided tour of the psychic centers in Tara's body represents a series of initiations that purify his mind and give him the power and wisdom needed to reach Shambhala and receive his lama's teachings. The vari-ous deities he sees in each center appear in standard tantric visualizations of the psychic nervous system. A common Tibetan saying refers, in fact, to the body as the mandala abode of the Buddhas and tutelary deities. Since the nerves he sees in the var-ious centers have the shapes of the mythical continents sur-rounding Mount Meru—square, triangular, and so forth—they probably form part of a further visualization of the body as the universe itself.

The flight that follows evidently symbolizes a mystical leap of transcendence that takes Khamtul into new and unfamiliar realms of heightened awareness. He and his guide first pass over countries he knows with shapes that we can recognize. The "nar-row, pointed end" of China, for example, apparently refers to the

Chinese province of Sinkiang, which lies just north of Tibet. As the flight continues, Khamtul enters a region of mythical geography that seems to represent the passage into a transformed and magical perception of the world. The fabulous lands of gold and jewels that he sees appear in at least one of the guidebooks to Shambhala. Kangden, the country flecked with white, is a remote region of snows far to the north of India and Tibet. Ravana, whom the girl mentions earlier in connection with Ceylon, or Sri Lanka, is the well-known demon King of the Hindu epic the *Ramayana*.

The bridges that lead into the center of Shambhala obviously represent an important step of the journey. In the mythology of many cultures, such bridges often link earth to heaven, symbolizing the transition to a higher state of being. Here they seem to symbolize the final passage into the realm of the innermost mind. The water poured on Khamtul's head by the maiden at the far end of the bridge clearly represents an initiation that attests to the successful completion of this difficult passage. This conclusion is supported by the fact that his guide then takes him to the east side—the side by which an initiate enters a mandala. The three bridges themselves—upper, middle, and lower—may symbolize the Hinayana, Mahayana, and Vajrayana stages of Tibetan Buddhism. We can safely guess that Khamtul has to take the lowest one because he has not reached a stage advanced enough to make use of the other two, which he cannot even see.

The rock he comes to next, the one shaped like a door, has the primordial quality of the innermost mind. As Khamtul describes it, "Its nature was like the crystal that comes from very old mountains." The weapons and soldiers stored inside it represent the dormant powers of the innermost mind, which will eventually awaken to destroy the encroaching forces of illusion. The mantra written on the rock reveals that it embodies the essence of Avalokiteshvara, the Bodhisattva of Compassion. The flowers that grow nearby evidently symbolize the pure awareness that unfolds in the depths of the mind.

The blue horse that Khamtul spies in the distance has a special significance. We have already seen the important role that supernatural horses play in carrying people to Shambhala. The girl tells him that this one will carry Rigden Dragpo (Rudra Cakrin, the future King of Shambhala) in the final battle against the forces of evil. In fact, some Tibetan paintings of the subject actually show this King of Shambhala riding a horse of the same blue color (see Plate 4). In the dream the girl adds that the horse is an incarnation of Avalokiteshvara and an emanation of Buddhahood itself. As such, it symbolizes the compassionate energy and wisdom of the innermost mind, the realization of enlightenment that shatters all illusions. Its blue color shows it to be a manifestation of the Primordial Buddha, who embodies the ultimate nature of reality, vast and formless as the sky.

The old lama whom Khamtul meets at the end of the journey turns into one of the multi-armed forms of Avalokiteshvara (see Plate 24). The body of enjoyment that he assumes, complete with the ornaments of a King, refers to one of three basic bodies a Buddha or Bodhisattva is supposed to possess: a physical one seen by ordinary people, known as the body of transformation; an ethereal one visible only to advanced yogis, known as the body of enjoyment; and an absolute, formless body, known as the body of truth.[12] The old lama who first appears to Khamtul evidently represents Avalokiteshvara in a physical body of transformation. In tantric practices a yogi is supposed to regard his human teacher as a manifestation of his tutelary deity. So when the old lama reveals himself to be an embodiment of Avalokiteshvara, Khamtul finally realizes that the old lama represents the real essence of his three teachers back in Tibet.

According to Khamtul, the lama in the form of the Bodhisattva taught him the complete path of meditation on Avalokiteshvara, showing him the practices leading from the beginning stages to the final goal of complete enlightenment. The mantra that he was told to recite one hundred million times was meant to enable him to maintain contact with Avalokiteshvara and the power and wisdom he embodies. In the prophecy he gave him, in addition to personal matters, the lama showed Khamtul how the Khambas of eastern Tibet would mount an unsuccessful revolt against the Chinese occupation of their country and how the

Dalai Lama would flee to exile in India—events that actually happened about ten years later, in 1959. He also revealed that in the future Tibet would once again be free and explained how Mao Tse-tung had come to power through the actions and wishes of his previous lives.

Khamtul felt that he had actually gone to Shambhala but did not insist that others agree: "After all, it was only my dream, so why should other people believe in it?" In his opinion, his mind left his body, "like a second self," and flew with the girl to Shambhala. Other knowledgeable Tibetans who heard about the dream agreed that this was possible and had quite likely happened. Chophel Namgyal thought that the way Khamtul described losing his physical body and flying over various countries suggested that his mind had, in fact, traveled there in another, more refined body. From a Tibetan point of view, the description of his return—"at the end I felt as if I were absorbed back into my flesh body"—reinforces this interpretation of what took place.

For the symbolism to have appeared in the dream, however, Khamtul need not have actually gone to Shambhala. Ever since he was young, he had had a deep interest in the kingdom and had even seen a relic at Litang Monastery that was thought to be the fruit brought back in the story of the cook who went there hanging onto the horse's tail. He was familiar with texts describing Shambhala and had practiced visualizations involving the deities and psychic centers he saw in the dream. His teachers had also given him oral teachings on the subject, which may account for differences between his version of the kingdom and standard written descriptions of it. When he fell asleep—or slipped into a vision—his mind had all the material needed to produce the dream with all its incredible detail.

Whether or not he actually went to Shambhala, it seems evident that Khamtul did take a journey into the depths of his mind. There, far beneath the surface consciousness of his usual waking life, he found an inner source of wisdom and guidance in the person of the old lama who turned into Avalokiteshvara. The teachings that Khamtul received from this figure—an obvious embodiment of the innermost mind—became the basis of Khamtul's daily spiritual practice. The prophecies that the lama also gave Khamtul in his vision of the kingdom altered the course of his life: As a result of them, he left his monastery just in time to escape from Tibet to India. All these suggest that the symbolism of the journey to Shambhala might be able to help others find a similar source of inner wisdom and guidance that they could use in their own lives. With this in mind, having looked at various stories of the journey to the hidden kingdom, we will now turn to the guidebooks for their more complete descriptions of the way to Shambhala.

8

The Guidebooks

Ever since Indian yogi-scholars were supposed to have gone to the hidden kingdom in search of the Kalacakra, Tibetans have shown an interest in the journey to Shambhala. The possibility of reaching a mysterious country of Bodhisattvas where one might speedily attain enlightenment has always appealed to a few adventurous spirits. Over the centuries various lamas and mystics have composed a number of guidebooks to aid such people in their quests. Most of these authors brought together directions from older texts, but some drew on their own dreams and visions of the journey, and a few even described routes they claimed to have actually followed on foot. Unfortunately, many of the guidebooks they wrote have been misplaced and lost; Tibetans have tended to consult only the later works, which they found easier to understand, and to neglect the earlier ones, which contained archaic language. Since there were not many copies of the older texts to begin with—most of them having been hand-copied rather than printed from wood blocks—they were easily lost or left to molder away in dank corners.

In this chapter we will look at four guidebooks that have managed to survive. The first one, perhaps the oldest, appears as an anonymous fragment of a larger manuscript. It gives a brief, but fairly realistic, description of the route to Shambhala, which seems to provide the basis for the other guidebooks. The most popular and widely read guidebook, entitled *Shambhalai Lamyig* or *The Description of the Way to Shambhala*, was written in 1775 by the third Panchen Lama, Lobsang Palden Yeshe. When speaking about the journey to the hidden kingdom, Tibetans usually refer to this text, which has tended to supersede all others. It closely follows the route description of an older guidebook found in the *Tengyur*, the commentary section of the Tibetan Canon. The *Tengyur* text bears the title *Kalapar Jugpa* or *The Entrance to Kalapa*—the capital city and palace of the King of Shambhala—and was translated from Sanskrit into Tibetan in the seventeenth century by the lama-scholar Taranatha. The most beautiful and moving description of the journey appears, however, in *Rigpa Dzinpai Phonya* or *The Knowledge-bearing Messenger*, a long poem composed in the form of a letter by a sixteenth-century Tibetan prince named Rinpung Ngawang Jigdag.[1]

Lamas also speak of other guidebooks to Shambhala, but they are difficult to find and may no longer exist. In a Preface to his version of the journey, the Panchen Lama mentions a guidebook written by a certain Menlung Lama. According to the Panchen Lama's summary of it, it describes a route that leads from western Tibet northward through the region of the upper Hor and the Sog—probably Mongol and Uighur peoples of the Tarim Basin area. The journey to Shambhala is supposed to take two or three years along this route. The Panchen Lama points out, however, that Menlung Lama received the contents of his guidebook from a dream, which he himself regarded as a possible source of delusion.[2]

The Sakya Trizin mentioned to me that a yogi friend of his once told him about a guidebook written by a lama of the Nyingmapa sect. The author of that guidebook claimed to have gone to Shambhala on foot and wrote a very exact and detailed description of the route he followed. According to his version, the journey should take about three months, starting from Mount Kailas in western Tibet. The lama described the route as straightforward but warned that after his death, without his personal guidance, it would become difficult, if not impossible, to follow his directions. When I asked if we might be able to get the guidebook from the yogi who had told him about it, the Sakya Trizin replied that his friend had gone to meditate somewhere in the mountains of Bhutan and added, "He's the kind of person who doesn't have an address."

Among the guidebooks available to us, the one with an anonymous author is the shortest and simplest: It presents the basic outline of the journey with a minimum of magical embellishment. A German scholar, Berthold Laufer, found it imbedded in a larger manuscript and translated it into German around 1907. Since the surrounding text describes Peking and the imperial palace as they appeared during the reign of the Mongols who conquered China after Genghis Khan, Laufer concluded that the guidebook must date back at least to that time, the thirteenth century, if not earlier. The following section describes the journey to Shambhala:

> When one travels far to the north, where Queen Khom Khom lives, there are, so they say, beautiful forests and waters. From there, farther to the north, the kingdom of Li is the largest among the six countries found in that region. One has to travel on the great road that goes along the Iron Mountains for six days' journey. There is the River Sita, which flows from west to east and along which live the Hor. Generally they do not have houses but simply live in felt tents. The tents of the important people have two and even three roofs. For transportation they use camels; a group of 110 make up a caravan.
>
> At the foot of the southern side of the outer snow mountains surrounding Shambhala is a big city in which all the people, men as well as women, have sexual intercourse in the following manner: The penis is located on the inside of the right upper thigh muscle, while the female genital organs are located on the opposite side, on the left upper thigh. The fetus remains three months in the left upper thigh, and then the birth takes place, so they say.
>
> About the extent of the land of Shambhala, in the south it is about half the size of a small Jambudvipa [either an island conti-

nent or India]. On the north, however, it is a big country, Yo Sum, with the usual name of Shambhala. It is surrounded by snow mountains five hundred yojanas long. Three inner mountain ranges cut it into eight petals that have the form of a lotus so that the edges of the outer and the inner mountains touch each other.

In the southwest there is water and a road that is passable for people on foot. It is said that Sogpos, merchants, and newly wed women, as well as others, frequently travel back and forth along this road. In the east there is not only a river and birds, but also a pass, which has never been traveled by people, not even in ancient times.[8]

With the exception of the city of the hermaphrodites, the guidebook describes a routine Central Asian journey through fairly ordinary places that we can identify without too much trouble. The land of Queen Khom Khom apparently refers to "Kho Khom" or "Kho Bom," an old Tibetan name for Kathmandu, the capital of Nepal. As we saw in an earlier chapter, Li corresponds to the region around Khotan in the Tarim Basin. Because the Sita runs from west to east, Laufer identified it as the Tarim River. The Hor who live along its banks are probably nomads of Turkish origin, while the Sogpos who travel along the road leading into Shambhala are either Mongols or Sogdians from West Turkestan. The straightforward account of the journey makes it sound as if one could simply join a group of merchants and go to Shambhala in a camel caravan. A passage from the guidebook suggests that the author himself may have gone this way or else in a dream or vision: "Once, when the King gave religious teachings to many people, I, too, beheld his countenance and heard his words."[4]

The other guidebooks seem to have taken certain basic features of this text and incorporated them into much longer and more magical versions of the journey. As we shall see, they all describe routes that lead north across the River Sita and over a great wall of snow mountains to Shambhala. In one of them, the traveler must also pass through a city of hermaphrodites that lies on the edge of the kingdom. But in between these major landmarks, the longer guidebooks add burning deserts that no ordinary mortal can cross, forests filled with supernatural creatures, and mountains populated by gods and demons. This curious blend of realistic and fantastic features suggests that the authors of these texts may have overlaid the description of an actual journey with mythical symbolism intended to convey mystical insights. In any case, the journeys they describe require more than physical stamina and the money needed to pay for passage on a camel caravan: One needs the power and the vision that come from the practice of meditation.

The most widely read of these magical guidebooks, *Shambhalai Lamyig* by the third Panchen Lama, Lobsang Palden Yeshe, probably owes much of its enduring popularity to the stature of its author. Many Tibetans consider the Panchen Lamas to be spiritually higher than the Dalai Lamas, whose political supremacy they have sometimes challenged. After the Dalai Lama fled Tibet in 1959, for example, the Chinese temporarily set up the present Panchen Lama as the nominal Chief of State. In any case, Tibetans believe that the Panchen Lamas have a special connection with Shambhala that makes them unique authorities on the kingdom: An earlier incarnation of the line was supposed to have been Manjushrikirti, the King who unified the castes of Shambhala, and a future incarnation is supposed to be Rudra Cakrin, the King who will destroy the forces of evil. Lobsang Palden Yeshe himself took a deep interest in Shambhala and quizzed foreign visitors and travelers about places mentioned in texts describing the way to the hidden kingdom.

In 1775, at the request of some lamas he was visiting, Lobsang Palden Yeshe wrote his guidebook to Shambhala. The first part of the text deals with the general geography and history of Asia and India; the remaining sections focus on the journey to Shambhala and include a description of the kingdom itself, along with its history and prophecy. In writing his book, Lobsang Palden Yeshe drew material together from various texts of the Kalacakra Tantra and from commentaries composed by various lamas. By his own admission, his description of the journey itself closely follows that of the guidebook he considered the best—the one found in the *Tengyur* section of the Tibetan Canon. Since this older text uses ancient Sanskrit place names that are no longer in use, it becomes very difficult to identify most of the places mentioned along the way to the kingdom. Lobsang Palden Yeshe evidently preferred to have it this way: According to a more or less contemporary lama, he wanted to keep the route vague in order to keep the wrong kind of people from following it to Shambhala.[5]

Taranatha, a prominent lama-historian born in 1575, translated *Kalapar Jugpa*, the guidebook in the *Tengyur*, from a Sanskrit text he found in Nepal (see Plate 20). At the end of his translation, he mentions that a Brahmin scholar helped him, but he does not specify who composed the original or when. The guidebook takes the form of a dialogue among various sages and Bodhisattvas in a supernatural setting. One of them, a sage named Arya Amoghankusha, describes the journey to the others. Since the Buddha does not appear in this dialogue, as he usually does in early dialogues, the text could be a fairly late work, composed well after his death around 500 B.C. We can guess that it was probably written sometime after the Kalacakra teachings appeared in India in the tenth century, but there always remains the possibility that it dates back to an earlier period. Taranatha must have taken a personal interest in the contents of the text: His secret autobiography mentions a dream he had in which a small white boy led him to Shambhala, where he found the kingdom populated almost entirely by women.[6]

The Panchen Lama took his version of the journey straight from the *Tengyur* guidebook and paraphrased it in more contemporary Tibetan with only a few changes, the most important being the addition of the land of hermaphrodites on the edge of Shambhala. The two guidebooks differ much more in their descriptions of the kingdom itself, and the older text does not even mention the prophecy of the final battle and the golden age to come. Lobsang Palden Yeshe got his information on these subjects from other sources. Since the *Tengyur* text is closer to the original Sanskrit, we will look at a condensed translation of it and note where the Panchen Lama's guidebook deviates from it.[7]

After the usual invocations, the *Tengyur* text begins with the setting of the dialogue. Once Manjushri, the Bodhisattva of Wisdom, and Avalokiteshvara, the Bodhisattva of Compassion, were residing on a beautiful mountain with a vast host of Bodhisattvas, gods, men, and other beings. Hearing that they were there, five hundred sages came to request teachings for the degenerate times of the future when people would become so deluded that spiritual practices would lead them only to suffering. "Where in those times," they asked, "will one be able to find the true path to perfection?"

In reply, Avalokiteshvara told them of the city of Kalapa to the north, a place of wealth and happiness, where the true teaching would still be found. "Those who wish to go there without returning," he said, "in search of the great meaning, can go and obtain what they seek from the Master and sages of Shambhala."

Then the goddess Ekajati, the Bodhisattva who destroys all obstacles, said to Avalokiteshvara, "O Lord, in the future, in the degenerate times to come, there will be some who wish to seek enlightenment for the benefit of others. For their sake, to guide them away from those who are deluded, please explain the way to the city of Kalapa."

And the noble Amoghankusha, speaking for Avalokiteshvara, said:

> Listen to my words, you of the five hundred. Whoever wishes to go to Shambhala must enter the right path and practice meditation. He must have faith and the irresistible urge to attain enlightenment for the benefit of all beings. He also needs to have received an initiation into the mandala, to know the science of ritual, and to have embarked on the study of tantra. In addition, he should have a clear mind together with understanding and a truthful nature.
>
> One who has these qualifications must first meditate on his tutelary deity, and after a while Shambhala should appear to him, either in reality or else in a dream. If he has received this sign of permission from the deity, then he can set out on the journey to Kalapa. If he tries to go without such a sign, however, he will encounter great suffering, and all his efforts will

come to nothing. Those who attempt the journey without the necessary preparation and qualifications are like foolish children who try to reach the moon by climbing a pile of mud.

The seeker who has received permission in this way should recite the mantra of Manjushri eight hundred thousand times and make eighty thousand fire offerings of flowers. In order to overcome demons and evil spirits, he needs to recite the mantra of Amritakundali one hundred thousand times and offer more blossoms. In order to eradicate all hatred and aggression, he must chant the mantra of the Great Wrathful One, Yamantaka, the Conqueror of the Lord of Death. After making more fire offerings of flowers, he should prepare offering cakes for these Bodhisattvas and pray to them for the successful completion of his quest.

Whoever performs these rituals without sin or slander, doing them only to obtain the power needed to help others, will surely reach Shambhala. But if the rituals are disordered, or the person performing them has evil inclinations, then he will be attacked and punished by all manner of wrathful gods and demons. Those who are accomplished in the tantras do not need to use these methods: They can go more quickly and easily by means of mantras and energy meditation. But through the practice of these rituals, even people of little attainment can accomplish the impossible and go to Shambhala.

The seeker can now enter the path to Shambhala by making offerings at the bodhi tree in Bodhgaya, where all the Buddhas have attained enlightenment. From there he should go to the ocean that lies to the west and take a boat north to an island called Treasure Island. He must avoid the barbarian city on its western side and proceed directly to the town on the eastern side, where he will find the stupa of Kanakamuni, the Buddha of an earlier aeon. The seeker should circumambulate this relic mound five thousand times, all the while reciting the one-hundred-syllable mantra of the Buddhas.

After staying on the island six months, he should take a boat to the shores of western India. Many countries lie north of there, but they are not to be enjoyed: If the seeker ventures into them, he will lose himself in aimless wandering. Avoiding the wrong direction, he should go northeast. Then, going north to north, he will have to travel for six months past numerous cities until he reaches a great river named Satru and the snow mountains of

Kakari. He must cross these, but he will have nothing to fear as he goes: The people who live in the surrounding countries have a good and truthful nature.

Two kinds of medicinal herbs grow on the mountains there. One, called tujanaya, is very sweet and has sharp thorns, leaves like the teeth of a battle-ax, and red flowers the color of sunset. It always grows on rocks that face toward the south. The other, called tilaka, has a very bitter taste, milklike drops, and a white flower shaped like a buffalo's nipple. It hangs on the sides of ravines. The seeker should make a dagger out of the wood of a patali tree and use it to dig up the roots of these herbs, chanting the powerful Vajralanka mantra seven times. After drying the roots for seven days and reciting another mantra, he should put them in a rock cave.

Around that place there are minerals of five different colors— white, yellow, red, black, and green. After gathering and washing these minerals in snow water, the seeker should use them to paint a picture of Marici, Goddess of the Dawn, on a flat white stone. The figure should be orange with three red eyes and six arms. She has two faces: the right red and the left a black pig's face with an angry expression. She wears a blue-striped cloth over her shoulder and carries various things in her hands, such as a flower arrow and a skullcup. The boar she rides is trampling evils beneath its hooves. As he paints her image, the seeker must recite a mantra to her and make offerings of red flowers. This ritual is not for the person who engages in misconduct; it is only for one who has gained mastery over himself and developed the power of compassion.

Then the seeker should take the roots from the cave, grind them up, and boil the powder in the milk of wild cows who live in the snow mountains. The resulting potion should be placed in front of the picture of Marici. At the end of each recitation of the mantra he has been reciting, the seeker should add the words, "Provide drops of nectar." After repeating this a thousand times and receiving power, he can drink the potion. Then he should place the image so that it faces north and cover it with fruit and flowers. By doing so, he will gain immunity from hunger, thirst, and fatigue. The power of the goddess will enable him to overcome the obstacles that lie ahead.

He will then have to walk for twenty-one days to the north

across a desert without a trace of grass, trees, or water. Beyond that, the path runs through a great forest filled with poisonous snakes, tigers, and other dangerous animals. It will take him twelve days to cross it. On the far side rises an enormous mountain, a King of mountains called Gandhara. Winged lions live there, and every day they kill scores of magic creatures with bodies of changing shape.

Using the blood of one of these creatures slain by a lion, the seeker must draw a picture of the demoness named Mandeha on a slab of black rock. Red in color, she should look fierce with protruding fangs, a human skin wrapped around her loins, her left hand brandishing a sword, and her right holding up a cowhide filled with blood, flesh, and hearts. The seeker should place offerings of blood and flesh in front of the image he has drawn and visualize himself as Yamantaka, the Conqueror of the Lord of Death, riding on a buffalo. The recitation of that Bodhisattva's mantra will make the demoness come forth. When she appears, the seeker should offer her the flesh and immediately subjugate her with the power of the Great Wrathful One, Yamantaka. Then she will ask what he desires and he must reply, "O Demoness, since I wish to go to Kalapa to benefit all sentient beings and make them happy, provide food for me in these empty lands." After consenting to do so, she will vanish. Thereafter, every night when the seeker stops, at the foot of an arjuna tree, he will find delicious food of a white color with the taste of honey.

To the north lies a great snow mountain filled with ascetics, sages, and various kinds of demons. If he has developed the power to subdue others, the seeker should go and play with them, and after a while, they will put him on their shoulders and fly him straight to Kalapa. But if he lacks this power, he must not go there; he must hurry away along an obvious path that runs north in the direction of the wind.

From that snow mountain a great river rushes down to the east and west. As it reaches lower ground, it mixes with thousands of springs and slows down so much that it takes on the appearance of a motionless lake. On account of its white color, it is called the Sita or the "White." It flows for thousands of miles and empties into the seas of poison to the east and west. It is several miles wide, and its water is so icy that no fish, birds, nor crocodiles live in it—only hell beings. Indeed, it is so cold that it overpowers the touch of wind and snow and never freezes, not even in the middle of winter.

On the near side of the river is a copper-colored mountain with a thousand caves and many kinds of trees. A demoness named Flashing Lightning lives there. The seeker must perform the same kind of ritual for her as he did for the previous demoness. The image should show her gray, riding an elephant, and holding a pestle. It should be drawn with marijuana, roses, and the blood of wild bullocks and elephants, all of which should also be used for offerings. The seeker should visualize himself as Yamantaka with a body the color of black clouds, six legs, and twelve hands holding various weapons as well as a skullcup brimming with blood (see Plate 22). After he has recited the proper mantras, the demoness will appear, and he must ask her to show him the way across the river. Through her power she will cause the water to freeze into a sheet of ice strong enough for him to walk over it with ease.

On the far bank of the Sita is a forest of many different kinds of lovely trees. The seeker should rest there a month and eat the fruit and roots that grow in that place: They are very tasty and will make him strong. He should also recite the mantra of the goddess Cunda, this mantra having been blessed by seven million Buddhas. As a consequence, he will see black blood dripping from his limbs, either in reality or else in a dream. This means that his body has lost all sickness and has become very light and powerful.

The seeker should now gather as much of the golden fruit that grows there as he can find; no matter how much he carries, it will not weigh him down. Across the path that lies before him runs a range of small snow mountains. All the streams originating there flow south and are clear and good to drink, but beyond these mountains, for several hundred miles to the north, he will find nothing potable. Because of the golden fruit he has collected, however, he will not suffer from hunger nor thirst, and the new power and lightness of his body will enable him to cross that desolate plateau in only seven days. By the time he reaches the far side, no matter how much fruit he started with, it will all be gone. West of that region, visible from a great distance, rises a white mountain with beautiful forests, but the seeker must not go there: If he does, the inhabitants of the place, five hundred demonesses with copper lips, will do him great harm. He should take the straight path that leads to the north.

After a day's journey he will come to a mountain called Ketara, of a black and frightening appearance. It rises like an awesome pillar over a thousand miles high, and is filled with gold and silver. Four lakes of flowers surround the mountain, and beautiful birds with lovely voices float on their waters. Sometimes the Protector of the World, Virudhaka, Guardian King of the South, comes to Ketara to play. Many daughters of the gods and thousands of beautiful serpent maidens worship him there. While reciting the appropriate mantra, the seeker should make an offering of fish and meat and burn incense made from tree sap, herbs, and flesh. In this way he will propitiate the harmful demigods, goddesses, flesh eaters, hungry ghosts, and demons.

After that he can proceed north to a mountain called Menako, surrounded by a forest of sandalwood and other trees. There dwell the daughters of titans and serpent deities as well as the horse-faced daughters of demons.[8] They spend all their time in play, always singing, dancing, and making music. The seeker must not let himself be attracted to the maidens nor allow himself to enjoy their songs and music. He should simply take provisions and go on with his journey.

Beyond Menako he will come to the River Satvalotana, which flows from east to west with great turbulence and is extremely difficult to cross. It has fish of many colors with the faces of humans, tigers, lions, panthers, cows, monkeys, parrots, and other creatures. The branches of trees that grow on either bank reach over the water and intertwine. The seeker can cross the river by hanging from these branches or else with the help of the fish. If he goes the second way, he must gather rice and grains from the surrounding hills, and honey that drips from nearby trees. Mixing these ingredients together and cooking them, he should purify them with the mantra of the exalted treasure of space. Then he should pray to his tutelary deity and offer this food to the fish. Having recited another mantra, he should cry out, "O King of the Fish, I am going to Kalapa for the benefit and happiness of all sentient beings. Please help me over this river." After that the King of the Fish will appear and carry the seeker across the water.

Along the paths that lead north from the snows of Kakari to

this river, there are no human inhabitants—only nonhumans and ferocious demons. On either side, hundreds of miles to the east and west, are towns and cities, but if the seeker strays off in their direction, he will lose the way and never reach Kalapa, not even if he travels for a hundred years. The region just north of the River Sita is filled with snow mountains, but they will not block his path. Beyond them, on the far side of the river he has just crossed, lie the cities of northern Jambudvipa [either Asia or the world].[9] The people of these places are happy and prosperous and live without fear or sadness. There the seeker will find many countries graced with beautiful rivers, valleys, lakes, and forests. He will pass by magnificent palaces of Kings, and marketplaces filled with all kinds of goods and luxuries. But he must not pay attention to any of these things: They can only distract and hinder him in his quest. He must think of Kalapa and go on, across China, Great China, and the northern lands, always going north. He who has the power of mantras will not take more than six months to cross all the countries of these vast and far-off regions.

Along the way the seeker will pass many springs, some of them poisonous, that issue from mountains filled with heaps of gold, silver, copper, iron, and other metals. Trees and meadows and layers of earth and jewels cover these heaps and hide them from view. The water that comes from the mountains of gold causes death, the water from the mountains of silver drives men mad, and the water from the other mountains brings sickness and the loss of skin and hair. But the seeker with the power of mantras will find the waters of these springs beneficial to drink. The water of gold will grant him long life, the water of silver will give his skin a fresh and healthy complexion, and the remaining waters will cure him of whatever sickness he may still have.

Passing beyond these springs, the seeker will come to five mountains covered with lovely flowers, trees, and jewels. Fabulous beings, both male and female, live happily there, playing with beautiful objects.[10] They will sing enticing songs and make sweet music to seduce the seeker. If that fails, they will change into frightening forms and threaten him with terrifying sounds; or else they will produce various kinds of dismal smoke to make him sad and depressed. The seeker must not let himself become attracted, scared, or saddened. By remaining unmoved in the contemplation of emptiness, he can overcome these manifestations and go on. If he attempts to do otherwise, he will succumb to terrible suffering.

Having overcome these fears and temptations, he can now venture into the countries where the Vajra Dakinis, the skygoing goddesses, live in magic forms. He should neither be excited nor terrified by the sight of their beautiful and frightening bodies. They who possess the diamond eye are known to have virtue and compassion for all. Because he has abandoned his sins, the seeker will experience great happiness in that place. He should stay there and pray to the Vajra Dakinis for seven days. At the end of that time, they will ask him, "What do you need, O Seeker?" and he should reply, "Please take me quickly to Kalapa." Then, lifting him on her shoulders, one of these ladies of miraculous power will carry him for an hour through the sky over hundreds of miles of mountains piled deep with glaciers and snow. At the end of the flight, she will deposit him in a beautiful valley of medicinal herbs at the foot of Candrakala, a forested mountain on the edge of Shambhala.

A wrathful form of the goddess Ekajati, one with a single tuft of plaited hair, dwells in that place. The seeker should make fire offerings of flowers and pray to her for spiritual power and attainment. Then he should pick lotus blossoms of snow and recite her mantra five thousand times. By tying the flowers on top of his head, he will gain power over harmful demons and awaken the unimpeded wisdom that penetrates all things. Now he can proceed through the last few countries and forests that remain between him and his destination.

After going north for several hundred miles, he will reach a valley called Samsukha, where all the different kinds of trees found in the world grow together. From there he will go on through the Forest of Perpetual Happiness. And passing beyond that, he will come at last to the great city of Kalapa and enter the presence of the King of Shambhala.

After instructing the seeker on how to obtain teachings from the King, the last few pages of the guidebook describe the wonders of Shambhala. This description of the kingdom differs most strikingly from the Panchen Lama's in making no mention of any eight-petaled lotus shape. The *Tengyur* text does, however, say

that the country is round and that roads fan out from the center
to the eight points of the compass, where guardians are posted.
In his adaptation of the journey itself, the Panchen Lama makes
only a few slight changes, mostly in the way of minor additions.
For example, he identifies the great snow mountain with the
sages and demons who can fly the seeker directly to Kalapa as
the abode of one of the sixteen major disciples of the Buddha.
He also attempts to correlate the ancient place names of the
Tengyur text with places familiar to contemporary Tibetans.
When the seeker comes to the cold River Sita, the Panchen
Lama also adds the warning that if he touches the water, it will
turn him to stone. But his most significant addition, which makes
his version of the journey approach that of the anonymous thirteenth-century guidebook, occurs at the valley of Samsukha on
the edge of Shambhala. According to the Panchen Lama's text,
the same hermaphrodites described in the earlier work, the ones
with male and female genitals on either thigh, live there. As we
shall see, this adds something of importance to the symbolism of
the journey to Shambhala.

Now we turn to a guidebook of a somewhat different and
deeper nature—the poem by the Tibetan prince Rinpung
Ngawang Jigdag. Rinpungpa, as we shall call him, was the last of
a dynasty of ministers who ruled over much of Tibet during the
fifteenth and sixteenth centuries. Considered one of the finest poets of the Tibetan language and given the literary distinction of
being called "The Scholar-King," he was, unfortunately, not as
good at governing. He evidently spent too much time on poetry
and not enough on administration because in 1565, only eight
years after he composed his guide to Shambhala, he was over-
thrown by one of his governors. The poem vividly describes the
turmoil and corruption that tormented him in the years preceding
his downfall.

Rinpungpa composed *The Knowledge-bearing Messenger* in
1557 as a letter to his dead father, whom he believed to have
been reborn in Shambhala. In this missive he pours out all his
woes and asks for help and guidance in dealing with the problems that confront him. The part of the poem that concerns us

consists of the directions he gives to a visualized messenger for taking the letter to his father in Shambhala. Although Rinpungpa himself never claimed to have gone to the kingdom physically, he may well have had dreams or visions of taking the journey there. In any case, as a well-read poet and scholar, he was certainly familiar with Kalacakra texts that describe the way to Shambhala; however, since he wrote his poem at least forty years before Taranatha found and translated the guidebook in the *Tengyur*, he probably did not have access to that particular text. As we shall see, he, more than the authors of the other guidebooks, treated the journey to Shambhala as a metaphor for conveying mystical teachings. Although he was not officially recognized as an incarnate lama, Tibetans regard him as highly enlightened and take his writings as products of true insight rather than as mere fantasy.

The poem is written in a complex and ornate style derived from the Sanskrit poetry of India. It piles subordinate clause on subordinate clause and makes abundant use of lavish epithets and technical terms that even Tibetans have difficulty in recognizing. For this reason, rather than present a long and convoluted translation of the poem itself, I will condense and retell it in a form that reads more easily but still gives a taste of the original wording.[11]

The poem opens with an invocation of various deities of wisdom such as Manjushri and the Kalacakra. Then it goes on to praise Rinpungpa's father and lament his death. He has passed on to the peaceful land of Shambhala, leaving his son alone in the midst of troubles, feeling sad and helpless without him. Each day since his death has seemed like a year of unending misery. Life in this world of sorrows is vicious and unpredictable. Only the universal respect held for his father's name has enabled Rinpungpa to cope with the problems that beset him from all sides.

The thought has come to him that if he writes him a letter, his father may be able to respond and help him with the power of his great compassion. But how can he send the message to him in Shambhala? Standing on the roof of his palace, Rinpungpa looks up at the sky and sees the sun and the moon: Their light reaches Shambhala, but they cannot deliver the letter. He spies clouds passing lightly by and thinks, they can go there but they cannot carry my message. Various birds fly overhead, going north: He appeals to them to take the letter, but without success. No one else can deliver the message: In these degenerate times nobody has the miraculous powers needed to reach the kingdom, and the deities who might otherwise help are no longer available, having been driven away by the delusions that now fill the minds of most people. Going to Shambhala under these conditions is like trying to see a star at noon.

Suddenly a new idea occurs to Rinpungpa: to visualize a messenger, a kind of yogi endowed with the power and wisdom needed to make the journey, and to have him deliver the letter to his father.[12] Seeing him appear out of his own mind, he says to this yogi, whom he recognizes as himself, his companion of many lives:

> Take this message and go to my father in Shambhala. May my words of truth, conquering the mountains of dualism, guide you along the way and help you to overcome the obstacles that lie before you.
>
> Go first to the shrine of my father in the palace of Rinpung and pray for his blessings. Then go toward Shigatse, to the place of my tutelary deities, and ask them for help in the journey to Shambhala. After that you must travel across central Tibet, visiting shrines and monasteries along the way and seeking the audience of lamas who can bless you in your undertaking. Pay homage at the Monastery of Zalung Trubu to the great image of Maitreya, the Buddha to come. Stop also in the mountains of Nepal, at the holy shrine of Muktinath, and bathe there in the hot springs filled with scented flowers.
>
> Then turn to the north and west and take the high plateau to the sacred mountain of Kailas, where the knowledge holders dwell. To those who see them with uncommon sight, these sages appear as tutelary deities with their diamond consorts. There, in the place of golden caves, lives the Elder Angaja, one of the sixteen disciples of the Buddha, surrounded by a thousand saints.

If you listen carefully, you will hear, to the sound of bells and cymbals, the music of their enlightened teachings.

From Kailas continue northwest to Ladakh and go down through mountains and forest to the vale of Kashmir. There, scattered among green meadows, beautiful groves of saffron and sandalwood provide cool shade and fill the air with sweet scent. In that delightful place are over three million towns, all filled with houses made of jewels, surrounded by walls of crystal. Beside and between them you will find busy shops selling emeralds and rubies, coral and pearl, gold and silver. Crowds of happy people, dressed in white and singing songs, fill the streets like drifts of snow. Beautiful women with dark blue eyes and lovely breasts will send you seductive glances. Although they give nectar to the eye, they will burn the mind with the fires of passion: They are the flower arrows of the god of desire. Be careful and avoid attachments; remember your aim and go on.

Now the journey becomes more difficult. You will have to follow narrow paths that wind north through a maze of treacherous mountains. Many of these paths lead off into valleys from which the traveler can never return. If you take the wrong one, you will become hopelessly lost. But if you take heart and dedicate your efforts to the benefit of others, you will pass safely through and come out in the land of the Paksik, horsemen who wear white turbans and quilted robes filled with cotton. Although they have broad chests and look very fierce, they are quite friendly and will do you no harm. You will see much wealth in their possession, many jewels and other treasures.

Leave them behind and go north across the plains. After many days of travel, you will enter a deep forest with trees so tall that they touch the clouds. Because of that, everything below lies in utter darkness. Although you will have no light to see by, you must pass through the forest. On the far side of this dark and gloomy passage, you will come to a wild foaming river called the Sita.[13] Its splashing water makes such a great noise that it sounds like the wind that roars when the world comes to an end. Whatever its spray touches turns to stone. Beware. Taking hold of a tree branch, carefully pull it back, and let it fling you through the air so that you fly like a bird across the river.

On the far bank you will find yourself in a tranquil park where elephants play beneath a mountain lush with grass the bluish-green tint of a peacock's neck. Branches of sandalwood, moist with drops of dew, arch overhead like cobras to form canopies of cool shade. A delicious fruit of golden color, which smells of saffron, hangs from the trees, waiting to be plucked and eaten. Does have left milk for their fawns in leaves shaped like saucers, as if the gods themselves had set it out for you to drink. Stay there and rest a while.

Rest well, for many days of trying journey through a dark and terrible forest lie ahead. Packs of killer animals with eyes like sparks of fire and shaggy manes of bloody, matted fur roam the woods, drunk on their victims' fat and blood. All around, as you go, you will hear them growling and breaking bones with a horrible noise like the sound of axes chopping wood. Pieces of flesh and bone, still warm from recent kills, lie strewn along the path. From the darkness on either side, demons' eyes, red like copper, will spy on you as you pass. During the daytime witches appear there in human form but take on the shapes of lions and tigers by night. Like messengers from the Lord of Death, hordes of ghostly night travelers who feed on flesh will try to feed on yours. By directing a deep and inexhaustible compassion toward all these threatening monsters, you can subdue their rage to kill and pass safely through the forest.

After that you will come to a great body of water that looks as vast and boundless as the open sky. By luck born from your store of merit, a boat will be waiting to carry you across the water. The virtue of your past deeds will also cause a fair wind to spring up, and if you handle the boat with skill, it will blow you to the far shore, where you wish to go.

From there to the north, a barren desert devoid of water will stretch away before you like the desolate paths of suffering that run through this world of illusion. Glaring off sand, the relentless heat of the sun will roast you as if it were the fire of a furnace melting silver into drops of molten liquid. If you try to cool off by fanning yourself with branches of dried-out leaves, you will only succeed in searing your flesh with burning air. The mournful whistle of wind blowing through parched grass will make you sigh with sadness and despair. Remember your mystical knowledge and use it to rub your tonsils so that cool nectar drips out from the secret moon within you. If you know how to drink this stream of soothing liquid, your thirst and hunger will vanish, along with old age and death.

After the desert, which takes many days and nights to cross, you will have to pass over a range of lofty mountains. As you climb, a tremendous wind will hurl rough sand and bits of leaves and twigs against your face, cracking the skin and causing great pain. Again, use your knowledge to prepare the secret ointment that shields your flesh from the wind. This medicine is very powerful and will also clear your vision and brighten your eyes.

Beyond the mountains the path leads down into the fearful Copper Forest, the lair of great serpents with jaws the size of a house. They have copper eyes and awesome black bodies that loom like mountains. Six months of the year they sleep and then they wake to kill and eat. When they breathe, poisonous steam spews out a mile and more, and whatever it touches turns to dust. But if you prepare the right antidote, it will restore your body and allow you to pass through their deadly breath unharmed.

Then you will come to a high mountain with three pointed peaks. Sharp thorns and stones cover its slopes, making it impossible for anyone with ordinary footgear to cross it. Using your secret knowledge once again, you can make the soles of your feet as hard as copper plates and walk easily over this painful obstacle.

A few miles to the north rises another peak, called Incense Mountain. From a distance its green meadows and lush foliage make it look like a heap of luminous emeralds. Medicinal herbs and incense trees grow all over its gentle slopes, filling the air with a delightful scent. Numerous sages, powerful yogis, live on the mountain in jewel-like caves. They sit erect in constant meditation, gazing straight ahead with never a flicker of their deep blue eyes. Their skin is gold and a slight smile graces their lips. As soon as you see them, prostrate yourself in homage and give them offerings of beautiful flowers. Then ask for their aid and advice in reaching Shambhala. Since they are able to accomplish whatever they wish, they can protect you from the dangers of the path and help you to overcome the obstacles that lie ahead.

Before you lies a long journey through a dangerous region of red dust storms that shoot up like fire offerings into the sky. Thunder and lightning will strike all around you, bombarding the ground with deadly showers of diamond hail. At any moment flocks of shrieking eagles can drop out of the sky with claws extended to rip you to shreds. Demons with red eyes and beings who embody nameless fears lurk in ambush, waiting to feast on your flesh. But the power and teachings of the sages will ward off these threats to your life and permit you to follow the path that leads to the north, toward Shambhala.

After many days of harrowing travel, you will come out in a beautiful land of gold and jewels—the country of fabulous beings who are neither men nor gods.[14] Everywhere in that land there is fresh, clear water sparkling in lovely pools made of gems. You will also see houses built of precious stones, surrounded by walls of shining crystal; and in their gardens you will find wish-fulfilling trees that can grant whatever you desire. The fabulous maidens who dwell there, always happy and singing songs, have lovely moon faces, beautiful as lotus blossoms, with eyes like blue flowers. Sashes of fine cloth decorated with pearls adorn their golden bodies. Their graceful, jeweled limbs move like tree branches swaying in a gentle breeze.

As soon as the maidens see you, they will go wild with passion and swarm around you like excited bees craving honey. Smiling and looking at you out of the corners of their eyes so that it feels as if your minds merge in one, they will embrace you and wrap their seductive limbs around your body like vines around a tree. Why not take pleasure with these maidens who have attained the purity and spiritual power of enlightened dakinis? Taste the honey of their breasts, extended toward you like flowers offering you their nectar.

As you do, a great surge of joy and bliss will carry you soaring beyond all bodily sensation. The heat of an inner fire, like the fire that blazes on the southern edge of the universe, will rise through your body, burning away the thickets of mental obscurations. When it reaches the crown of your head, it will melt the mystic syllable *hum* into drops of liquid the color of a molten moon. A stream of silver nectar will cascade down into your psychic centers, causing their knots to loosen and open. As it spreads out through the thousands of nerves and channels that radiate from the centers, it will purify your body and transform it into the indestructible diamond body of bliss. In what other way can you so quickly attain it? Now that you have this marvelous body, you are certain to reach the Pure Land of Shambhala.

Now go on across the beautiful countries that lie ahead. Your path runs through idyllic towns that look like pieces of heaven dropped to earth. You will pass by mountains gleaming with the light of precious jewels and cross over rivers shining with masses of pearl-like bubbles. Go through all these lands with ease and joy in your heart.

Then you will come to the last great obstacle of the journey —a wall of mountains piled so high and deep with snow that not even the eagles can fly over it. Piercing the sky with their summits, the mountains rise like enormous demons threatening to block the way and destroy your hopes. Do not be dismayed but remember the compassionate omnipotence of the Buddha's mind and cast aside all doubts. Bring the clear light of awareness to bear on your fears and illusions so that they vanish like the mirages of darkness in the glow of a dust-free dawn. Then, to the music of golden ankle bells, the noble ones will lift you on their shoulders in a sedan chair of the gods and carry you like a load of cotton over the wall of snow mountains. Through their miraculous power you will float like an umbrella in the sky, putting even the eagles to shame.

After crossing the mountains, you will have to go through one last forest filled with snakes and wild animals, but if you show friendliness and compassion to whatever creatures you meet, you will have no trouble. Although you feel exhausted and sick from the rigors of the journey, hold onto your aim and continue to dedicate your efforts to the benefit of all beings.

Then you will see, at last, the cities of Shambhala, gleaming among ranges of snow mountains like stars on the waves of the Ocean of Milk. Flowers of light, the sight of them will remove all ignorance from your mind and leave you happy and refreshed, completely recovered from the hardships of your journey. Now you can drink and rest and enjoy the fruits of all your efforts. . . .

Compared to the other guidebooks, this one gives us a much more vivid and intimate picture of the journey to Shambhala. Rinpungpa manages to accomplish this by using striking imagery to focus our attention on the inner feelings and experiences of his yogi. We not only see the dangers and beauties of the journey, but we also feel the fear and delight they inspire. In addition, while the *Tengyur* guidebook focuses on the performance of external rituals, such as the painting of pictures to summon deities, Rinpungpa's poem delves deep into the inner experiences of meditation. In this regard, it seems to be written for the more advanced yogis mentioned in the *Tengyur* text, the ones who can go by another method that makes use of the power of mantras and psychic energy.

All three guidebooks we have examined in this chapter describe physical journeys that follow roughly the same general route to Shambhala. Along the way both the seeker of the *Tengyur* text and the yogi of Rinpungpa's poem also go through mental and spiritual transformations that amount to a kind of parallel inner journey. Each one overcomes his own weaknesses, acquires various powers, and attains a new body or higher stage along the path to enlightenment. By looking at the interplays among the places they pass through and what happens within their minds, we can read the guidebooks they follow not only as descriptions of physical journeys, but also as allegories for an inner journey to greater freedom and awareness. This we will do in the next chapter. According to Dudjom Rimpoche, the texts do describe actual journeys to be taken in the body, "but the most important thing in the guidebooks to Shambhala is the practice of mind."

9

The Inner Journey

If Shambhala symbolizes the end of a journey into the hidden
depths of the mind, India—or Tibet—represents its beginning in
the familiar realm of the surface consciousness. This in turn suggests that the vast expanse of intervening countries described in
the guidebooks to Shambhala symbolizes another part of the
mind, which we have not yet considered. So far, in looking beneath the surface consciousness, we have examined only the innermost mind and the deeper levels around it. But the unconscious, as we shall call all of the mind outside the range of
ordinary awareness, holds much more. It includes a vast and
mysterious region similar to the little-known lands between India
and Shambhala with all their demons and deities—a region filled
with deluded passions and sublime insights, repressed desires
and altruistic impulses, a confusing blend of the demonic and
the divine.

The unconscious consists, in fact, of two major parts, which we
shall call the superconscious and the subconscious. The superconscious is the pure region symbolized by Shambhala—the
realm of the innermost mind together with the deeper levels that
surround it. We use this term for it because it contains a clear
and purified awareness that can penetrate to the true nature of

things as they are. The great distance separating Shambhala from India and Tibet indicates that the superconscious is hidden deep in the mind, far from the illusions of the surface consciousness.

The subconscious, as its name suggests, lies just beneath the surface consciousness in the gap between it and the superconscious. We find the subconscious symbolized by the vast expanse of lands that lie between the beginning and the end of the journey to Shambhala. As we shall see in our interpretation of the guidebooks, the subconscious contains a mixture of different elements, some of which come from the superconscious and some of which come from the surface consciousness. The former provide bright rays of illuminating awareness, while the latter generate dark clouds of delusion. The surface consciousness unwittingly contributes its share to the subconscious by repressing those parts of itself—passions, fears, and so forth—that do not fit the ego, its symbol of itself. As a result, they become unconscious and mix with elements from the deeper levels of mind that are rising toward consciousness, trying to awaken. Because of this, when we dip beneath the surface consciousness, we find ourselves in a fluid region of shifting states of mind where things have a double-edged nature that can both help and hinder us in our quest for liberation.

Although repressed and out of sight, the alienated parts of the surface consciousness continue to function, often in warped and chaotic ways. Without control or direction, they can spread like cancerous growths through the subconscious, appropriating the energy of various elements of the deeper levels of mind that are there. In the process, they gain power over the rest of the surface consciousness, producing inexplicable quirks of thought and emotion. Unseen conflicts between repressed impulses struggling blindly against each other can break out in the form of bizarre and contradictory behavior, ranging from the symptoms of mild neurosis to those of severe psychosis. Although usually hidden from view, the contents of the subconscious occasionally pop up into awareness, only to vanish back into the depths from which they have come, leaving their startled possessor with the impression that they belong not to him but to someone totally alien.

In our examination of Khamtul Rimpoche's dream of going to Shambhala, we saw how its features embodied deeper parts of his mind that he found strange and unfamiliar. The girl who guided him, the countries he flew over, the bridge he crossed, the blue horse he saw, and the old lama he met all evidently symbolized various contents of the unconscious that lay outside his normal, waking consciousness. The dream revealed to him—and to us—his subconscious fears and hopes as well as his inner resources of power and wisdom. Now, if such a dream can use the features of the journey to Shambhala to reveal hidden aspects of the mind, it makes sense to suppose that the guidebooks can do the same. The Buddhist tradition behind these texts makes little distinction between what we see while awake and when asleep; according to a well-known saying of the Buddha, "The variety of things is like a hair net, a mock show, a dream." In any case, it seems clear that the features of the journey described in the guidebooks to Shambhala reflect the consciousness of the traveler who sees and experiences them. As a Tibetan text says, "Observing outer objects, I find but my own mind."[1]

In other words, we can read the guidebooks to Shambhala as instructions for taking an inner journey from the familiar world of the surface consciousness through the wilds of the subconscious to the hidden sanctuary of the superconscious. From this point of view, the deities, demons, mountains, rivers, and deserts described by the texts symbolize the various contents of the unconscious that we have to face and master—or make use of—on the way to awakening the innermost mind. These contents include a number of inner obstacles or psychological blocks of two general kinds. Some come from repressed parts of the surface consciousness: They include the hidden fears, desires, illusions, and habits that keep us confined to our usual state of limited awareness. Others have their source in elements of the deeper levels of mind that act as barriers to keep the superconscious from being overrun by the impure and chaotic contents of the subconscious.

Much of the inner journey consists of bringing the contents of the subconscious—especially the repressed and alienated parts of the surface consciousness—to awareness in order to face and master them. This happens when we begin to awaken elements from the deeper levels of mind. Since repressed material from the surface consciousness has attached itself to these elements, it comes up too, giving us the characteristic experience of discovering something that seems bad for everything good that we uncover in ourselves. Many of the horrifying demons of the journey, for example, embody the horror we feel at finding hidden failings in ourselves that we despise others for having. Not only does this threaten the integrity of our egos, but even worse, it threatens to release an agonizing flood of self-loathing. As a result, we see these alienated parts of the surface consciousness—and the awareness of their existence—as dangerous and terrifying monsters that we must avoid. They become obstacles that we dare not face, much less attempt to overcome. Yet only by doing so can we dispel our illusory images of ourselves and proceed along the path to liberation. In facing our inner obstacles, and the pain and dismay they entail, we purify our minds and clarify our perceptions of reality.

But the journey to Shambhala consists of more than demons and deserts. The traveler also comes to pleasant groves with refreshing fruit and meets sages and benevolent deities who help him toward his destination. These symbolize the elements of the deeper levels of mind that lie hidden in the subconscious. They embody such positive forces as spiritual aspirations, true insights, promptings of compassion, reserves of energy, and feelings of inner tranquillity. In bringing the negative aspects of ourselves to consciousness, we open the way for these positive forces to awaken. Since they are mixed together in the subconscious, when one enters our awareness, so does the other.

The guidebooks to Shambhala project the contents of the subconscious onto an outer landscape where we can more easily see and deal with them. Within the mind they have an amorphous and insubstantial nature that makes them elusive and difficult to perceive. Having directed most of our attention outward, we are used to dealing with tangible things of the external world, not with the ghostly entities of the unconscious. By giving them concrete forms that we can see and recognize, such as mountains and rivers, demons and deities, the guidebooks symbolize the contents of the subconscious in a way that can give us deeper insights than we could get from direct descriptions of them that would give us, at best, only an intellectual awareness of their existence.

Having set up a framework for their interpretation, we can now turn to the specific symbolism of the guidebooks themselves. The rituals that characterize the *Tengyur* text, the first guidebook we will consider, give us a useful means of tracing the course of the inner journey. As we saw in our examination of Tibetan Buddhism in Chapter 5, the deities visualized in these rituals, such as Manjushri and Yamantaka, symbolize the stages and experiences of the path to liberation. Through them—and the demonesses also invoked by the seeker—we can discern the contents of the subconscious that we must confront on the way to awakening the innermost mind. The order in which the guidebook presents these rituals gives us the basic outline of the inner journey to Shambhala.

In a kind of Preface to its instructions for the journey itself, the *Tengyur* text opens with a plea for guidance to Shambhala in the future, when widespread delusion will make spiritual practice impossible in the outside world. We can interpret this to mean that the inner journey can begin only after we have become aware of the deluded nature of the surface consciousness. Until that time the surface consciousness seems fairly reliable: We do not see the illusions that distort our awareness and limit the possibility of progress along the path to liberation. When we do, we finally turn away from our reliance on the surface consciousness and begin to seek a way to awaken the deeper levels of mind. In other words, we reach a point at which we realize the impossibility of further progress in our usual state of awareness.

In order to reach this point and safely embark on the dangerous journey to Shambhala, the seeker of the text must fulfill certain prerequisites. He needs to develop the overriding aim of attaining enlightenment for the benefit of others; otherwise his efforts will simply go into building up his ego, rather than transcending it. If he has not entered the right path, one leading to the innermost mind, he runs the risk of getting lost in the wilderness of the subconscious. To distinguish and follow this path, he needs to possess a clear mind, understanding, and a truthful nature. These will enable him to recognize and avoid the delusions and spurious paths that lie in wait to lead him astray. The need for initiation and background in tantric teachings indicates that he will have to know how to handle the psychic energy his quest will inevitably release. He will have to have faith in the reality of his goal in order to endure the turmoil and hardship of the inner journey, especially the painful dismay of seeing negative aspects of himself. This must be a faith based on the conviction of knowledge and insight, not on the weak sentiments of wishful thinking.

According to the text, the seeker must then meditate on his tutelary deity until he sees Shambhala in a dream or a vision. In this way he directs his attention toward the innermost mind and opens himself to its guidance. The dream or vision shows that he has succeeded in establishing contact with it and has reached a stage advanced enough to be able to complete the inner journey. In tantric practices such dreams come as signs that the meditator has begun to receive transmissions of power and wisdom from his tutelary deity, the embodiment of the innermost mind. Since in the waking state the surface consciousness tends to block these transmissions, they usually happen first in sleep. The necessity for having a dream or a vision of Shambhala indicates that the impetus for the inner journey must come from the innermost mind, not from the desires of the surface consciousness. If the seeker attempts to go before receiving a sign that shows he is ready, if he still harbors selfish inclinations and performs the subsequent rituals for his own sake, repressed fears and passions symbolized by demons and monsters will overwhelm him and tear his consciousness apart, producing the fragmented personalities of schizophrenia. To negotiate the dangerous passage of the subconscious, one needs the power and guidance of the deepest mind.

The repetition of mantras and offerings to Manjushri, Amrita-kundali, and Yamantaka that the seeker must perform next serve to arouse and focus the deeper forces symbolized by these Bo-dhisattvas. Manjushri, who holds a sword in one hand and a book in the other, embodies the transcendent wisdom that enables one to cut through the delusion and ignorance of the subconscious (see Plate 23). The seeker also invokes the power of Amrita-kundali, "The Coil of the Nectar of Immortality," to counteract the self-destructive and suicidal impulses that will appear when-ever the sight of his own failings overwhelms him with despair. According to legend, Yamantaka once subdued Yama, the Lord of Death, when a hermit assumed the form of Yama and ran amok, killing every living creature he spied.[2] As a wrathful form of Manjushri, Yamantaka embodies the wisdom that compre-hends the illusory nature of death and overcomes the hatred and aggressive tendencies that spring from the fear of it. The seeker will need this wisdom to face truths about himself that seem to threaten his life by threatening the illusions of his ego.

The guidebook speaks of accomplishing the impossible and going to Shambhala. In order to reach the zone of the supercon-scious symbolized by the kingdom, the seeker must transcend the limitations of his ego. But since he has identified himself with these very limitations, this will seem to be an insurmountable task. He needs the assistance of some outside force. By going ahead and attempting what seems beyond his power to achieve, he can reach a point at which the deeper levels of mind will emerge to overcome the limitations of his present state of awareness. We can see this process symbolized each time the seeker comes to an obstacle he cannot cross and summons a deity to help him over it. The ego—or the surface consciousness identified with it—can play a useful part in the inner journey by making the efforts that prompt the deeper levels of mind to arouse themselves.

The actual journey begins with a visit to Bodhgaya, the place where the Buddha was enlightened. This suggests that the seeker must start out with a glimpse or insight into the nature of his goal—the awakening of the innermost mind. The rest of the inner journey will then be a gradual realization in himself of what the Buddha attained at Bodhgaya. What the seeker sees for a moment outside his normal consciousness will develop and grow until it permanently transforms his awareness of reality. The innermost mind lies hidden at the beginning as well as the end of the journey, but he must become truly aware of this fact and realize it in actual experience.

The first stage of the journey leads to an island in the middle of the western ocean. Now, oceans with their vast expanses, mysterious depths, and sunken treasures make natural symbols for the unconscious. The voyage into this one suggests that the seeker now leaves the surface consciousness behind and ventures into the fluid and hidden regions of his mind. The island he reaches typifies the mixed nature of much of what he will encounter on his journey through the subconscious. The barbarian city on the western side of the island represents a repressed part of the surface consciousness that has attached itself to an element of the innermost mind symbolized by the stupa of the Buddha Kanakamuni on the eastern side. The seeker must develop the ability to distinguish between the two and make use of the latter. He does so by staying on the island to circumambulate the stupa and recite the mantra of the Buddhas. The contact with the relics of Kanakamuni, which embody traces of the innermost mind, gives him the blessing this Buddha bestows—the power of fearlessness.

Back on the mainland, a long but easy journey leads past many attractive countries where the seeker can lose himself in aimless wandering if he goes in the wrong direction. Passing by a clear and pleasant zone of the subconscious, he must not let himself get distracted by its delights nor lulled into a false sense of ease or overconfidence. For beyond this easy passage lies the first serious obstacle of the journey—a great desert that he can only cross with the aid of a special potion that eliminates hunger and thirst.

The ritual the seeker must perform to prepare this potion gives him a concrete means of focusing his attention and arousing the deeper levels of his mind. In collecting herbs and other ingredients, he gathers together and combines various contents of the subconscious in order to extract energy from them. The part of this energy he needs comes from elements of the deeper levels of mind embodied in the goddess Marici. By painting her image on a stone and reciting her mantra, he allows these deeper levels to well up into his consciousness. Tibetan yogis commonly paint such pictures as a way of concentrating on deities and invoking their powers; they call on Marici, in particular, to prepare special pills they use for fasting. Here the seeker uses this technique to activate the energy of the subconscious contents he has brought together in his awareness. In this way he produces a kind of inner elixir that gives him the strength to ignore the demands of insistent desires symbolized by hunger and thirst. With its power, the power of Marici, he can pass through the desert before him—a barren region of the subconscious that stimulates powerful cravings but provides no means for their satisfaction.

The seeker must also withstand the attack of aggressive and predatory impulses symbolized by the wild beasts of the forest that lies beyond the desert. He paints Marici in a ferocious form to give him the power to overcome these hostile forces of the subconscious through a clear awareness of their nature. As the Bodhisattva of the Dawn, she brings the light of wisdom to bear on the darker regions of the mind. The seeker uses the bright awareness she inspires to see through the repressed passions of the surface consciousness that obscure the path to enlightenment and threaten to divert him from it.

The seeker needs additional energy to sustain the efforts he must make to reach the innermost mind. With the help of tantric rituals, he can obtain it from the very passions and illusions that block his way. The magical creatures of Gandhara with their shifting forms represent illusory hopes and desires that are always changing, flitting from one object to another. The seeker uses the flesh and blood of these creatures as offerings to attract Mandeha, a demoness who embodies the subconscious forces of despair that feed on the demise of such hopes and desires. She symbolizes hatred, rage, jealousy, and other forms of resentment that spring from frustration. These passions suck off a great deal of energy from elements of the deeper levels of mind. In order to recover and make use of this energy, the seeker must subjugate the demoness. As with Marici, he paints her image on a stone as a means of bringing the hidden forces she embodies up into awareness. By visualizing himself as Yamantaka, a powerful manifestation of the innermost mind with an appearance as fierce as hers, he gains control over Mandeha and the deadly passions she symbolizes. Now tamed, they provide him with the energy he needs in the form of a white food with the taste of honey, reminiscent of the manna provided the Children of Israel during their journey through the wilderness of Sinai.

Lamas sometimes perform this kind of ritual to subjugate demons and use the evil forces they embody for good ends. But the process is considered tricky and dangerous: The intense passions it arouses can easily take over the practitioner instead. The visualization of a wrathful Bodhisattva such as Yamantaka tends to counteract the power of these evil forces, but the most important safeguard is purity of intent. The seeker must tell the demoness that he wishes to go to Shambhala for the benefit of all sentient beings. If he tries to subdue her for his own sake, the energy she provides will go into building up his ego until he becomes a demon himself.

The sages and demons of the snow mountain that lies ahead represent even more powerful contents of the subconscious—a highly charged mixture of deeper levels of mind and deeply alienated passions of the surface consciousness. If he can handle the sudden awareness and energy they will release, the seeker can make use of them to fly directly to Shambhala, the zone of the superconscious. But if he cannot, they will shatter his sanity: The sages will reveal more than he can stand to see, and the demons will overwhelm him with the fury of repressed emotions. He will be torn apart by the opposing forces of the superconscious and the surface consciousness. The guidebook recommends that he avoid them and take a slower, but safer, path to his goal.

The next obstacle, the River Sita, represents an inner barrier that freezes all spontaneity and initiative. It consists of the paralyzing kind of self-condemnation that torments the inhabitants of the cold hells, who are the only beings able to live in the icy river. It appears when the seeker realizes with horror and self-loathing how he fails to live up to the exalted standards of his ego. To see himself as he truly is, he must overcome his tendency to freeze at the sight of his failings. He does so here by stimulating a flash of repressed anger symbolized by the demoness Flashing Lightning. Through the visualization of Yamantaka, he gains control over this anger and uses it to neutralize the immobilizing forces of self-condemnation: The demoness freezes the river so that it will not freeze him as he crosses over it.

Having overcome this barrier to greater awareness, the seeker finds himself in a zone of inner calm and spiritual renewal symbolized by the forest with its nourishing fruit. Here he gets a refreshing taste of the deeper levels of mind he will experience more fully in the peaceful groves of Shambhala. Cunda, the goddess whose mantra he now recites, is a manifestation of Vajrasattva, the Bodhisattva of Emptiness. Tibetan yogis commonly visualize Vajrasattva as a means of purifying their awareness by emptying their minds of defilements. The dream the seeker has after reciting Cunda's mantra comes as a sign that most of his impurities—his delusions and deceptive passions—have drained out of him like black blood dripping from his limbs. Rid of their weight and inhibiting effects, he feels light and powerful, his mind and body cleansed and revitalized.

The golden fruit that the seeker collects in the forest contains the magical power of the deeper levels of mind. No matter how much he gathers, it does not burden him down, nor does it last longer than needed. With the fruit to nourish him, he can cross the barren plateau that lies ahead. Its power gives him the strength and inspiration to go through the feelings of inner desolation he will experience as a result of having lost cherished illusions that have sustained him up to this point. By the time he gets to the other side of the plateau, however, he will have reached a stage at which he will no longer feel a need for something to replace these illusions—and all the fruit will be gone.

The seeker now approaches Ketara, an awesome mountain frequented by Virudhaka, the Guardian King of the South. In Tibetan mythology this deity protects Buddhism from demonic forces and guards the southern entrance to the heavens above Mount Meru. Here in the guidebook he seems to symbolize a powerful element of the deeper levels of mind that bars the way to the superconscious. The seeker can go on only if this inner guardian lets him pass. The four lakes that surround Ketara form an apparent mandala with the mountain as its center. In stopping there to recite a mantra and make offerings, the seeker evidently undergoes an initiation that gives him the permission and power needed to venture on into the deeper regions of the mind. This enables him to pass safely by dangerous forces of the subconscious symbolized by flesheaters, hungry ghosts, demigods, and goddesses.

The seeker must then gather provisions at Menako, a mountain inhabited by supernatural maidens who pass their time in song and dance. The guidebook warns him not to let himself be drawn to them or their music. Like Circe and the Sirens of *The Odyssey*, they threaten to lure him away from his quest, perhaps to his death. As daughters of demons, serpents, and titans, they represent sexual desires of a perverse and harmful nature. He must draw energy in the form of provisions from the place of these desires without, however, stimulating them.

In doing so, he stirs up turbulent emotions that threaten to sweep him away. They appear in the form of the next obstacle— a raging river named the Satvalotana. The fish that live in its waters represent various contents of the subconscious that these emotions bring up into awareness. In the animal and human faces of the fish, the seeker can recognize parts of himself that he has rejected: tendencies to become imitative like a parrot, bovine like a cow, scatterbrained like a monkey, and so forth. As long as he refuses to accept them and denies that they even exist, the emotions that brought them up will, like the river, block his progress. He will not be able to get past the seething resentment and frustration caused by their rejection. By making offerings to the fish, however, he acknowledges the existence of these repressed parts of himself and assimilates them into his consciousness. In this way, he recovers the energy they have appropriated and obtains their help in overcoming the inner barrier of turbulent emotions symbolized by the river.

Up to this point the seeker has had to travel through uninhabited regions filled with ghosts and demons. In them he experiences shadowy fears that spring from a foreboding sense of loneliness and isolation from all human contact. Although he may be tempted to seek companionship in cities to the east and to the west of his path, the guidebook warns him not to: If he heads toward them, even if he travels a hundred years, he will never reach his goal. He must now face his deepest fears of loneliness and recognize that their source is in the isolation of his ego, which insists on its own independent existence. Unless he overcomes this illusory sense of separation from everything else, no matter how far he goes into the subconscious nor how many mystical experiences he has, he will never succeed in awakening the innermost mind.

Having eliminated, or at least reduced, his tendencies toward self-isolation, the seeker finds himself more open to the world, able to relate to it with greater warmth and interest. This is reflected in the happy people and desirable things of the countries north of the River Satvalotana. The guidebook warns him, however, not to let these external attractions divert him from his goal; he must continue north without stopping. If he lingers to enjoy his new appreciation of the world around him, his openness will become as great an obstacle as his earlier tendency to set himself apart from everything else. He must follow a middle course between the two extremes.

Along the way he passes springs whose waters sicken and kill ordinary people but give him health and long life. Here the guidebook uses a common tantric analogy to show that the seeker has reached a stage at which he can transmute poison into the nectar of immortality—that is, he can transform the passions and illusions that still bind him into means of liberation. He now realizes that these passions and illusions have their source in the deeper levels of mind, symbolized by the gold and other precious metals hidden in the mountains from which the springs flow. As a result, he can make use of the pure energy and awareness that the poisonous waters actually represent. If an ordinary person who lacks this realization indulges in these passions and illusions, they will lead him astray—into suffering, madness, or even death. In any case, since the pure energy and awareness concealed in the springs threaten to dissolve the illusions of the ego, with which he still identifies himself, if such a person should accidentally awaken them, they would seem to him like deadly poisons.

The fabulous beings who try to seduce and terrify the seeker at the next juncture of the journey embody his deepest fears and desires. Now that he has access to the pure energy and awareness hidden in them, he can penetrate to their roots and free himself from their grip. In a scene reminiscent of the Buddha's enlightenment, when Mara, the god of delusion, sent seductive maidens and terrifying armies to deflect the Buddha from his goal, the seeker withstands the temptations and attacks of the fabulous beings by meditating on emptiness. In this way, he realizes once and for all the empty nature of his fears and desires: They spring from the illusions of his ego and have no reality of their own. Once he has transcended these illusions, they can no longer exert any influence over him.

The seeker is now ready to cross the last major obstacle on the way to Shambhala—the great snow mountains surrounding the kingdom. They represent an inner barrier that keeps the superconscious from being overrun by the chaotic contents of the subconscious. Whoever still harbors any of these contents and has not yet realized the emptiness of their nature cannot surmount this final barrier. The white snow and the great height of the mountains show that they embody the pure and impregnable power of the deeper levels of mind.

The seeker can cross this obstacle only by leaving behind whatever attachments to his ego he may still possess. This happens when one of the Vajra Dakinis takes him on her shoulders and flies him over the snow mountains. These goddesses are used in tantric meditation to inspire the irresistible urge to attain enlightenment. Their beautiful female bodies arouse a powerful impulse latent in sexual desire—the impulse to lose oneself in the ecstasy of release. The seeker uses the force of this impulse to transcend the last illusions of the surface consciousness and merge with the deeper levels of mind. He does so in a leap of spiritual ecstasy symbolized by the magic flight over the snow mountains to the edge of Shambhala. With the help of the Vajra Dakinis, he makes full use of the energy tied up in sexual desires to liberate himself from any remaining attachments to his ego—something he was not ready or able to do earlier when he encountered the maidens of Menako.

The seeker lands in a beautiful valley filled with medicinal herbs that represent the healing qualities of the deeper levels of mind. There he performs a ritual dedicated to Ekajati, a powerful form of Tara, the Savioress. Tibetans meditate on this female Bodhisattva in order to remove obstacles from the path to liberation. As a result of reciting Ekajati's mantra and placing her flowers on top of his head, the seeker gains power over obstructing demons—impeding impulses of the unconscious—and the ability to understand and see into the nature of all things. Having overcome the obstacles of the subconscious, he can enter the zone of the superconscious and proceed toward enlightenment without further hindrance.

According to the Panchen Lama's version of the journey, before reaching the capital of Shambhala, the seeker must pass through a lovely valley inhabited by hermaphrodites. This strange addition to the *Tengyur* text reflects the state of inner harmony the seeker has attained by uniting the male and female aspects of his nature. Thought and feeling, for example, no longer war within him, producing the inner tensions that afflict so many people. At a deeper level he no longer experiences any difference between his energy and his awareness—the male and female expressions of the mind. He has reached an advanced stage of tantric practice in which the paths of form and emptiness have come together. In him compassion and wisdom have become one. He has achieved the inner unity needed to awaken the innermost mind and penetrate to the ultimate nature of reality. Now, at last, he can go into the presence of the King of Shambhala.

We can discern a similar, but deeper, journey in the poem by Rinpungpa. The focus on the experiences of meditation and the abundant use of mystical metaphors encourage an inner reading of this guidebook to Shambhala. As we noted at the end of the previous chapter, the poem describes what seems to be a more advanced kind of journey for one who has mastered the higher levels of tantric practice. At these levels the usual distinctions between external and internal experience fade away: The world and the mind come to reflect and embody each other. As a result, the outer journey to Shambhala naturally acquires an inner meaning that can give us additional and deeper insights into the process of liberation.

Rinpungpa's version of the journey begins with a search for someone able to take a message to Shambhala. After failing to find anyone outside himself, Rinpungpa turns his attention inward and visualizes a yogi with the power and the wisdom needed to reach the hidden kingdom. Like the deities more commonly visualized in tantric meditation, the yogi apparently embodies a deeper and purer part of the meditator's mind. In other words, the one taking the journey described in the poem is actually Rinpungpa himself—but not in his usual state of awareness. His failure to find a suitable messenger in the external world suggests that there is no part of the surface consciousness that has the energy and awareness needed to reach Shambhala. Only by awakening something deeper can he overcome the obstacles along the way.

Rinpungpa starts his visualized messenger on the journey to Shambhala by sending him on a pilgrimage through Tibet. Having awakened the deeper awareness embodied in the yogi, he focuses it on the familiar contents of his surface consciousness.

There he gradually discerns the pervasive influence of his culture and environment. He sees how they have shaped his perceptions of himself and the world and how they determine the characteristic ways in which he thinks, feels, and acts. In this way he acquires the kind of self-knowledge that will enable him to penetrate to the roots of his ego and eventually free himself from its illusions. At the same time, he picks up insights and inspiration from certain contents of his surface consciousness, such as religious ideas and feelings, that reflect the influence of the deeper levels of mind on Tibetan culture and society. This happens when the yogi receives blessings from the shrines and lamas he visits in Tibet. Mount Kailas, in particular, and the image of Maitreya, the Buddha to come, infuse him with the aspiration to attain enlightenment, an aspiration that gives Rinpungpa the motivation and direction needed for the inner journey. Whoever wishes to reach and awaken the innermost mind must begin by examining the conditions that have made him what he is. He cannot afford to ignore the contents of his surface consciousness: They contain valuable sources of wisdom and power, as well as things he needs to know about himself in order to undo the illusions of his ego.

The next stage of the journey takes the yogi beyond the borders of Tibet to the lovely vale of Kashmir. The poem's description of fabulous cities filled with houses made of jewels and graceful people dressed in white has the quality of a beautiful half dream experienced by someone drifting into sleep. Here Rinpungpa apparently leaves his surface consciousness behind and enters a delightful state of reverie on the edge of the unconscious. Since he can easily become attached to it and lose his motivation to go on, this idyllic state of mind represents the first major obstacle he must overcome on the inner journey. The poem tells the yogi to remember his aim and ignore the seductive glances of beautiful women with dark blue eyes. They embody sexual fantasies that threaten to arouse powerful desires that he will not be able to control. Only later, when he meets the maidens in the country of fabulous beings, will he have reached a stage at which he can safely make use of the energy contained in such desires.

Leaving Kashmir behind, the yogi enters a bewildering maze of mountains full of deceptive paths that can lead him astray. Rinpungpa now plunges into the unfamiliar and disorienting world of the subconscious itself. Not knowing his way around, he runs the risk of wandering off into regions of the mind from which there is no return. If he takes a wrong path, he might easily lose himself in the byways of madness. At this stage he can only open himself to a mysterious inner guidance that comes when he drops egotistic ambitions and dedicates all his efforts to the welfare of others. As the dark forest ahead makes clear, he must travel blind until he gets used to the turgid darkness of the subconscious and acquires the awareness needed to see where he is going. The fierce but friendly horsemen along the way reveal the reassuring fact that much of what seems hostile in the unconscious can actually be quite helpful—if recognized for what it is.

The river beyond the forest seems to combine the freezing and the turbulent qualities of the Sita and the Satvalotana in the *Tengyur* text. Like Medusa's glance, the touch of its spray turns people to stone. This fate represents the most complete form of bondage imaginable, the ultimate end of all attempts to lock the mind in an immutable image of itself. It comes from the ego's misguided desire to attain a kind of static immortality in material form that is actually the death of the spirit. The river therefore embodies the essence of all unconscious forces working against liberation; in its turbulence we can see the rough and impure nature of the terrific energy these forces possess. The yogi manages to cross this imposing barrier with the help of tree branches that fling him over its deadly spray. As natural symbols of life and growth, the trees represent a source of inner vitality that Rinpungpa taps to overcome the deadening forces of bondage that he finds within himself.

As a result of flying over this barrier in a leap of transcendence, he passes into a blissful state of inner calm and ease symbolized by the tranquil park on the far bank of the river. Everything now seems to come spontaneously without the need for effort: deer's milk, nourishing fruit, and cool shade lie waiting to satisfy the yogi's wants. Such states of apparent attainment occur on the inner journey whenever one overcomes some major obstacle of the subconscious and allows a deeper level of mind to emerge. But they do not last for long: After the tranquil park comes a terrible forest. The journey seems to consist of a series of dismaying setbacks: Just when one thinks one has finally attained a state of permanent tranquillity, up surges more inner chaos, often worse than anything previously experienced. This happens because these states bring a clarified awareness that soon reveals even more deeply repressed contents of the subconscious that have to be dealt with next. Thus the apparent setbacks actually represent signs of progress on the inner journey.

The terrifying creatures of the forest beyond the park symbolize the ferocious contents of the subconscious that Rinpungpa must now confront. Predatory and destructive impulses of repressed rage, greed, and envy rise up in the form of killer animals, demons, and other eaters of flesh. The slaughter taking place in the forest symbolizes the inner carnage wrought by these warring impulses—inner conflicts that sap Rinpungpa's energy and cut off his awareness. The witches who take the shape of men by day and lions and tigers by night reveal the illusory and changing nature of the subconscious forces that now attempt to tear his consciousness apart. Rather than try to get rid of these forces, which would only repress them and increase their power over him, Rinpungpa welcomes them as his own impulses. No longer enraged at being suppressed, nor hidden where they can fester, they lose their ferocious character and cease to wreak their debilitating vengeance on him. By directing compassion toward the creatures that menace him, the yogi dissipates their rage to kill.

Emerging from the confines of the forest, he comes to the shore of an enormous body of water that seems to have no end. No longer hemmed in by the fear of savage impulses within himself, Rinpungpa suddenly experiences the vastness of the subconscious and is momentarily overwhelmed by it. How can he possibly traverse the immense regions of the mind that lie ahead? As a consequence of virtuous actions done in the past, the yogi finds a boat and a fair wind waiting to speed him across the water. According to a common Buddhist metaphor, the images of a boat and wind symbolize the body and the force of karma. By using the latter two with wisdom and skill, one can cross over the waters of illusion—the vast and deceptive reaches of the subconscious that separate Rinpungpa from the pure awareness of the innermost mind.

The desert crossing that follows symbolizes a characteristic stage of all mystic quests: the unbearable sense of spiritual thirst and desolation that comes when one has to abandon inspiring ideas and feelings that have outlived their usefulness and become hindrances to further progress on the inner journey. Here the yogi suffers from the terrible heat of the sun—the searing awareness of his own shortcomings. With the external protection of comforting illusions no longer possible, he must look inward for the means to endure this painful passage. The secret moon he activates by mystically rubbing his tonsils refers to a visualized drop of silver-white semen that embodies the impulse to enlightenment. When Rinpungpa awakens the energy of this impulse, it feels like a cool, soothing liquid flowing through his body and reviving his spirits. A kind of nectar of immortality, it gives him the strength to face his shortcomings and go on toward liberation.

At this point, subconscious forces opposed to the inner journey burst forth in the form of a mountain wind that lashes the yogi's face with sand and bits of leaves and twigs. Rinpungpa now experiences the terrific energy bound up in his own resistance to seeing himself as he is. The savage onslaught of the wind prompts the yogi to make a protective ointment for his face that also clears his vision and brightens his eyes: The confrontation with negative forces of the subconscious leads to the awakening of a deeper and purer awareness. As we have noted before, by stimulating the development of spiritual powers needed to overcome them, such forces can actually play a positive role in the inner journey to Shambhala. Approached the right way, they provide natural opportunities for awakening deeper levels of mind.

We can see this process at work in the next two obstacles. The first, the deadly breath of the giant serpents, represents destructive forces of the subconscious that seem to threaten Rinpungpa's very existence. The knowledge that they can destroy only his illusions about himself, not his real nature, acts as the antidote to these lethal forces. It gives him the courage to confront them and undergo a death-and-rebirth experience that frees him from much of his identification with his ego. In the next obstacle, the mountain of sharp thorns, his loss of illusions leads to the painful recognition of more repressed parts of the surface consciousness. The secret knowledge the yogi uses to protect his feet symbolizes a deeper understanding that allows Rinpungpa to face these parts of himself without piercing reactions of disgust and shame.

Having made great efforts to overcome all these obstacles, the yogi comes, at last, to a resting place—the beautiful Incense Mountain. The sages who meditate there in an atmosphere of sublime sanctity embody elements of the subconscious that come from the deepest and purest levels of the mind. In fact, they symbolize the essence of his true nature, which Rinpungpa does not yet have the awareness to experience directly. At this point he can only catch intimations of it through the sight of the sages. By having the yogi make prostrations to the sages, Rinpungpa surrenders the whims and desires of his ego and acknowledges the supremacy of the innermost mind. In this way, he gains access to the wisdom and power needed to complete the inner journey.

With the help of the sages, the yogi is able to survive the perils that lie ahead—the awesome storms and deadly attacks of birds and demons. Having let go of his ego and the reassuring sense of identity it gave him, Rinpungpa experiences the terrifying fear of sudden annihilation. At any moment, with the swiftness of an eagle dropping out of the sky, he could cease to be. Vague anxieties that lurk in the depths of the subconscious now appear as demons with red eyes and beings who embody nameless fears. Only the awareness of his real nature, however dim or remote, gives him the sense of inner unity needed to go on without succumbing to terror and disintegrating into madness.

After many days of harrowing travel, the yogi comes out in a heavenly land of fabulous beings. The clear water and sparkling jewels that abound there reflect the pure and gemlike awareness of the deeper levels of mind. Having transcended the fear of losing himself, Rinpungpa discovers a paradise in the depths of the subconscious. Since he no longer clings to the grasping tendencies of his ego, he can enjoy objects of desire without the risk of becoming attached to them: He has found a true wish-fulfilling tree in the deeper levels of his mind. Because of this, the yogi can safely take pleasure with the fabulous maidens—something he could not do with the seductive women of Kashmir. Having achieved the purity of enlightened Dakinis, rather than give rise to attachments, the maidens inspire the impulse to attain enlightenment. Rinpungpa has reached a stage advanced enough to make full use of the energy contained in sexual desires.

We can see this quite clearly in what happens when the yogi makes love with the maidens. The sudden heat of an inner fire shoots up through his spine to melt a mystical syllable on the crown of his head and cause nectar to stream down through his body, purifying and transforming it into the diamond body of bliss. We have here a clear reference to the visualization and effects of an advanced kind of tantric meditation meant to generate psychic heat. Those who practice it visualize just such a fire and syllable, as well as the same kind of nectar flowing down through their bodies. As a physical side effect, they are supposed to produce so much bodily heat that they can go out naked in the snow, at temperatures well below zero, and dry towels that have been soaked in icy water and draped around their shoulders. Some meditation texts even tell the practitioner to visualize the kind of love-making Rinpungpa's yogi performs with the fabulous maidens.[3]

Rinpungpa visualizes a drop of semen in the form of the mystical syllable on the crown of the yogi's head. When the energy of sexual desire causes it to melt and spread through the psychic

nervous system, the impulse to enlightenment, which it embodies, fills up the mind and drives out all other, distracting
aims. Having focused his energy and attention completely on the
attainment of liberation, the yogi feels himself physically transformed, endowed with a new and indestructible body capable of
reaching Shambhala. Only by reaching the level of purity represented by the diamond body of bliss can Rinpungpa enter the
zone of the superconscious. Cleansed of all murky defilements,
his ego has become a transparent window that gives him a view
into and out of the depths of his mind. This brings with it a
transformed perception of the world, reflected in the beautiful
lands that lie ahead. Everything now appears in the light of its
true and divine nature, as if pieces of heaven had fallen to earth.

As in the *Tengyur* text, the great wall of snow mountains surrounding Shambhala represents an inner barrier thrown up by
the deeper levels of mind to keep out the impure contents of the
subconscious. Like fierce guardian deities, the peaks take on the
wrathful appearance of demons who seem to bar the way and
crush all hopes of reaching Shambhala. The sight of them brings
out the last of the yogi's fears—the fear that he will not be able
to transcend the limitations of his mind. How can he go where
not even the eagles can soar? As the poem makes perfectly clear,
he must see this fear for the illusory obstacle it is. Then, as it
vanishes like the mirages of darkness in the glow of a dust-free
dawn, the deeper levels of mind will emerge in the form of the
noble ones—Bodhisattvas or Dakinis—to carry him over the snow
mountains in a mystical flight of transcendence that puts even
the birds to shame.

The royal ease with which the yogi rides over the final obstacle in a sedan chair of the gods shows that Rinpungpa has
reached the stage of effortlessness; he can now proceed smoothly
toward liberation. No longer will he have to struggle against
himself: He has gone beyond the conflicts of the subconscious
and attained a state of lasting unity with the deeper levels of his
mind. Nothing, not even the snakes and wild beasts of the forest
ahead, can impede his further progress: The compassion and

friendliness that now radiate from him spontaneously remove the hostility of whatever he might encounter. The way lies clear to the shining cities of Shambhala.

We have used the symbolism of the guidebooks to interpret the journey from an inner, psychological point of view. The meditation and rituals they tell the traveler to perform, as well as their descriptions of the experiences he will have, strongly suggest that the texts are meant to be read in this way. There is certainly a clear basis for this kind of interpretation in the tantric view of the world as a reflection of the body and mind—the correspondence of macrocosm and microcosm. But the question remains whether Tibetans themselves would read the guidebooks as we have—or in some similar way.

Most Tibetans who are familiar with the texts take them as literal descriptions of an outer journey to Shambhala. They do not usually speak of them as instructions for an inner journey into the mind. This is not surprising, since such an interpretation would belong to the secret part of the Kalacakra, which initiates, those who would know, have taken vows not to reveal. In any case, relatively few Tibetans would have the background to read the guidebooks in this way.

When I asked, however, if the texts were meant to be read from an inner point of view, a number of lamas agreed that it was possible. The Sakya Trizin felt that one could view the journey to Shambhala as a way of purifying the mind and the meetings with deities as stages in that process. Chopgye Trichen Rimpoche, a master and teacher of the Kalacakra, said that he could not reveal details but, depending on the level of the person going, the journey could be more or less similar to the path leading to enlightenment. He felt that Rinpungpa's poem, in particular, referred to the inner experiences of meditation on the way to liberation, which was symbolized by Shambhala. In Kalu Rimpoche's opinion, the obstacles of the journey—snow mountains, rivers, winds, demons, and so forth—were probably the same as the negative tendencies of the mind that have to be overcome in order to attain enlightenment.

Two lamas—Chugyal Rimpoche and Samdong Rimpoche—offered more detailed interpretations of the guidebooks. According to Chugyal Rimpoche, the journey to Shambhala represents a yogi's progress through the successive stages of Hinayana, Mahayana, and Vajrayana Buddhism—which we examined in Chapter 5. The obstacles described in the texts symbolize various mystical practices along the way that lead to the realization of tantric meditation in the kingdom itself. He added that the snow mountains surrounding Shambhala represent worldly virtues, while the King in the center symbolizes the pure mind at the end of the journey.

According to Samdong Rimpoche, one can read the guidebooks to Shambhala as instructions for going into the mind without going to the kingdom itself. He expressed the opinion that the outer journey they describe bears a close relation to the stage of completion according to the Kalacakra—the higher stage of meditation leading to final enlightenment.[4] In his view the physical obstacles on the way to Shambhala represent inner barriers that must be faced at the psychic centers. These barriers form the knots that block the proper flow of energy through the psychic nervous system; as such, they correspond to mental defilements, such as ignorance and lust, that limit our awareness. Thus the outer journey to Shambhala symbolizes the inner process of working one's way through the psychic centers until one has opened them all and liberated the innermost mind from its imprisonment in the last center reached—the heart center. A yogi might do this by taking the deities the *Tengyur* text tells the seeker to invoke and visualizing them in the appropriate centers in order to undo the knots that impede the smooth flow of energy through the psychic nervous system. In the process, he would automatically purify his awareness and awaken the deeper levels of mind.

As we can see, lamas interpret the guidebooks to Shambhala in a number of different ways. Drawing on some of their interpretations, we have approached the journey from a psychological point of view that makes it more accessible to someone with a modern Western background. Ultimately, the validity, or usefulness, of our interpretation does not depend so much on whether it corresponds to the way Tibetans might read the texts, as on whether it can help give us meaningful insights into the nature and possibilities of our own minds. This the reader will have to experience and decide for himself. The beauty and richness of the guidebooks to Shambhala lie precisely in the way they leave themselves open to a variety of interpretations.

10

The Inner Prophecy

Having looked into the inner meaning of Shambhala and the journey to it, we can now turn to the last major theme of the myth: the prophecy of the final battle and the golden age to come. Like the preceding two themes, it speaks of a liberation that occurs within as well as without. According to the prophecy, the future King of Shambhala will come not only to deliver the world from the external tyranny of the barbarians, but also to liberate its inhabitants from the internal bondage of their own delusions. The main purpose of the final battle and the golden age is to bring about the conditions and teachings needed to attain enlightenment—to help people awaken the innermost mind and know the true nature of reality. Since the events of the prophecy lead up to this end, it makes sense to examine them in some detail to see what their symbolism can reveal about the path to liberation.

In the texts themselves the account of the prophecy usually begins with the history of Shambhala. The final battle and the golden age to come do not happen in isolation; they emerge from and depend on the events of the past. Without the previous existence of Shambhala and the introduction of the Kalacakra, there would be no King to liberate the world from the forces of evil and no teaching to free people's minds from delusion. If we want to look into the meaning of the prophecy, we need to examine the history of the kingdom as well. If the events of the future have an inner significance, so must those of the past; at the very least, they tell us something about what precedes whatever the former symbolize. The history and prophecy of Shambhala form a whole process that we need to consider in its entirety.

We will begin, therefore, with the mythical origins of the kingdom itself. Although the Kalacakra texts do not go into its history before the life of the Buddha, various lamas believe that Shambhala existed previously as a hidden country but had neither Kings nor teachings that could lead its inhabitants to enlightenment. According to legend, sometime after the Buddha's birth, an Indian King attacked and killed thousands of the Buddha's clan, the Shakyas. One of the Shakyas, Shakya Shambha, happened to be off hunting and escaped the massacre. When he sought refuge with the Buddha, the Buddha advised him to go to another country. Following his advice, Shakya Shambha fled over snow mountains to a distant land of the north. When he arrived there, the inhabitants asked him who he was and where he was from. "I have come from India," Shakya Shambha replied. "I am a messenger of the great King Shakya Shambha, and many of his soldiers are coming behind me to conquer this country."

"How powerful are they?" they asked.

Drawing out his sword, he sliced a rock in two and said, "I have this much power and am only a messenger, so you can imagine how powerful the soldiers are!"

At this the people took fright and surrendered to Shakya Shambha, giving him their land and begging for his mercy and protection. Thereafter the country became known, after him, as Shambhala. According to one source, disputed by the Panchen Lama, Shakya Shambha was the father of Sucandra, "Good Moon," the first religious King of Shambhala.[1]

The recorded Tibetan history of Shambhala begins with the preaching of the Kalacakra at the stupa of Dhanyakataka in southern India. At the age of about eighty, just before he passed away, the Buddha went to this great relic mound, shaped like a mandala, and gave various mystical teachings—in particular, those of Manjushri, the Bodhisattva of Wisdom. At that time, King Sucandra of Shambhala came to Dhanyakataka with his ninety-six vassal princes and a retinue of assorted deities. After listening to the other teachings, he rose and asked the Buddha to teach the Kalacakra, the highest of all. Delighted with his request, the Buddha took on the form of the main Kalacakra deity and gave the complete teaching to the entire assembly. Sucandra then flew back to Shambhala with his followers and wrote down the sermon in what became the basic text of the Kalacakra Tantra.[2] In addition to introducing his subjects to the new

Fig. 13   *Sucandra, the first religious King of Shambhala.*

teaching, he also composed thousands of verses of commentary and built a great three-dimensional mandala studded with jewels. The texts regard him as an incarnation of Vajrapani, the Bodhisattva of Power and Master of Secret Teachings.

Two years after he received the Kalacakra in India, Sucandra died and was followed by six religious Kings, each of whom reigned for a hundred years. According to the texts, they descended in a line from the Buddha's clan, the Shakyas, and were the incarnations of various Bodhisattvas, such as Yamantaka, the Conqueror of the Lord of Death. Making use of their wisdom and the writings left by Sucandra, they taught and initiated their subjects into the mysteries of the Wheel of Time, and under their enlightened rule the kingdom prospered and developed into an important center of mystical teachings.

The son of the seventh King—counting Sucandra as the first—was Manjushrikirti, "The Renowned and Glorious Gentle One." As his name implies, he was an incarnation of Manjushri, the Bodhisattva of Wisdom. Tibetans also regard him as the second in the line of incarnations of the Panchen Lamas. According to certain sources, he came to the throne of Shambhala around 200 B.C.[3] During his reign Manjushrikirti united the various castes or religious factions of the kingdom into one diamond caste and won for himself and his successors the title of Kulika or Rigden, meaning "Holder of the Castes." This came about through an incident that the texts treat as an event of particular importance in the history of Shambhala.

Near the end of his reign, Manjushrikirti summoned the sages of his realm together and asked them to explain their views and practices. They responded with so many conflicting opinions that they became utterly confused and fell to the ground in a daze. "What can be done with all these discordant views?" he asked. "Next month, on the full moon, I shall give all the people of this realm an initiation into a single, diamond caste. If you wish to enter that path, stay here, but if you do not, then leave and go elsewhere; otherwise the doctrines of the barbarians will come to spread even in Shambhala."

After talking it over among themselves, the sages said, "We

are not happy about entering a path other than our own. Since we are also unable to go against your commands, O Master of Men, we will go to India."

Fig. 14 *Manjushrikirti, the first Kulika King of Shambhala.*

After they had left and journeyed twelve days to the south, Manjushrikirti began to have misgivings and thought: When the people of Shambhala see how these seekers of wisdom have had to go to India, they will think that the tantric teachings are false. Realizing that wrong impressions might arise from their banishment, he stunned the sages with his magic power and sent great birds to fetch them back and deposit them beside the mandala built by King Sucandra. When the sages woke from their stupor, they were so amazed that they immediately made an offering of gold to Manjushrikirti and asked him for his teachings. He then condensed and simplified the Kalacakra Tantra and initiated them into the new diamond caste. After meditating on the revised teaching for a month, the sages finally attained the wisdom they had been seeking.[4]

Manjushrikirti's son, Pundarika or "White Lotus," further clarified the Kalacakra Tantra and composed the basic commentary on it, called the *Vimalaprabha* or "Stainless Light." An incarnation of Avalokiteshvara, the Bodhisattva of Compassion, he was the second in the line of twenty-five Kulika Kings, the "Holders of the Castes," who are supposed to preserve and teach the Kalacakra in Shambhala. With the possible exception of two, each of these divine monarchs is supposed to rule for a hundred years. According to the prophecy, the line of Kulika Kings will culminate in Rudra Cakrin, "The Wrathful One with the Wheel," who will come out to vanquish the barbarians and establish the golden age.[5]

The Kalacakra texts also give another line of teachers, who are supposed to originate and spread the barbarian doctrines of materialism throughout the world. In this list we can recognize the names of such figures as Abraham, Moses, Jesus, and Mani—the last being the founder of the gnostic religion of Manicheism. But the texts focus most of their attention—and consternation—on Mohammed, whom they call Madhumati or "Honey Intellect." They describe the rise of Islam under him in the "country of Makha," or Mecca, during the reign of the tenth Kulika King of Shambhala in the seventh century A.D. According to the texts, the barbarians and their doctrines will take over one nation after another and eventually put an end to the practice of Buddhism outside of Shambhala.[6]

Although some scholars have identified the barbarians as Muslims, we can see from the list of their teachers that they also include the followers of other religions, such as Judaism, Christianity, and Manicheism. Actually, the texts seem to refer to any foreign doctrine that threatens Buddhism as *mleccha* or "barbarian." At the time the Kalacakra appeared in India in the tenth century, the greatest threat was Islam, which had destroyed Buddhism in most of Central Asia and was in the process of doing so in India as well. For that reason Islam seems to have become the symbol—for that time—of all doctrines opposed to true spirituality, as Buddhists saw it. But the term used by the texts, *mleccha*, actually refers to any materialistic barbarians, whatever their religion. According to Chopgye Trichen Rimpoche, "There are many kinds of barbarians. They all lack spiritual values, they are materialistic, and they don't mind killing millions of people just for the sake of gaining a name for themselves and their countries."

During the reign of the twelfth Kulika King, as Islam was taking over Central Asia, the Kalacakra came to India from Shambhala and shortly thereafter found a refuge in Tibet that was to last for almost a thousand years. In an earlier chapter we looked at stories of the Indian yogi-scholars who were supposed to have gone in search of the teaching and to have brought it back to their homeland in the tenth century. Whether or not they actually got it from Shambhala, centers for the study of the Kalacakra did develop in Kashmir, and in Bengal in eastern India. From these places various Buddhist missionaries took the teaching to Tibet and established a number of lineages of teachers and disciples to pass it on and preserve it. Later on, the Kalacakra spread with Tibetan Buddhism to Mongolia and southern Siberia, where the people developed a particular interest in the mystical northern kingdom of Shambhala.[7]

During all this time, the Kings of Shambhala are supposed to have continued teaching the Kalacakra to their subjects, untouched by events in the outside world. According to most sources, the twenty-first Kulika King, Aniruddha or "The Unstoppable One," assumed power in 1927 and will rule until the year 2027. So far during his reign, in accordance with prophecy, Buddhism and the Kalacakra have nearly come to an end in Tibet, Mongolia, China, and much of Asia. This trend will continue through the reigns of three more Kulika Kings until the twenty-fifth, "The Wrathful One with the Wheel," comes to the throne in 2327 to defeat the rampant barbarians. Some lamas believe, however, that this may happen much sooner, perhaps even in the very near future. They argue that not all the Kings of

Shambhala have ruled a hundred years. Chogyam Trungpa Rimpoche, for one, thinks that the reigns of a few were shortened by the premature deaths of Dalai Lamas in Lhasa. In any case, the Buddha's death, the starting point for calculating the advent of the golden age, varies in Tibetan sources from 2422 to 546 B.C., giving a wide range of dates to choose from, including the present.[8]

Before the final battle takes place, however, conditions will become much worse. According to the prophecy, drought, famine, disease, and war will sweep the world. People will no longer have any religion to which they can turn for solace or liberation: The doctrines of materialism will overwhelm their minds and drive them to struggle for their own selfish ends. The lust for power and wealth will prevail over the teachings of compassion and truth. Nations will fight nations, and the larger will devour the smaller. The victorious barbarians will take over and begin to squabble among themselves. According to various versions of the prophecy, two groups that have conquered most of the earth between them will attack each other in what some Tibetans believe will be the Third World War. At the end of this conflict, an evil King will emerge as the victor and master of the world—or at least of all regions south of the River Sita. Unaware of the existence of Shambhala, he will think that there is no one as powerful as he.

By this time, however, Rudra Cakrin, the twenty-fifth Holder of the Castes, will have come to the throne and have been ruling for a number of years in Shambhala. According to one Tibetan commentary, a wheel of iron will fall from the sky to mark the beginning of his reign—hence his name, "The Wrathful One with the Wheel."[9] This attribute identifies him as a Universal Emperor of Buddhist mythology and symbolizes his temporal and spiritual powers. In some versions of the prophecy, Rudra Cakrin actually uses his iron wheel like a spinning discus to cut down his enemies. It also symbolizes the power he has to spread the teachings of Buddhism: When the Buddha preached his first sermon after attaining enlightenment, he is said to have "turned

Fig. 15 *Rudra Cakrin, the future King of Shambhala.*

the Wheel of Truth." According to most sources, Rudra Cakrin will be the incarnation of Manjushri, the Bodhisattva of Wisdom.

There are various versions of how the barbarian King, whose name means "Childish Intellect" or "The Intelligence of Doing," will become aware of Rudra Cakrin and his hidden kingdom.[10] Most of them agree, however, that this will happen only after the barbarian King thinks he has conquered the world and eliminated all possible rivals. At that time, according to Khempo Tsondu, a lady, who happens to be an incarnation of the Savioress Tara, will come to the arrogant monarch and show him a vision of Shambhala in the smoke of burning incense. On seeing Rudra Cakrin and the splendor of his palace, the barbarian King will become enraged that there exists anyone of comparable power and magnificence, and in a fit of envy, he will lead his army forth to attack Shambhala.

In another, related version of the prophecy, Palden Lhamo, a fierce goddess who protects the teachings of Buddhism, will take birth as the Queen of the barbarian King. After the tyrant has conquered most of the world, he will run wild with pride, like a mad elephant. Sharing in his arrogance, the King's ministers will boast to all that there is no one more powerful than he. Then the Queen will say to them, "O proud and childish ministers, I have witnessed an even greater world than this. If we do not conquer it, then your pride will be nothing more than childish boasting."

Stung by her words, the ministers will reply, "If such a world exists, we will certainly conquer it."

Then they will conduct an aerial surveillance of the earth, and when it reveals the existence of Shambhala with its incomparable wealth and happiness, their jealousy will surpass all limits, crashing up like waves of the sea. Incensed that there could be such a land outside their control, they will gather an army together and set out to conquer it.[11]

The sources disagree over whether the barbarians will actually reach Shambhala. Many lamas believe that they lack the spiritual power needed to overcome the barriers protecting the hidden kingdom. The third Panchen Lama's version of the prophecy tends to support this belief: According to his guidebook, when the barbarians finally become insufferable, Rudra Cakrin will emerge to defeat them in a great battle south of the River Sita in the land of Rum—probably Iran or Turkey. According to Khamtul Rimpoche, who had the dream of going to Shambhala, the final confrontation will take place on the banks of the Sita itself. The main Kalacakra text does not specify the location of the battle, but it does imply that Rudra Cakrin and his army will come out of the hidden kingdom to fight against the barbarians.[12]

Some lamas believe, however, that the barbarians will actually get into Shambhala, either through scientific or other means. According to Khempo Lodu Zangpo, they will fly over the snow mountains in aircraft and engage in aerial combat above the kingdom itself. Some of the airplanes involved in the clash will fall into a river that flows past the palace at the center of Shambhala, turning the water red with blood. Outraged at the sight of this, Rudra Cakrin will storm out to destroy the invaders who have desecrated his kingdom.

Another lama, Dardo Rimpoche, heard the following prophecy from his teacher in Tibet. After the barbarians become united, an evil spirit whom they worship will tell them that they are not the greatest power on earth, that there also exists the realm of Shambhala. Having discovered where it lies hidden, they will proceed to cut a road through the snow mountains that surround the kingdom. By that time much of the snow will have melted, making their task much easier. When the barbarians reach Shambhala, their invasion will not bother the King until, one day as he is walking on the terrace of his palace, they attempt to stab him in the heart with a javelin. Uninjured but angry, he will walk three times around the offending weapon and then initiate the final battle.

According to Samdong Rimpoche, the barbarians will use vehicles made of iron to fly over the outer ring of snow mountains surrounding Shambhala. After taking over the outer part of the kingdom with its eight petal-shaped regions, they will turn their attention toward the center and try for many years to cross the higher, inner ring of snow mountains that hide the central region from view. After much experimentation and many accidents, they will finally overcome this barrier and reach the capital city of Kalapa. Being compassionate and wishing them no harm, Rudra Cakrin will welcome the barbarians and invite their King to rule jointly with him. For a number of years, the two of them will sit on equal thrones, but then the barbarian King will try to kill Rudra Cakrin and make himself the sole ruler of Shambhala. At that point the inevitable confrontation will finally take place. Samdong Rimpoche thought that the whole process—from the initial invasion to the final battle—would take about fifty years.

Since the barbarians will have the ultimate in material weapons and power, Rudra Cakrin will have to defeat them through spiritual means. According to a commentary on the Kalacakra, "Becoming motionless as a mountain, he will enter the meditation of the Best of Horses."[13] Out of his concentration will come a magical army composed of war elephants, golden chariots, stone horses with the power of wind, cavalry, and millions of warriors. We can now appreciate the significance of the horse that Khamtul Rimpoche saw in his dream of Shambhala: Not only does Rudra Cakrin ride it in the final battle, but he also meditates on it to get the spiritual power needed to destroy the forces of materialism. As for the stone horses with the power of flight, lamas tend to interpret them as airplanes. According to Chopgye Trichen Rimpoche, the stone refers to petroleum fuel that comes out of rocks in the ground. Others think that the texts are talking about metal used in the construction of aircraft. In any case, the spiritual power that comes from the meditation of the Best of Horses will enable Rudra Cakrin to materialize whatever weapons and vehicles the barbarians have built with the aid of science and technology.

The army of Shambhala will also include the reincarnations of many high lamas of Tibet as commanding officers. The abbot of Reting Monastery near Lhasa, for example, is supposed to be reborn as the general in charge of the right wing of mountains protecting the hidden kingdom. Another, more intriguing reincarnation will be a lama from Amdo, in eastern Tibet, who will become a commander of the barbarian forces and lure them into defeat at the hands of Rudra Cakrin. The lama himself will be killed, but his sacrifice will help liberate the world from the forces of evil. The lama seems to have a role in the prophecy similar to that of the goddess who reveals Shambhala to the barbarian King and encourages him to try to conquer it.[14]

The two armies will clash in a great battle that ends in the destruction of the barbarians and their doctrines of materialism. As we saw in the Panchen Lama's prayer to Shambhala, elephants will overwhelm elephants, horses will trample horses, chariots will smash chariots, and warriors will slay warriors. Even the gods will rise up to defeat the antigods attacking Shambhala. Rudra Cakrin himself will thrust a spear through the heart of the barbarian King, while Cakrin's General Hanumanda stabs the commander of the barbarian army (see Plate 4). Everyone killed in the battle, including the evil tyrant, will attain liberation, or at least a good rebirth in a Pure Land. The death administered by the King of Shambhala will turn out to be in reality the greatest of blessings. For this reason some Tibetans even pray to be reborn as insects to be squashed in the final battle.

Following his victory, Rudra Cakrin will extend his rule over the entire world and establish the golden age. All fighting will come to an end, and the earth itself will become a peaceful extension of Shambhala. People will no longer have to work for food; fruit will appear on trees, and grains will grow without the need for cultivation. Everyone will live a hundred years—without threat of disease or war. According to the main text of the Kalacakra Tantra, the human lifespan will, in fact, increase to eighteen hundred years. Although people will still die, they will have no fear of death, since they will know that it brings liberation or rebirth in an even better place than Shambhala. Under the rule of Rudra Cakrin, the teachings of Buddhism in general and of the Kalacakra in particular will spread and flourish throughout the world. Whether or not these teachings lead people to enlightenment in that lifetime, all will make great spiritual progress and acquire marvelous powers, such as the ability to walk extremely long distances in a day. They will also become very proficient in science and technology—but know how to use them for peaceful ends. During this time various sages of the past will come back to life and guide many fortunate people to liberation —so many, according to the Panchen Lama, that they will be "as dust on the land."[15]

Tibetans disagree over whether the golden age of Shambhala will come to an end. Some believe it will last forever; others say it will endure only a thousand years—or eighteen hundred at most. The texts do not clearly resolve the dispute. According to most of them, after Rudra Cakrin passes away, eight Kings will follow him, making forty in all from the time of the Buddha. (Interestingly enough, among these eight we find the names of incarnations of Vishnu who precede Kalki, Rudra Cakrin's equivalent in Hindu mythology. Since seven religious Kings precede the line of twenty-five Kulika Kings, Rudra Cakrin, the twenty-fifth Kulika King, is actually the thirty-second King of Shambhala.) The main Kalacakra text says that the human lifespan will decrease in stages from eighteen hundred years under the first two successors of Rudra Cakrin to one hundred years under the last. But it fails to specify what will happen thereafter—either to the world or to Shambhala.[16]

According to the more usual Buddhist prophecy, the teachings of Gautama Buddha will gradually deteriorate, lasting for only five thousand years at most. After that Buddhism will vanish, depravity will triumph, and life will become short and miserable. Then conditions will begin to improve slowly until, after many thousands of years, the next Buddha, Maitreya, will come to establish a golden age and enlighten the world. He will be the fifth in a line of one thousand Buddhas, each of whom brings his own teaching to replace the defunct teaching of his predecessor. Like the Hindu view of time, this prophecy foresees repeated cycles of degeneration and renewal.[17]

Most lamas combine the two prophecies into one and say that the golden age of Shambhala will come to an end with the demise of Buddhism five thousand years after the death of Gautama. Then the true teachings will once again be lost until the coming of Maitreya. Since thirty-two Kings of Shambhala, each with a reign of a hundred years, are supposed to come before Rudra Cakrin defeats the barbarians, the golden age will commence about thirty-two hundred years after the death of Gautama Buddha, leaving eighteen hundred years for it to endure. By predicting that Rudra Cakrin's successors will rule less of the world than he and that human lifespan will gradually decrease, the Kalacakra texts do suggest a definite decline of the golden age. Thubten Norbu, the present Dalai Lama's brother, has described one version of the end of the golden age of Shambhala in the following passage from his book *Tibet*:

> For a thousand years religion will be taught, but then will come the end of the world. Fire will be followed by wind, destroying all we have built; then will come water to cover everything we know. Only a few will survive, in caves and in the tops of trees. The gods will come from Ganden Paradise and take those people

back with them. They will be taught so that religion will not die, and when once again the winds blow the milk-ocean and once again the world is formed, these same enlightened ones, saved from the world before, will be the stars in the sky.[18]

Other lamas, a minority, tend to downplay the prophecy of Maitreya and to put more emphasis on the prophecy of Shambhala. They seem to view the former as an addition to the latter, which they consider older and more authoritative. They point out that the Kalacakra texts predict no specific end to the golden age and make no mention of Maitreya and his coming. According to Chopgye Trichen Rimpoche, the texts say nothing about what will happen after the fortieth King of Shambhala because Gautama Buddha prophesied only that far into the future. When Rudra Cakrin comes to power, he will make a further prophecy about what will take place thereafter. We should not, therefore, take the fortieth King to be the last—nor the end of his reign to be the end of Shambhala. The Tengboche Rimpoche, in agreement with this view, felt that whatever happens in the world outside, whether or not the golden age fades away, in the kingdom itself prosperity and bliss will continue without end. In any case, those who have attained enlightenment as a result of the defeat of the barbarians will have entered the changeless state of Nirvana beyond all possibility of further corruption; for them the golden age of Shambhala will last forever in the serenity of their hearts.

Now that we have a detailed overview of the history and prophecy of Shambhala, we can look into the inner meaning of the events leading up to the golden age and its aftermath. The final battle in which Rudra Cakrin comes out to defeat the barbarians clearly symbolizes a decisive inner conflict that results in the emergence or awakening of the innermost mind. In order to uncover the nature of this conflict and what gives rise to it, we need to establish a framework for interpreting this part of the myth. As we did with the features of the journey to Shambhala, we will treat the figures of the history and prophecy as embodiments of various contents of the mind. Viewed in this way, the sages, warriors, Kings, and Queens become actors in an internal drama that takes place in the mind of a single person on the path to liberation. In their lives and struggles we can see the activity and conflicts of thoughts, emotions, impulses, and other contents of the mind. The barbarians of the outside world, for example, symbolize egotistic contents of the surface consciousness, while the inhabitants of Shambhala represent the deeper levels of mind hidden in the superconscious.

From this point of view, the beginning of the history of Shambhala in the period before the advent of Buddhism symbolizes a preliminary stage in which the deeper levels of mind lie dormant and neglected. The lack of teachings that can lead to liberation indicates that the person seeking enlightenment has not yet begun his quest. He does not know that he has deeper levels of mind to awaken, nor does he have access to the means of doing so. Since his superconscious lies dormant, some outside influence must come to jolt him out of his state of ignorance. It comes in the form of Shakya Shambha, the member of the Buddha's clan who conquers Shambhala and founds its line of divine Kings, thereby preparing the kingdom for the advent of Buddhism. His conquest symbolizes the shock of an external idea or experience that penetrates to the superconscious and awakens the impulse to seek liberation. Stirred by this impulse, but not necessarily aware of its nature, the seeker becomes dissatisfied with his present state of being and begins to search for some way out of it.

The impulse to achieve liberation emerges in the form of King Sucandra and his retinue, who come out of Shambhala to ask the Buddha in India for the teachings of the Kalacakra. At some point early in his quest, the seeker catches a glimpse of the awakened state and the way to attain it. This may come about through a spontaneous mystical experience or through contact with a spiritual teacher. The teaching of the Kalacakra in India symbolizes such a moment of awakening and the energy and insight it brings. The Buddha embodies the teacher or situation that gives the seeker a taste of liberation. As we saw in our interpretation of the kingdom itself, the Kalacakra teachings represent the awareness of the deeper mind, which the seeker now experiences for a brief moment. Tibetan lamas generally transmit their power and wisdom through initiations that are supposed to arouse the recipients' deeper levels of mind and give them a glimpse of the state they will someday attain. The teaching of the Kalacakra at the stupa of Dhanyakataka, a relic mound in the shape of a mandala, represents such an initiation and the momentary awakening that goes with it.

As the incarnation of Vajrapani, master of secrets and inspirer of tantric teachings, King Sucandra represents the innermost mind in the role of inspirational guide and inner teacher. His return to Shambhala to write down the Kalacakra Tantra and compose commentaries on it symbolizes the way in which the innermost mind registers and assimilates the insights the seeker has received. In the jeweled mandala Sucandra builds, we can see the precious memory in which the seeker enshrines his first glimpse of enlightenment and the way to it. Sucandra also teaches the Kalacakra to the inhabitants of Shambhala: The innermost mind now conveys the insights of this glimpse to the deeper levels of mind in order to arouse their awareness. Although the innermost mind may seem to lie dormant while these levels awaken first, it actually guides the entire process of liberation and only appears to emerge last.

The first glimpse of enlightenment also stimulates the delusions of the surface consciousness. Dazzled by what he has glimpsed in himself, the seeker attributes the power and wisdom of the deeper mind to his ego and concludes that he has become the person he has always dreamed of being. If he has wished to be a great leader, now he is that leader; if he has aspired to be a selfless saint, now he is that saint. Whatever glorified image he may have had of himself now rises up to take over the surface consciousness. Without realizing it, he substitutes this image for the actual experience of his real nature. Rather than strive to awaken the awareness he glimpsed in the depths of his mind, he develops a superficial imitation of it—a deluded picture of himself and of reality.

We can see this process reflected in the rise of the barbarians after the teaching of the Kalacakra at Dhanyakataka. Their doctrines of materialism symbolize the illusions of power and wisdom that take over the seeker's surface consciousness. Enthralled by his glorified image of himself, he embarks on a campaign to establish the supremacy of his ego and suppress anything that might oppose it, or reveal its illusory nature. Just as Buddhism and the Kalacakra disappear before the onslaught of the barbarians in the outside world, so the insights he gained from his first glimpse of enlightenment fade from his surface consciousness, driven out by delusions of power and glory. Eventually he no longer even remembers the insights he once had: Like the Kalacakra teachings, which are concealed in Shambhala, they have become hidden in the depths of his mind.

For a while, despite the growing power of his illusions, the seeker still gets flashes of insight from the superconscious: Around the tenth century the Kalacakra comes from Shambhala to India and Tibet. A few parts of the surface consciousness that have not yet succumbed to delusions of power and glory manage to find and retain the deeper awareness symbolized by the teaching. We see them embodied in the Indian yogi-scholars who get the Kalacakra from Shambhala, and the Tibetan lamas who transmit it in Tibet. But the eventual loss of religion in Tibet through internal corruption and external invasion shows that the deluded views of the rest of the surface consciousness eventually take over even its more enlightened parts and distort the insights they have managed to preserve. The barbarian doctrines of materialism are destined to take over the outside world and subvert all spiritual values. The famine, disease, and misery that ensue represent the suffering the seeker experiences as a result of losing touch with his inner nature. His sterile quest for power and glory ravages the surface consciousness and turns it into a mental wasteland.

Meanwhile, unknown to the seeker, the deeper levels of his mind are gradually awakening. While Buddhism succumbs to barbarian doctrines in the outside world, the kings of Shambhala continue to teach and simplify the Kalacakra in order to guide their subjects toward liberation. This symbolizes the way in which the innermost mind clarifies the awareness of the deeper levels of mind so that they can awaken from their state of dormancy. The story of Manjushrikirti, the first Kulika King, and the sages who leave Shambhala represents an important step in this process. As a means of clearing up their confusion, Manjushrikirti initiates all the sages into a single diamond caste: In the course of purifying their awareness, the innermost mind gives the deeper levels of mind a unified view of reality so that they can work together toward the seeker's eventual liberation. Without this kind of inner unity, the superconscious would disintegrate and fall prey to the delusions of the surface consciousness. Manjushrikirti warns the sages that if they do not get rid of their discordant views and enter the single diamond caste, "the doctrines of the barbarians will come to spread even in Shambhala."

A parallel kind of unification takes place in the surface consciousness. We can see its progress in the wars that lead to the emergence of an evil King who unites all the barbarians under his rule. The barbarians in their struggles against each other represent conflicting self-images or egos that fight among themselves to dominate the seeker's mind. Eventually one ego, symbolized by the evil King, manages to subdue the others and bring them under its control. In this way the seeker suppresses the internal conflicts of the surface consciousness and attains a kind of inner unity. But despite the appearance of peace it creates, this unity requires constant tension to hold the antagonistic egos in check. If the victorious ego should relax its grip, all the tumultuous impulses it has repressed would break out again, shattering the calm it seems to have attained. Just as the evil King must hold onto his power through a regime of tyranny, so the seeker has to maintain a dictatorial control over his thoughts and feelings. The unity he has achieved in the surface consciousness is an unstable façade that can fall apart at any moment. It is, in fact, a superficial imitation of the real unity that develops in the deeper mind.

By unifying the seeker's illusory images of himself, the triumphant ego inadvertently makes it easier for the innermost mind to destroy them: The evil King unwittingly gathers all the barbarian forces together in one place so that the King of Shambhala can defeat them in a single decisive battle. The innermost mind makes other, similar uses of the ego's pride to free the seeker from his illusions. In one version of the prophecy, a goddess who protects Buddhism tells the barbarian ministers about Shambhala and goads them into trying to conquer it. In another version, the Savioress Tara reveals the hidden kingdom to the evil tyrant and lets his jealousy do the rest. In both cases elements of the deeper mind, symbolized by these female deities, use the ego's pride to lure it into a fatal confrontation with the superior power of the superconscious. The Amdo lama who is supposed to reincarnate as a commander of the barbarian army and guide it into defeat embodies another element of the deeper mind that infiltrates the surface consciousness and uses the ego's arrogance to lead it to its own destruction—and the seeker's liberation.

After learning of the existence of the hidden kingdom, the evil King tries to conquer Shambhala and impose his own barbarian doctrines on its inhabitants. Having become aware of the superconscious, the ego tries to take it over and extend its own illusions into the deepest reaches of the mind. The disagreement among lamas over whether the barbarians will or will not be able to penetrate into Shambhala itself reflects differing views as to whether the ego possesses the power to delude the deeper levels of mind. Whether or not it does, its boundless arrogance eventually awakens a reaction that overwhelms and destroys it. This happens when the ego tries to subjugate even the innermost mind and reduce it to its own superficial level of awareness.

The barbarian King's attempt to conquer Shambhala prompts Rudra Cakrin to come out to liberate the world from the forces of materialism: The deluded energy of the ego provides the shock needed to galvanize the innermost mind so that it emerges to free the seeker from his illusions. Chopgye Trichen Rimpoche pointed out that by forcing Rudra Cakrin to come out to establish the golden age, the barbarians actually help to spread Buddhism, despite their attempts to destroy it. He compared their role in the prophecy to the use of ignorance in certain tantric

practices: "Those who seek enlightenment normally avoid ignorance, but sometimes ignorance itself supports their meditation."

The evil King's attempt to invade the hidden kingdom ex-
emplifies the wrong way of taking the journey to Shambhala. As
we have seen, the guidebooks tell the traveler to go for the
benefit of others, but the barbarian King goes solely for the sake
of his own aggrandizement. Instead of seeking the teachings of
the King of Shambhala, he sets out to destroy them and plunder
the kingdom of its riches. The ego embarks on the inner journey
not to awaken the innermost mind and obtain its guidance, but
to subjugate it and appropriate its powers. Whereas the traveler
of the guidebooks overcomes the barriers guarding Shambhala
with the help of deities, the barbarian King has to rely on material means of his own devising, such as aircraft. In other words,
the ego attempts to break into the superconscious without the
approval or assistance of the deeper levels of mind. As the fate
of the barbarians shows, even if the ego succeeds in reaching its
goal, its efforts will have only led it to its own destruction.

Even so, the wrong kind of journey can still have beneficial
consequences. The barbarian attempt to invade Shambhala results in the death of the evil King and the liberation of the outside world from the doctrines of materialism. Although the seeker
takes the inner journey the wrong way, it nevertheless releases
him from identification with his ego and frees the surface consciousness from its illusions. Even the evil King benefits from his
misguided attempt to invade Shambhala: The death he finds at
the end of his journey gives him either liberation or rebirth in a
Pure Land ideally suited for making spiritual progress. The inner
journey transforms the ego from an illusory image that shuts out
awareness into a transparent window that reveals the innermost
mind. The death of the evil King symbolizes a transformation of
consciousness in which the seeker discovers the wisdom inherent
in his illusions.

The happy rebirth or liberation of the barbarian King suggests that the seeker finds what he was really seeking in his
quest for power and glory. Whether or not he realized it, he was
trying to establish the supremacy of his ego in order to free him-

self from bondage and suffering by putting himself beyond their reach. But in building up an illusory image of omnipotence that he had to guard against all possible threats, such as the innermost mind, he succeeded in doing the opposite: He bound himself instead to a source of constant anxiety and inevitable frustration. Only when the seeker gives up his quest for power—when the evil King meets defeat in the final battle—does he attain the real goal of his striving. Then he finds the inner peace and freedom that he was really seeking—and realizes that he has no need for the power and glory that seemed so essential.

The final battle itself symbolizes the decisive inner confrontation that must eventually take place between the ego and the innermost mind. It follows the resolution of lesser conflicts between opposing impulses of the surface consciousness—the barbarian wars in the outside world. In this culminating confrontation, the pure awareness of the innermost mind finally overcomes the delusions of the ego. Rudra Cakrin, the incarnation of Manjushri, the Bodhisattva of Wisdom, defeats the barbarian King whose name means either "Childish Intellect" or "The Intelligence of Doing"—the latter meaning referring to the superficial activity of the surface consciousness. Since the seeker has identified himself with his ego, embodied in the evil tyrant, the final battle represents a death-and-rebirth experience that he must undergo on the way to liberation. In order to awaken to his real nature, he must die to his illusory image of himself.

In the final battle Rudra Cakrin uses spiritual means to vanquish the forces of materialism. Through meditation on the Best of Horses, he creates a supernatural army capable of defeating even the invincible barbarians. This implies that instead of descending to fight the ego on its terms, the innermost mind transfixes it with the direct awareness of its illusory nature. If the innermost mind were to do otherwise, it would sink to the level of the ego, and in conquering it, simply give rise to another ego—a new and even more powerful tyrant. To break free from the delusions that blind him, the seeker needs more than new ideas and inspiration, however true they may be: He needs the transcendent awareness of the deeper mind.

After defeating the barbarians, Rudra Cakrin extends his rule over the outside world. The golden age he establishes symbolizes the state of inner harmony the seeker attains when the innermost mind finally emerges to take over the surface consciousness. The split between the conscious and unconscious regions of his mind vanishes—and with it the conflicts and illusions it spawned. The process of awakening that had been taking place unknown to him in the hidden depths of the superconscious now spreads to the surface consciousness. Similarly, many great teachers appear in the outside world to guide countless numbers of people to enlightenment. The golden age represents the stage or stages at which the inner journey becomes completely conscious. Now the seeker can devote himself wholly to the task of achieving liberation, without working against himself. Since the outside world becomes an extension of Shambhala, our earlier interpretation of the kingdom itself gives us a good idea of the state he has attained.

Depending on how we read the prophecy, this state of attainment may or may not come to an end. The version that says the golden age will last forever suggests that the seeker has completely transcended the illusions of his ego and cannot fall back under their spell. On the other hand, the versions of the prophecy that predict an end to the golden age suggest that the seeker is fated to slip away from the state he has attained. But in their additional predictions of the coming of the next Buddha, Maitreya, they also imply that he will regain what he loses. This opens up interesting insights into the cyclical nature of the inner journey.

Nearly a thousand Buddhas are supposed to follow Maitreya, each coming after his predecessor's teachings have faded out of the world. This suggests that the golden age of Shambhala represents a temporary state of attainment that recurs over and over on the inner journey. The seeker gains it each time the innermost mind liberates him from an illusory self-image that has come to dominate the surface consciousness. The people who attain enlightenment during the golden age symbolize elements of the mind that are freed from the delusions of that particular ego. As a result, the seeker enjoys a period of inner freedom and clarity, but like the sojourns in pleasant groves along the way to Shambhala, it cannot last. The seeker harbors other images, latent egos, that have also been liberated from the bondage of the defeated ego. Eventually the next one rises to take over the surface consciousness and obscure his awareness with its illusions. The golden age comes to an end until the coming of the next Buddha or savior equivalent to the King of Shambhala.

We can see the cyclical nature of the inner prophecy even more clearly through the related Hindu myth of Kalki, the last incarnation of Vishnu. There, each time the world goes through its cycle of four declining ages, this equivalent of Rudra Cakrin returns to destroy the forces of evil and bring back the golden age. As this cycle repeats itself on an inner level, the innermost mind gradually frees the seeker from one illusory image after another until he is free of them all. Approached this way, the history and prophecy of Shambhala reveal not only the course of the inner journey, but also the nature of the particular stages that make it up. In other words, we can view each stage as a recapitulation in miniature of the entire path to liberation.

Whereas the guidebooks focused our attention on the efforts of the seeker to reach the superconscious, the history and prophecy of Shambhala bring out the other side of the inner journey: the role of the innermost mind in actually motivating and guiding it. They correct a tendency to regard the process of liberation as the artificial work of the ego, rather than as a natural unfolding of the deeper mind. The history and prophecy of the kingdom contribute a sense of growth and inevitability to our interpretation of the guidebooks. Just as the King of Shambhala comes out to defeat the barbarians only when he is prophesied to do so, the innermost mind emerges only when its time has come. The seeker cannot force his own liberation: If he tries, he will only succeed in building up his ego and binding himself ever more tightly in its grip. All he can do is help the process along in a natural way, understanding that the innermost mind, not he, is really doing it. When the innermost mind finally acts to dispel his illusions, he will see Shambhala in the world around him. As Khetsun Zangpo remarked, "Just as flowers blossom in the spring when heat, fertilizer, and water meet together, in the same way Shambhala will be visible to all when the time is right."

11

Beyond Shambhala

So far we have treated Shambhala as a hidden kingdom of Central Asia that symbolizes a hidden region of the mind. While such an interpretation helps to uncover the deeper meaning of the myth, it also tends to inspire escapist fantasies: If we do not treat this interpretation carefully, it can lead us off into daydreams of an idyllic state of bliss and tranquillity far from the problems of everyday life. A Shambhala hidden deep in the unconscious is as remote from our usual experience of the world as any mythical kingdom of Central Asia. Being so distant and unreal, such a version of Shambhala can easily become a paradise that we merely imagine in the depths of our minds—an illusory inner sanctuary to which we go to escape from the unpleasant realities of the world around us. In the myth itself, this is clearly not the purpose of Shambhala: The seeker goes to the kingdom not to escape reality but to find it—to obtain the teachings that will enable him to see things as they really are. To remain true to the myth and avoid using it as another source of illusion, we need to relate the myth to the world in which we live: We need to see how we can experience it in the ordinary events of everyday life.

Although the hidden nature of Shambhala has a tendency to

stimulate escapist dreams, it does give the myth much of its power and appeal. The idea of a mysterious country concealed behind distant snow mountains has a special fascination: It stirs something deep within us that longs to feel itself in the presence of the unknown. As much as anything it might conceal, we seek the sense of mystery evoked by a hidden place like Shambhala. The unknown itself has a freshness and promise, a depth and richness that nothing we find seems able to match. In its presence we feel a sense of awe and wonder that only it has the power to inspire.

In addition, by virtue of its hidden nature, Shambhala possesses a purity that cannot be corrupted by the outside world. According to the myth, only those who have rid themselves of any inclination to desecrate the kingdom can find it—at least until the barbarians try to conquer it. This gives Shambhala a special quality that sets it apart from other idyllic places, which although remote are nevertheless accessible and vulnerable to exploitation. Unlike Hunza, a peaceful valley in the Karakoram Mountains of Pakistan that may have inspired James Hilton's idea of Shangri-la, it is difficult to imagine Shambhala ever turning into a resort for wealthy tourists. In our minds the kingdom lies far beyond the reach of anyone who might use it in such a way. The powerful appeal of Shambhala reflects a yearning we have for some pure and uncorrupted place that neither we nor others can ever defile.

Such a place, imbued with the sense of mystery and purity we seek, lies closer than we think. The hidden kingdom of Shambhala symbolizes, in fact, the hidden nature of the world right here, all around us. As long as we remain attached to the delusions of the ego, we lack the awareness needed to perceive it. A screen of preconceptions thrown up by the surface consciousness obscures our view of what surrounds us. Instead of seeing the world as it is, we see it as we picture it to be. Only when we awaken the direct awareness of the deeper mind do our actual surroundings appear before us, no longer concealed behind a mist of illusions. Because the surface consciousness cannot perceive it, the world revealed by the deeper mind can never be touched and defiled by the selfish desires of the ego. Since it lies beyond all conception, accessible only to immediate experience, it always possesses a fresh and mysterious quality. We cannot describe the world as it is nor fit it into any system of established knowledge. Even when we know it, it remains in the deepest sense unknown.

Myths of hidden places like Shambhala help to remind us, if only subconsciously, that there is much more to the world than we imagine. We need such a reminder to counteract the tendency of the surface consciousness to cut us off from immediate experience and lock us up in the illusions of the ego. Without something to inspire a sense of the unknown, of a realm beyond conception, our lives become closed and static, limited by the superficial views we hold. Rather than being just a form of escape, our interest in Shambhala actually reflects a deep longing to experience reality itself. We might say that the kingdom represents the place in each of our lives where we make contact with the world in which we really live. Such a place could be a forest in moonlight, a dewdrop struck by the sun, the smile of one we love—anything that awakens a deeper and more intense awareness of what lies within and around us.

When this awareness appears, it brings back the forgotten memories of childhood experience. It reminds us of a time when we did not know what the world was like, when everything seemed as unknown and mysterious as Shambhala. At that age we had no preconceptions to cover up and dull our perceptions. Rather than fitting things into fixed ideas of how they should be, we experienced them directly, with all the sense of awe and wonder they inspired. As a result, the world around us had the fresh and magical quality of a hidden kingdom. We were open to whatever it might contain, no matter how strange or fantastic it might seem.

In taking the inner journey to Shambhala, we strive to regain this direct awareness of a child with all its sense of wonder and awe. But we cannot do so by retreating into the past and attempting to become children again. We have lost the innocence that enabled us to experience the world directly. We cannot simply ignore or wish away the screen of preconceptions that now obscures our vision. We have to face ourselves and see what we have done to our minds. Only by becoming aware of our illusions and how we cling to them can we free ourselves from their power and awaken a fresh and direct awareness of the world around us. Rather than go back, we have to go forward to a new and wiser innocence—one that combines the wonder of a child with the wisdom of a sage.

Our interpretation of the guidebooks to Shambhala suggests that we can do this by living our lives as journeys toward a deeper awareness of ourselves and the world around us. By treating the ordinary events of daily life as we did the magical features of the journey to Shambhala, we may be able to uncover the hidden aspects of ourselves that we need to know in order to awaken the deeper mind. Like the demons and deities, mountains and rivers encountered by the traveler in the guidebooks, the people and things we meet each day reflect various contents of the subconscious that we have projected onto our surroundings. Because of this, if we approach them as features of the path to Shambhala, these objects of external perception can act as symbols that reveal the illusions and insights concealed within our minds. In other words, we can use the events of daily life as means of actually taking the inner journey symbolized by the guidebooks to Shambhala.

Our interpretation of the guidebooks can help us to see the symbolism inherent in the events of everyday life. If we treat frustrating incidents, for example, as obstacles of the journey to Shambhala, they take on a new significance that directs our attention toward inner barriers of resentment and anger that block our access to greater awareness. In a similar way, enticing people and situations can act as the seductive maidens of the guidebooks, giving us valuable insights into the nature of our desires and the attachments they create. Like insurmountable snow mountains on the way to Shambhala, problems that seem insoluble can bring out feelings of inadequacy that we need to acknowledge and overcome. The barking of a dog on a dark street at night can become the ferocious howling of the killer animals in the terrible forest of Rinpungpa's poem, making us aware of the power and extent of the irrational fears that lurk in the depths of our minds.

Like the features of the journey to Shambhala, the events of daily life can also reveal the energy and insight of the deeper mind. Certain people we meet in the course of our lives inspire and teach us in ways that make a particularly deep and lasting impression. Through them, as through the sages of the guide-books, we can become aware of our own inner resources of wisdom and power. Sometimes, if we stop to face a problem instead of trying to avoid it, a burst of inspiration will emerge, apparently out of nowhere, to solve it for us, like the deities who suddenly appear to carry Rinpungpa's yogi over the snow mountains to Shambhala. On such occasions the confrontation with an obstacle serves to awaken the awareness of the deeper mind. At other times, a moment of contentment on accomplishing a difficult task or just the experience of the world on a beautiful morning can act as a peaceful grove on the way to Shambhala, reminding us of a deep calm that lies hidden beneath the turbulence of our emotions.

Whether or not we ever reach the ultimate goal, treating our lives as expressions of the inner journey has value in itself: It enables us to appreciate and make use of those sides of our experience that we tend to neglect or repress. When viewed as necessary steps of the inner journey, even the most trivial events of daily life, such as the simple act of walking to the corner, take on meaning and significance. We begin to see that they, too, have something of importance to show us about ourselves and our habitual ways of thinking and acting. By revealing the deeper passions and illusions that bind us to our egos, even negative experiences of disappointment and failure can become positive opportunities for developing greater freedom and awareness.

In other words, living life as a journey can serve to redeem it and fill it with meaning. By giving the events of daily life a symbolic dimension, it makes them in a sense transparent, turning them into windows that open up fresh views into ourselves and the world around us. As a result, our lives become richer and deeper, filled with a growing awareness of reality. In this way, rather than merely stimulating escapist fantasies of the mind, the symbolism of the journey to Shambhala can help us to live more fully right here in the world of everyday life.

In living life as a journey, we can also treat it as the unfolding of a prophecy—the prophecy of eventual liberation from the bondage of our illusions. Viewing our lives this way makes it easier for us to experience the process of awakening symbolized by the history and prophecy of Shambhala. We can make use of our interpretation of the rise and fall of the barbarians, for example, to gain a deeper understanding of the way our illusions develop—how they spread and grow until they collide with something more powerful that shatters them and reveals their empty nature. The symbolism of the barbarian King, in particular, helps to focus our attention on the tyrant within us—the ego that tends to take over the surface consciousness and encroach on the territory of the deeper mind.

We can see the prophecy repeated each time we have a fresh insight into the nature of reality. At first it has a striking depth and vitality, opening new vistas filled with meaning, but then, just as barbarian doctrines supplant the teachings of the Kalacakra in the outside world, our old ideas gradually take over and distort the original insight, turning it into something flat and lifeless. Instead of using the insight to see things as they are, we use it to build up our egos: We take pride in being a person who has had such a deep and meaningful insight—and lose sight of its meaning. Intoxicated by the resulting arrogance and delusion, like the barbarian King of the prophecy, we eventually blunder into a situation we cannot handle, which exposes our pretenses and leaves us devastated. This apparent calamity, however, clears the way for the emergence of fresh insights, symbolized by the teachings that appear in the golden age of Shambhala.

The symbolism of the prophecy helps us to distinguish the impulses of the ego from the promptings of the deeper mind. In any given situation we can examine our actions to see whether they reflect the motivation of the barbarian tyrant or the King of Shambhala. This gives us a perspective on ourselves that tends to keep us from succumbing to our own desires and illusions. In particular, it helps us to avoid falling into the delusion of thinking we are liberating ourselves when we are only building up the power and illusion of our egos. At the very least, we develop a skeptical view of our motivations, which helps to prevent us from doing things we might later regret. At the same time, we learn to recognize and heed the guidance that comes from the deeper mind—the liberating urges and insights symbolized by the Kalacakra teachings that emerge from Shambhala. As we come to rely on this guidance, we find ourselves less and less inclined to interfere with the process of awakening taking place in our lives. Instead of trying to impose liberation on ourselves, we allow it to unfold naturally, like the prophecy of Shambhala.

We can even see the history and prophecy of Shambhala as an allegory for the course of life as a whole, from the innocence of infancy to the maturity of old age. As an initiation, the Buddha's teaching of the Kalacakra in India symbolizes the birth of a baby with his fresh, new vision of reality. The loss of true religion in the outside world represents the child's loss of awareness and spontaneity as he grows up in a society that encourages him to ignore his inner nature and be false to himself. Just as the barbarian doctrines take over the world, so the values and concerns of others take over his mind, filling it with conflicting desires and illusions. He reaches the stage symbolized by the wars that the victorious barbarians fight among themselves. Most people never go beyond this stage; they remain caught in the conflicts of the surface consciousness, unable to get what they want or to see themselves as they are. Those who achieve worldly success manage to subjugate their desires and illusions under a single aim, which they succeed in accomplishing: They reach the stage of the King who unites all the squabbling barbarians under his dictatorial rule. The final battle and the golden age, on the other hand, represent the real fulfillment of life—the attainment of true maturity. If, after many years of struggle, a person manages to overcome his illusions and permanently awaken the deeper mind, he recovers the fresh vision of a child, enriched and deepened by the wisdom of experience. Whoever

achieves this kind of maturity lives his old age as the golden age
of Shambhala.

So far we have spoken primarily of the awakening of the individual, but the prophecy itself speaks of much more: It predicts
the coming of a golden age in which everyone will make great
progress toward enlightenment. This makes it clear that the purpose of the inner journey is not to withdraw from the world, but
to make it a place more conducive to the attainment of liberation
by all. In seeking to awaken the deeper mind, we seek a new
awareness that will enable us to help others to free themselves
from the bondage of their illusions. The prophecy counteracts a
tendency we have to view the inner journey solely in terms of
our own liberation. It encourages us to venture into the depths
of the mind in order to emerge, like the King of Shambhala, with
the power and wisdom needed to transform society and help establish the golden age.

The prophecy suggests, in fact, that only when we have awakened the deeper mind—or have access to it—can we really
change the world for the better. Only then will we possess the
awareness and compassion needed to create a just and humane
society in which everyone can be truly free. Just as the golden
age will emerge with the King of Shambhala, so the beneficial
changes we seek must issue from the inspiration of the deeper
mind. The prophecy implies that the solutions to the world's
problems will come from an inner source hidden within each of
us. As long as we continue to ignore this source and try to impose changes from without, experimenting with one idea or another, we will engage in the fruitless manipulations of the ego,
and all our efforts, like those of the barbarians, will end in failure. But when each of us, turning to the deeper mind, begins to
see the hidden nature of reality and to act on it, the world itself
will become an extension of Shambhala.

We have now seen what kind of insights the myth of Shambhala can give us. Myths with the power to inspire such insights—
with the power to awaken a deeper awareness of reality—are
more than superficial creations of the imagination or intellect:
Most of them seem to have their source deep in the unconscious.

A number of them come, in fact, from the dreams and visions of people who appear to have been in touch with the deeper mind, if only for a moment.[1] We saw an example of this in Khamtul Rimpoche's dream of going to Shambhala. The old lama he met at the end of his journey, the one who turned into a Bodhisattva and gave him teachings, evidently embodied the wisdom of the innermost mind. Although much of the dream reflected what Khamtul already knew about Shambhala, it added some new features to the myth, such as the three bridges leading to the center of the kingdom. Myths with this kind of origin have a special power that enables them to penetrate the illusions of the surface consciousness and awaken a response deep within us. They are the means by which the deeper mind conveys its insights to us and arouses an impulse to greater awareness.

Although such a myth originates in the depths of the mind, it has to emerge through the surface consciousness of the person who receives it. In doing so, it necessarily takes on a form that makes sense in terms of the particular culture that has shaped that person's view of the world. This means that despite its outward appearance, the myth of Shambhala is not just a Tibetan—or an Indian—myth; it is, rather, a Tibetan expression of something much deeper and more universal. Although it has assumed a form that has power and meaning for Tibetans in particular, the essence of the myth lies beyond the confines of any culture or religion. As we saw in Chapter 4, the underlying themes of the myth of Shambhala recur in the many different forms of related myths from other parts of the world.

Some of these myths exert a considerable influence on our lives, affecting not only what happens to us as individuals but also what happens to society and the course of history itself. In Chapter 4 we saw how the prophecy of the Messiah and the quest for the promised land merged and evolved into the modern myth of progress—the conviction that science and industry will transform the earth into a material paradise and establish a golden age of prosperity for all. This conviction lies behind much of the push for social reform and economic development that now determines the policies, as well as the fate, of governments throughout the world, regardless of their particular ideology. Even in countries that seem to have achieved a golden age of prosperity, the myth continues to have power, giving rise to expectations of constant improvement in income and quality of life. As recent events have clearly shown, governments that fail to meet these expectations find themselves in a great deal of trouble. In many ways the myth of progress is one of the most powerful forces at work in the world today.

This myth, which has driven us for so long, is now, however, reaching its limits. As we confront increasing shortages of energy and natural resources, we are beginning to realize that the endless growth the myth promises cannot continue. At the same time, we are becoming aware that our efforts to create a material paradise through science and technology are actually degrading and polluting more and more of the environment. If we continue to develop and industrialize as we have, we may even make the earth itself uninhabitable. In the name of progress and efficiency, the myth has also given rise to increasing dehumanization, reducing people to numbers that can be more easily shuffled and processed by computers. Even those who seem to have benefited, those who live in affluent suburbs or other oases of prosperity, are experiencing a growing sense of boredom and meaninglessness that drives many of them to random acts of violence and self-destruction. The myth of progress seems, in fact, to have led us into the degenerate period of materialism that is supposed to precede the golden age of Shambhala.

We have come to this quandary in large part because we have lost sight of the inner side of the myth of progress. In striving to create an earthly paradise, we have overlooked the needs and nature of those who must live in it. A fascination with the promise of ever-increasing material prosperity has led us to develop a one-sided view of the myth that emphasizes external progress at the expense of inner development. Failing to realize that the two must go together, we have attempted to transform the world without transforming ourselves. As a result, we have failed to develop the wisdom needed to see what really needs to be done. Like the barbarian doctrines of the Tibetan prophecy, an obsession with material progress for its own sake has taken over our minds and now threatens to drive us to our destruction.

We need to recover a balance and perspective that will enable us to use, rather than be used by, the power of the myth of progress. The kind of insights we have gleaned from the Tibetan myth of Shambhala may be able to help us do this by redirecting our attention toward the inner meaning of the myths that shape our lives. Through these insights we can gain a deeper understanding of the underlying nature of the myth of progress, in particular, and the way in which we have distorted it. With the help of such an understanding, we may be able to reverse the present course of events and begin to transform both ourselves and the world around us. We may even be able to use the myth of progress itself as a symbol to awaken the deeper mind and liberate ourselves from the bondage of our illusions.

Ultimately, however, each one of us needs to find and seek his own equivalent of Shambhala—that place, thing, person, or even idea that has the power to inspire us to take the inner journey to greater freedom and awareness. Such a symbol can give meaning and direction to our lives, as well as the strength and determination to endure the trials that lie ahead. For it to do so, it must, however, have the reality for us that a hidden valley has for the Tibetan yogi who seeks it. Our personal equivalent of Shambhala must be something genuine that grows naturally out of our own lives and experiences, something that comes, in fact, from the inspiration of the deeper mind. The myth of Shambhala is not a blueprint for us to copy: Its features are the symbols of another time and place. The myth is meant, instead, to encourage us to find a form of our own that reveals, rather than replaces, the essence of the kingdom itself.

In seeking the essence of Shambhala through whichever form we find to be ours, we come to realize that it lies hidden right here in the world around us. This realization opens us to a growing sense of the sacred in everything we see. People and things that we had regarded with scorn or indifference become sources of wonder and awe. What had seemed dead and meaningless comes alive with a mysterious significance that links it to us in deep and inexplicable ways. As we become aware of the sacred nature of all that surrounds us, we cease to see people and things as objects to be abused and exploited. We come, instead, to cherish them for what they are—and to treat them with the utmost care and respect. If we can awaken this sense of the sacred in the world around us, then we may have a chance of bringing about the golden age of so many myths and dreams.

Notes

The notes contain most Tibetan and Sanskrit terms in transliteration with diacritical marks. For the sake of simplicity, I have chosen to transliterate Tibetan words as syllables without intervening hyphens, unless they appear otherwise in published title pages. The names of contemporary Tibetans and a few important figures of the past, as well as some place names, are written according to the way they sound, as in the main text of the book. Sk. and Tb. stand for Sanskrit and Tibetan, respectively.

1: BEHIND THE RANGES

The Kipling quote comes from "The Explorer" in *Collected Verse of Rudyard Kipling* (New York: Doubleday, Page & Company, 1907), p. 19.

1. Sven Hedin, *My Life as an Explorer*, trans. A. Huebsch (Garden City, N.Y.: Garden City Publishing Company, 1925), p. 188.

2. Ibid., p. 186.

3. James Hilton, *Lost Horizon* (London: Pan Books, 1966), p. 128; ibid., p. 129.

4. The following description of Shambhala is drawn from a number of sources: Klong rdol bla ma ngag dbang blo bzang, *Dus kyi 'khor lo'i lo rgyus dang sham bha la'i zhing bkod bcas* (cited hereafter as *Sham bha la'i zhing bkod*) in Ven. Dalama, ed., *Tibetan Buddhist Studies of Kloṅ-rdol bla-ma Ṅag-dbaṅ-blo-bzaṅ* (Mussoorie: Ven. Dalama, 1963) 1:128–32; the Third Panchen Lama, Blo bzang dpal ldan ye shes, *Grub pa'i gnas chen po sham bha la'i rnam bshad 'phags yul gyi rtogs brjod dang bcas pa* (block print, 50 folios), fols. 41b–44a (commonly referred to, and hereafter cited, as *Sham bha la'i lam yig*), Tibetan text and German translation in Albert Grünwedel, ed. and trans., *Der Weg nach Śambhala,* Abhandlungen der Königlich Bayer-ischen Akademie der Wissenschaften 29, No. 3 (Munich, 1915), pp. 70–74; Gar-je K'am-trül Rinpoche, "A Geography and History of Shambhala," trans. Sherpa Tulku and A. Berzin, *The Tibet Journal* 3, No. 3 (Autumn 1978), pp. 6–8; *Rin spungs ngag dbang 'jigs grags kyis rang gi yab la phul ba'i zhu 'phrin rig pa 'dzin pa'i pho nya* (manuscript, 39 fols., reproduced and published in Dharamsala: Library of Tibetan Works and Archives, 1974), pp. 50–55 (hereafter cited as *Rin spungs pa'i pho nya*); Berthold Laufer, "Zur buddhistischen Litteratur der Uiguren," *T'oung Pao,* Ser. 2, Vol. 3 (1907), pp. 405–7.

5. K'am-trül Rinpoche, "Geography and History of Shambhala," p. 7.

6. The Tibetan for *Shambhala* (Sk. *śambhala*) is *bde 'byung,* "the source of happiness" (see Sarat Chandra Das, *A Tibetan-English Dictionary, with Sanskrit Synonyms,* rev. ed. [reprint ed., Delhi: Motilal Banarsidass, 1976], pp. 670 and 1,231). This trans-lation is not immediately evident from the Sanskrit. *Sham* (Sk. *śam*) does mean "happiness," but *bhala* is a term of uncertain meaning, possibly derived from the obscure verbal root *bhal,* which may mean "to give" (see Sir Monier Monier-Williams, *A Sanskrit-English Dictionary,* new ed. [1899; reprint ed., London: Oxford University Press, 1970], pp. 748 and 1,054).

7. For a reference to Kālacakra texts dealing with medicine and smallpox see the English Preface of Raghu Vira and Lokesh Chan-dra, eds., *Kālacakra-Tantra and Other Texts* (New Delhi: Inter-

national Academy of Indian Culture, 1966), Pt. 1, p. 12. On astrology and chronology see Robert Bleichsteiner, *L'Église jaune,* trans. J. Marty (Paris: Payot, 1950), pp. 249–61. For references on alchemy and the use of natural forces see the English introduction of Sonam Kazi, ed., *Encyclopedia Tibetica: The Collected Works of Bo-dong pan-chen Phyogs-les rnam-rgyal* (New Delhi: Tibet House, 1969), Vol. 2.

8. Mostly from an interview with the Bon lama Tenzin Namdak. On Bon and Olmolungring see Samten G. Karmay, ed. and trans., *The Treasury of Good Sayings: A Tibetan History of Bon* (London: Oxford University Press, 1972), pp. xxvii–xxxi, 15–26; id., "A General Introduction to the History and Doctrines of Bon," *Memoirs of the Research Department of the Toyo Bunko,* No. 33 (1975), pp. 171–76; David L. Snellgrove, ed. and trans., *The Nine Ways of Bon* (London: Oxford University Press, 1967), p. 14 and Illustration XXII.

9. Helmut Hoffmann, *The Religions of Tibet,* trans. E. Fitzgerald (New York: The Macmillan Company, 1961), p. 126.

10. On Tsilupa see Georges de Roerich, "Studies in the Kālacakra," *Journal of Urusvati Himalayan Research Institute of Roerich Museum* 2 (1931): 18–19. On the Kālacakra entering India see, for example, Hoffmann, *Religions of Tibet,* pp. 126–29.

11. Sarat Chandra Das, *Journey to Lhasa and Central Tibet* (London: John Murray, 1902), p. 181.

12. On Dorjieff and the Great Game see Sir Charles Bell, *Tibet: Past and Present* (Oxford: Clarendon, 1924), pp. 62–63. Grünwedel mentions the book tracing the Romanov Dynasty to Shambhala in *Der Weg nach Sambhala,* p. 4.

13. Song adapted from George N. Roerich, *Trails to Inmost Asia* (New Haven, Conn.: Yale University Press, 1931), p. 157. Quoted in C. R. Bawden, *The Modern History of Mongolia* (New York: Frederick A. Praeger, 1968), pp. 262–63. Hanamand is the general who will assist Rudra Cakrin, the future King of Shambhala, in the final battle against the barbarians—see Chap. 10.

14. See Roerich, "Studies in the Kālacakra," pp. 15–16.

15. See M. Huc, *Recollections of a Journey Through Tartary,*

Thibet, and China, trans. P. Smith (New York: D. Appleton Company, 1866), pp. 162–64.

16. Quoted in John MacGregor, *Tibet: A Chronicle of Exploration* (New York: Praeger Publishers, 1970), p. 60. In an interview in the *New York Times* (July 26, 1936), Pt. IX, p. 3, Hilton said he "cribbed" most of his Tibetan material from the British Museum Library, particularly from Huc. I have tried, without success, to find out if he had ever heard of Shambhala. The interview above certainly gives no indication of it.

17. Alexander Csoma de Koros, "Note on the Origin of the Kāla-Chakra and Adi-Buddha Systems," *Journal of the Asiatic Society of Bengal* (abbrev. *JASB*) 2, No. 14 (1833), p. 57. For Laufer and Grünwedel's translations see n. 4 above.

18. Nicholas Roerich, *Shambhala* (New York: Frederick A. Stokes, 1930).

19. Speech by Frances R. Grant in *The Roerich Pact and the Banner of Peace* (New York: The Roerich Pact and Banner of Peace Committee, 1947), p. 116. This publication also includes a draft of the pact and copies of news clippings about its signing, etc.

20. *Newsweek* (March 22, 1948), p. 28. On Wallace, Roerich, and the Guru Letters see this article and Arthur M. Schlesinger, Jr., *The Coming of the New Deal* (Boston, Mass.: Houghton Mifflin Company, 1959), pp. 31–34. Two of the Guru Letters published by Pegler mention Shambhala by name (Westbrook Pegler, "As Pegler Sees It," *New York Journal-American* [Mar. 10 and 12, 1948]). Wallace denied that he had written them, but Schlesinger seems to think they were genuine.

21. Translated from a prayer by Blo bzang dpal ldan ye shes, commonly referred to as *Sham bha la'i smon lam* (hereafter cited by that name), quoted by Klong rdol bla ma in *Tibetan Buddhist Studies* 1:150–51.

22. K'am-trül Rinpoche, "Geography and History of Shambhala," p. 11.

23. Remark by Geshe Rabten. H. Adams Carter told me this

story about the Anglo-American expedition of 1936, in which he participated, to Nanda Devi.

24. From Jacques Bacot, *Introduction à l'histoire du Tibet* (Paris: Société Asiatique, 1962), p. 92n.

2 : THE EXISTENCE OF SHAMBHALA

1. See Chap. 10 for more details.

2. *Srid pa* (Tb.) means "possible existence."

3. For a more detailed description of the mystical geography see W. Y. Evans-Wentz, ed., *The Tibetan Book of the Dead*, 3rd ed. (New York: Oxford University Press, Galaxy, 1968), pp. 61–66. The southern continent of Jambudvīpa actually has a semi-triangular shape, with the bottom corner cut off. On Meru as the Altai see R. G. Harshe, "Mount Meru: The Homeland of the Aryans," *Vishveshvaranand Indological Journal* 2, Pt. 1 (March 1964), p. 140.

4. Btsan po no mun han in his geography, *'Dzam gling rgyas bshad*—see Turrell V. Wylie, "Was Christopher Columbus from Shambhala?" *Bulletin of the Institute of China Border Area Studies*, No. 1 (July 1970), pp. 26 and 31.

5. For Sakya Pandita (Sa skya paṇḍi ta kun dga' rgyal mtshan) on Shambhala see *Sdom pa gsum gyi rab tu dbye ba* in Bsod-nams rgya-mtsho, ed., *The Complete Works of the Great Masters of the Sa Skya Sect of the Tibetan Buddhism* (Tokyo: Toyo Bunko, 1968) 5:312. According to Btsan po no mun han, the Third Panchen Lama wanted to keep the route to Shambhala vague (Wylie, "Christopher Columbus," p. 28).

6. See Chap. 8 on the guidebooks to Shambhala.

7. On the six zones see R. A. Stein, *Recherches sur l'épopée et le barde au Tibet* (Paris: Presses Universitaires de France, 1959), p. 309, n. 85. Klong rdol bla ma cites sources locating Shambhala in Great China (*Sham bha la'i zhing bkod, Tibetan Buddhist Studies* 1:128); the Third Panchen Lama puts it in Kailasha, the Land of Snow (*Sham bha la'i lam yig*, fol. 42a). On Ayushi see Stein, *Le Barde au Tibet*, p. 309, n. 83. Ekai Kawaguchi, *Three*

Years in Tibet (Benares and London: Theosophical Publishing House, 1909), pp. 497ff.

8. Hoffmann, *Religions of Tibet*, p. 125. Sir Charles Eliot, *Hinduism and Buddhism, an Historical Sketch* (London: Edward Arnold, 1921) 3:386.

9. On the names of Jesus, etc., see Helmut Hoffmann, "Kālacakra Studies I: Manichaeism, Christianity, and Islam in the Kālacakra Tantra," *Central Asiatic Journal* 13, No. 1 (1969), pp. 56ff. On numerical symbolism shared by Manicheism and the Kālacakra see id., *Religions of Tibet*, p. 52.

10. On the Uighurs and the kingdom of Khocho see Denis Sinor, *Inner Asia: History, Civilization, Languages; a Syllabus* (Bloomington: Indiana University Press, 1969), pp. 118ff.

11. Berthold Laufer and Paul Pelliot put Shambhala in the Tarim Basin around Khotan (Laufer, "Zur buddhistischen Litteratur," pp. 403–4; Paul Pelliot, "Quelques transcriptions apparentées a Çambhala dans les textes chinois," *T'oung Pao* 20, No. 2 [March 1920–21], p. 74, n. 2). On the Khotanese tradition see Kshanika Saha, *Buddhism and Buddhist Literature in Central Asia* (Calcutta: Firma K. L. Mukhopadhyay, 1970), p. 5. For the legend of Shakya Shambha see Chap. 10, n. 1.

12. Helmut Hoffmann's conclusions communicated in personal correspondence from him. On the location of Olmolungring see Chap. 4.

13. See Edgar Knobloch, *Beyond the Oxus: Archaeology, Art, and Architecture of Central Asia* (London: Ernest Benn, 1972), p. 54, on the Sogdian colony at Balasagun.

14. On Shambhala as Bactria see Sarat Chandra Das, *A Tibetan-English Dictionary, with Sanskrit Synonyms*, rev. and ed. G. Sandberg and A. W. Heyde (reprint ed., Delhi: Motilal Banarsidass, 1976), p. 1,231. For a discussion of the Kushan Empire and Buddhist art see Tamara T. Rice, *Ancient Arts of Central Asia* (New York: Frederick A. Praeger, 1965), pp. 140ff. On Uighur ruins north of the Tien Shan see ibid., p. 195. The late Shoun Toganoo of Koyasan University felt that Shambhala was in Kashmir or Uḍḍiyāna, according to his son, Shozui Toganoo.

15. See Aurel Stein, *On Ancient Central-Asian Tracks* (Chi-

cago: University of Chicago Press, Phoenix Books, 1974), pp. 278–82.

16. See *Encyclopaedia Britannica*, 14th ed., s.v. "Thug" and "Assassin"; also Arkon Daraul, *A History of Secret Societies* (New York: Citadel Press, 1961).

17. See Thomas Atkins and John Baxter, *The Fire Came By* (Garden City, N.Y.: Doubleday & Company, 1976).

3: THE HIDDEN VALLEYS

1. *Sbas yul mkhan pa lung gi lam yig* (incomplete manuscript, no author given, 31 fols.), fol. 31 (hereafter cited as *Lamyig A*). I have omitted references to the folio numbers of the following quotes from this text in this section of the chapter.

2. Padma gling pa, gter ston (discoverer), *Sbas yul mkhan pa lung gi gnas yig dang lam yig bcas* (copied from a text at the monastery of Gsang sngags chos gling in Bhutan, courtesy of E. Gene Smith, 35 fols.), fol. 12b (hereafter cited as *Lamyig B*). This text makes no mention of the route into Khembalung from Khumbu. Johan Reinhard has published the texts and translations of two other guidebooks to Khembalung that do describe this route in a section similar to that of *Lamyig A* (Johan Reinhard, "Khembalung: The Hidden Valley," *Kailash* 6, No. 1 [1978], pp. 15–35). In his article Reinhard describes an expedition he took in 1977 to a cave at the southern entrance to Khembalung, probably the cave that Oleshe was trying to reach when he encountered the yeti. The hidden valley itself would appear to lie north of this cave, in the region I entered in April 1976. My companions were Kent Obee and four Sherpas from Khumbu. We found trails and temporary hut foundations, which indicate that local people come up to graze animals in this region during the summer monsoon season. Other than Reinhard's article, very little has been published on Khembalung (see Alexander W. Macdonald, "The Lama and the General," *Kailash* 1, No. 3 [1973], p. 232, n. 28).

3. *Lamyig A,* fol. 27. *Lamyig B,* fol. 30a. Ling Gesar is the hero of the Tibetan national epic—see Chap. 4.

4. *Lamyig A,* fol. 29.

5. *Lamyig B,* fol. 33a.

6. Eva M. Dargyay, *The Rise of Esoteric Buddhism in Tibet* (Delhi: Motilal Banarsidass, 1977), pp. 62–67, describes the tradition of hidden treasures (*gter ma*) and treasure discoverers (*gter ston*). Lamas use the *Bar do thos rdol* (trans. in Evans-Wentz, *The Tibetan Book of the Dead*) to guide the dead to a good rebirth or Nirvana—see Chap. 7.

7. *Lamyig A,* fol. 6. *Lamyig B,* fol. 18a.

8. Adapted from trans. of *Padma thang yig* in Dargyay, *Esoteric Buddhism,* p. 147, and in Gustave-Charles Toussaint, trans., *Le Dict de Padma* (Paris: Ernest Leroux, 1933), p. 387. The *Padma thang yig* is a main source for prophecies of *gter ston,* discoverers of hidden treasures.

9. *Lamyig B,* fol. 32a.

10. Sbas yul 'bras mo ljongs in transliteration. This history of Sikkim comes from an interview with Khempo Tsondu. For further information on Rig 'dzin rgod ldem and Nam mkha' 'jigs med, see Dargyay, *Esoteric Buddhism,* pp. 129–32, 166–69.

11. Pemako (*Padma bkod*) means "lotus shape." On Sangye Thome see Jacques Bacot, *Le Tibet revolté: Vers Népémakö, la terre promise des Tibétains* (Paris: Hachette, 1912), pp. 10–12. Bacot refers to Pemako as Népémakö (the place of Pemako).

12. According to David Lichter, khemba (*mkhan pa*) is *Artemisia vulgaris,* or mugwort. Tibetans use the plant for incense. *Lung* means valley. An account of Kyimolung (*Skyid mo lung*) appears in Michael Aris, "Report on the University of California Expedition to Kutang and Nubri in Northern Nepal in Autumn 1973," *Contributions to Nepalese Studies* 2, No. 2 (June 1975), pp. 56–66.

13. Told to me by Chope Tsering.

14. Told to me by Sangye Dawa.

15. Told to me by Dudjom Khachopa Rimpoche of Sikkim.

16. Witter Bynner, trans., *The Jade Mountain: An Anthology* (Garden City, N.Y.: Anchor Books, 1964), pp. 166–67.

4: THE UNDERLYING MYTH

1. For sources see Chap. 1, n. 7.

2. Stein, *Le Barde au Tibet,* is a detailed study of the Gesar epic. On Thub bstan 'jam dbyangs grags pa's vision of Gesar's horse see id., *L'épopée tibétaine de Gésar dans sa version lamaïque de Ling* (Paris: Presses Universitaires de France, 1956), pp. 12–14. Alexandra David-Neel also describes the Gesar epic and its relation to Shambhala in *The Superhuman Life of Gesar of Ling* (New York: Claude Kendall, 1934), pp. 47–49.

3. From the *Viṣṇu Purāṇa* 4.24, trans. in H. H. Wilson, trans., *The Vishńu Puráña: A System of Hindu Mythology and Tradition,* ed. F. Hall (London: Trübner & Company, 1868) 4: 225–27.

4. Ibid., p. 229, trans. adapted.

5. For the Sanskrit reference to Rudra Cakrin as "Kalki" see Vira and Chandra, *Kālacakra-Tantra and Other Texts,* Pt. 1, p. 339. Klong rdol bla ma mentions Kings of Shambhala with the names of incarnations (Sk. *avatāra*) of Viṣṇu in *Sham bha la'i zhing bkod, Tibetan Buddhist Studies* 1:134–35.

6. For a summary of the Kalki Purāṇa see R. C. Hazra, *Studies in the Upapurāṇas,* Calcutta Sanskrit College Research Series, No. 2 (Calcutta, 1958) 1:303–8.

7. The best-known paradises of the Immortals are the palace of Hsi Wang Mu and the isle of P'eng lai (see E. T. C. Werner, *A Dictionary of Chinese Mythology* [Shanghai: Kelly and Walsh, 1932], pp. 163–64, 234, 372). On underground paradises see Wolfgang Bauer, *China and the Search for Happiness,* trans. M. Shaw (New York: Seabury Press, 1976), pp. 189ff.

8. Trans. in Homer H. Dubs, "An Ancient Chinese Mystery Cult," *Harvard Theological Review* 35, No. 4 (Oct. 1942), p. 231.

9. See Arthur Waley, trans., *Monkey* (New York: Grove Press, Evergreen Books, 1958), Chap. 5.

10. For the journey of King Mu see Bauer, *Search for Happiness,* p. 95. On Wu Ti and Hsi Wang Mu see Werner, *Dictionary*

of *Chinese Mythology*, p. 163, and Dubs, "Ancient Chinese Mystery Cult," p. 234, n. 43.

11. See Bauer, *Search for Happiness*, p. 95.

12. From Hedin, *My Life as an Explorer*, p. 121.

13. See Nicholas Roerich, *The Heart of Asia* (New York: Roerich Museum Press, 1929), pp. 136–38.

14. From the *Mahābhārata* 6.8, adapted from trans. in Pratap Chandra Roy, trans., *The Mahābhārata of Krishna-Dwaipayna Vyasa*, n. ed. (Calcutta: Datta Bose & Co., 1925) 4:18 (given as *Mahābhārata* 6.7).

15. See Harshe, "Mount Meru," p. 140; Buddha Prakash, "Uttarakuru," *Bulletin of Tibetology* 2, No. 1 (1965), p. 28; Nirmal C. Sinha, "Notes and Topics," *Bulletin of Tibetology* 2, No. 1 (1965), pp. 35–36; Shyam Narain Pande, "Identification of the Ancient Land of Uttarakuru," *The Journal of the Ganganatha Jha Research Institute* 26, Pts. 1–3 (1970), pp. 725–27.

16. Itinerary from the *Rāmāyaṇa* 4.42, trans. in Hari Prasad Shastri, *The Ramayana of Valmiki* (London: Shanti Sadan, 1957) 2:282–85 (given as *Rāmāyaṇa* 4.43). Arjuna's journey and the invisibility of Uttarakuru appear in the *Mahābhārata* 2.25, trans. in J. A. B. van Buitenen, trans. and ed., *The Mahābhārata* (Chicago: University of Chicago Press, 1975) 2:79–80.

17. On the Scythian myth see G. M. Bongard-Levin, *Studies in Ancient India and Central Asia*, Soviet Indology Series, Indian Studies, No. 7 (Calcutta, 1971), pp. 55–58.

18. On the Hyperboreans and Perseus see Edith Hamilton, *Mythology* (New York: Mentor, 1969), pp. 68 and 145.

19. N. K. Sandars, *The Epic of Gilgamesh*, rev. ed. (Baltimore, Md.: Penguin Books, 1975), pp. 103–4.

20. A very complete version of Perceval and the Holy Grail quest appears in Wolfram von Eschenbach, *Parzival*, trans. H. M. Mustard and C. E. Passage (New York: Vintage Books, 1961).

21. The Third Panchen Lama, *Sham bha la'i smon lam* in Klong rdol bla ma, *Tibetan Buddhist Studies* 1:150.

22. Dante Alighieri, *The Purgatorio* trans. J. Ciardi (New York: Mentor, 1961), p. 279.

23. See *Encyclopaedia Britannica,* 14th ed., s.v. "Mahdi" and "Eschatology."

24. Quoted in Mircea Eliade, *The Quest: History and Meaning in Religion* (Chicago: University of Chicago Press, Phoenix Books, 1975), p. 91. On the earthly paradise and the discovery and colonization of America, as well as the evolution of the myth of progress, see ibid., pp. 88–101.

25. Thomas More, *Utopia,* trans. P. Turner (Baltimore, Md.: Penguin Books, 1975).

5: THE WHEEL OF TIME

Much of this chapter is based on discussions with various lamas, such as Chopgye Trichen Rimpoche, Khempo Noryang, Khempo Tsondu, Lama Kunga Rimpoche, Namgyal Wangchen, the Sakya Trizin, and Samdong Rimpoche. I have tried to give a general impression of Tibetan philosophy and meditation, but there are in actuality many different schools of thought with conflicting views. For information on Buddhism in general and Tibetan Buddhism in particular, the reader can consult the following works in English: John Blofeld, *The Tantric Mysticism of Tibet* (New York: Dutton Paperback, 1970); Garma C. C. Chang, trans. and annot., *Teachings of Tibetan Yoga* (New Hyde Park, New York: University Books, 1963) and *The Practice of Zen* (New York: Harper & Row, Perennial Library, 1970); Edward Conze, *Buddhism: Its Essence and Development* (New York: Harper & Row Torchbooks, 1959); W. Y. Evans-Wentz, ed., *Tibetan Yoga and Secret Doctrines,* 2nd ed. (New York: Oxford University Press, Galaxy, 1970); Lama Anagarika Govinda, *Foundations of Tibetan Mysticism* (New York: Samuel Weiser, 1973); Helmut Hoffmann, *The Religions of Tibet,* trans. E. Fitzgerald (New York: The Macmillan Company, 1961); Lama Kunga Rimpoche and Brian Cutillo, trans., *Drinking the Mountain Stream* (New York: Lotsawa, 1978); R. A. Stein, *Tibetan Civilization,* trans. J. E. Stapleton Driver (London: Faber & Faber, 1972).

1. The Mādhyamika, the "middle way" that stresses the emptiness of all phenomena.

2. From "The Song of Mahamudra" by Tilopa, trans. in Chang, *Teachings of Tibetan Yoga*, p. 26. The Void refers to emptiness (Sk. *śūnyatā*).

3. I have taken the idea of deeper levels of mind from conversations with Samdong Rimpoche. This way of looking at the mind lends itself well to an explanation of Tibetan Buddhism and the interpretation of Shambhala in the next chapter—but it is only an expedient device and should not be taken too literally. Samdong Rimpoche referred to the innermost mind as *gnyugs sems* in Tibetan.

4. See Klong rdol bla ma, *Rgyal ba tsong kha pa'i lugs dang mthun pa rnams phyogs gcig tu btus pa'i dpal dus kyi 'khor lo'i ming gi rnam grangs* (hereafter cited as *Dus 'khor ming gi rnam grangs*) in *Tibetan Buddhist Studies* 1:162.

5. Adapted from a trans. of the *Cakrasambhāra Tantra* quoted in Evans-Wentz, *Tibetan Yoga and Secret Doctrines*, p. 45.

6. Most of this section on the Kālacakra is based on discussions with the lamas mentioned in the chapter note above. Very little has been written in Western languages on the Kālacakra. For a brief summary of the teaching, focused on the initiation itself, see Ngawang Dhargyey, "An Introduction to and Outline of the Kalacakra Initiation," trans. Sherpa Tulku, A. Berzin, and J. Landaw, *The Tibet Journal* 1, No. 1 (1975), pp. 72–77. The following works have discussions of the Kālacakra: the English introduction of Mario E. Carelli, ed., *Sekoddeśaṭīkā of Naḍapāda* (*Nāropā*) (Baroda: Oriental Institute, 1941); Shashi Bhushan Dasgupta, *An Introduction to Tantric Buddhism* (Berkeley, Calif.: Shambhala Publications, 1974), pp. 64–69; Hoffmann, *Religions of Tibet*, pp. 33–34, 123ff., and "Kālacakra Studies I," pp. 52–75; and Roerich, "Studies in the Kālacakra," pp. 11–22. One of the clearest and simplest explanations of the Kālacakra in Tibetan appears in Klong rdol bla ma, *Sham bha la'i zhing bkod* and *Dus 'khor ming gi rnam grangs* in *Tibetan Buddhist Studies* 1:125–81.

7. I have translated *bodhicitta* (the mind or thought of en-

lightenment) as "the impulse to enlightenment" to indicate that it denotes something more active and compelling than mere thought. The white and red drops of male semen and female blood, which symbolize the *bodhicitta* in Tantric Buddhism, are called *bindu* in Sanskrit (Tb. *thig le*).

6: THE INNER KINGDOM

The discussion of symbols and the interpretation of Shambhala are mine. The interpretation is based in part, however, on discussions with various lamas.

1. From "Auguries of Innocence" by William Blake in *The Poetry and Prose of William Blake*, ed. D. V. Erdman, rev. ed. (Garden City, N.Y.: Doubleday & Company, 1968), p. 481.

2. The term *Dharma* in Dharma Cakra has many meanings. In this context it is often translated as the "Law," referring to the Buddhist teachings. I have used "Truth" to indicate that it refers to the teaching of the true nature of reality.

3. From the *Muṇḍaka Upaniṣad*, trans. in Swami Prabhavananda and Frederick Manchester, trans., *The Upanishads: Breath of the Eternal* (New York: Mentor, 1957), p. 46.

4. This figure is based on a rough sketch by Khempo Noryang. A diagram in a Tibetan medical text shows the five kinds of sense consciousness served by one of four nerves issuing from the center of the heart; the fifth nerve in this diagram apparently corresponds to the central channel, which holds the innermost mind, referred to here as the *yid bzang ma rnam shes* (the consciousness of the good mind) (Rechung Rinpoche Jampal Kunzang, trans., *Tibetan Medicine* [Berkeley, Calif.: University of California Press, 1973], Pl. 3).

5. From *Sham bha lar skye ba'i smon lam rig 'dzin grong du bgrod pa'i them skas zhes bya ba* in *The Collected Works* (*Gsuṅ 'Bum*) *of Blo-bzaṅ-dam-chos-rgya-mtsho. Roṅ-tha Che-tshaṅ Sprul-sku*, reproduced by Ngawang Sopa (New Delhi: Ngawang Sopa, 1975) 6:467.

6. See Chap. 4, n. 22.

7. The Third Panchen Lama, *Sham bha la'i lam yig,* fol. 42b. Laufer, "Zur buddhistischen Litteratur," p. 407.

8. Klong rdol bla ma, *Sham bha la'i zhing bkod, Tibetan Buddhist Studies* 1:132; ibid., p. 129.

9. *Rin spungs pa'i pho nya,* p. 52; ibid.

10. Klong rdol bla ma, op. cit., p. 132; ibid.

11. Ibid., p. 131.

7: THE JOURNEY

1. See Evans-Wentz, *Tibetan Book of the Dead.*

2. See n. 3 inf.

3. On the yoga of consciousness transference (Tb. *'pho ba*) and its dangers see Evans-Wentz, *Tibetan Yoga and Secret Doctrines,* pp. 253–59.

4. Adapted from a trans. of "The Epitome of an Introduction to the Profound Path of the Six Yogas of Naropa" by Drashi Namjhal in Chang, *Teachings of Tibetan Yoga,* p. 93. Indra is the King of the gods. Amitabha and Vairocana are Buddhas.

5. This story of Dushepa (Tb. Dus zhabs pa; Sk. Kālacakrapāda) is based on a version in Roerich, "Studies in the Kālacakra," p. 19, and an account by Chopgye Trichen Rimpoche drawn from Bu ston.

6. Told to me by Garje Khamtul Rimpoche.

7. For a discussion of Shamanism and the role of the horse in mystic flights see Mircea Eliade, *Shamanism: Archaic Techniques of Ecstasy,* trans. W. R. Trask (Princeton, N.J.: Princeton/Bollingen, 1972), pp. 467–70 in particular.

8. Told to me by Lhakpa Drolmi of Junbesi.

9. Told to me by Tsetan Gyurme.

10. Trans. and ed. by Chophel Namgyal and myself.

11. Adapted from a trans. of *Urgyān gu ru padma 'byung gnas gyi rnam thar* in W. Y. Evans-Wentz, ed., *The Tibetan Book of the Great Liberation* (New York: Oxford University Press, Galaxy, 1969), pp. 132–33.

12. The Sanskrit terms for these bodies are the *nirmāṇakāya,* *sambhogakāya,* and *dharmakāya.*

8: THE GUIDEBOOKS

1. Laufer, "Zur buddhistischen Litteratur," pp. 404–7; the Third Panchen Lama, *Sham bha la'i lam yig* (Tibetan text and German trans. in Grünwedel, *Der Weg nach Sambhala*); *Kalāpāvatāra* (Tb. *Ka lā par 'jug pa*), trans. Tāranātha in *The Tibetan Tripitaka, Peking Edition,* ed. D. T. Suzuki (Tokyo-Kyoto: Tibetan Tripitaka Research Institute, 1957) 149:159–65; *Rin spungs pa'i pho nya.* For full references see Chap. 1, n. 4.

2. See the Third Panchen Lama, *Sham bha la'i lam yig,* fol. 34a.

3. Laufer, "Zur buddhistischen Litteratur," pp. 404–5, trans. and ed. from the German by Yolanda G. H. Gerritsen and myself.

4. Ibid., p. 406. For a discussion of "Hor" and "Sogpo" see Stein, *Tibetan Civilization,* p. 34. The peoples referred to by these terms have changed over time.

5. See Chap. 2, n. 5.

6. According to Helmut Hoffmann (personal correspondence), Ārya Amoghāṅkuśa (Tb. 'Phags pa don yod lcags kyus) may be a form of Avalokiteśvara. For Tāranātha's dream see Stein, *Le Barde au Tibet,* p. 277.

7. The following is a joint translation by Lama Kunga Rimpoche and myself. I have simplified the translation, summarizing the first section of the text, clarifying obscure passages, and omitting certain details, such as a number of place names and the exact mantras to be recited. Otherwise, the translation is fairly close to the original.

8. The itinerary to Uttarakuru in the *Rāmāyaṇa* (see Chap. 4, n. 16) mentions a mountain called *Maināka* with horse-faced women. Beyond it lies a river called the Śailodā, which can be crossed, like the Satvalotana of this text, with the help of branches —in this case, bamboo.

9. The text gives a long list of place names, which I have omitted.

10. The fabulous beings are kinnaras (Tb. *mia'm ci*).

11. This retelling is based on detailed summaries and explanations of the text provided by Chopgye Trichen Rimpoche and Lama Kunga Rimpoche. Ngor Thartse Khen Rimpoche (Sonam Gyatso) also helped to clarify certain difficult points. The journey itself runs through pp. 22–50 of the text.

12. At this point the text uses metaphors that are very difficult to figure out. According to Thartse Khen Rimpoche, Rinpungpa visualizes a figure who seems to be some kind of yogi (*Rin spungs pa'i pho nya*, p. 21).

13. The text does not specifically call this river the Sītā, but the location of the river and a note written in the manuscript imply as much (ibid., p. 42).

14. Kinnaras, the same fabulous beings mentioned in *Kalāpā-vatāra* (see n. 10 sup.).

9: THE INNER JOURNEY

1. Trans. from the *Laṅkāvatāra Sūtra*, vs. 157, in Edward Conze et al., eds. and trans., *Buddhist Texts Through the Ages* (New York: Harper & Row Torchbooks, 1964), p. 214. Trans. from "The Vow of Mahamudra" by Garmapa Rangjang Dorje in Chang, *Teachings of Tibetan Yoga*, p. 35.

2. On the legend of Yamāntaka see Lama Anagarika Govinda, *The Way of the White Clouds* (Berkeley, Calif.: Shambhala Publications, 1970), p. 249.

3. For a description of heat yoga (Tb. *gtum mo*) see "Six Yogas of Naropa" by Drashi Namjhal in Chang, *Teachings of Tibetan Yoga*, pp. 55–81. The following passage describes a visualization similar to Rinpungpa's visualization of lovemaking: ". . . one may apply the *Wisdom-Mother Mudra* by visualizing the sexual act with a Dakini, while using the breath to incite the Dumo-heat, to melt the white Tig Le, and so forth" (ibid., p. 68). The white Tig Le (Tb. *thig le;* Sk. *bindu*), a drop of semen symbolizing the impulse to enlightenment, corresponds to the mystic syllable that melts in Rinpungpa's visualization.

4. The Kālacakra and other higher tantras have two basic stages of meditation, known as the stage of production (Sk. *utpannakrama;* Tb. *bskyed rim*) and the stage of completion (Sk. *sampannakrama;* Tb. *rdzogs rim*). In the first, the yogi masters the visualization of deities and so forth; in the second, he goes on to the final realization of emptiness. For a discussion of these stages see Stein, *Tibetan Civilization,* pp. 180ff.

10: THE INNER PROPHECY

1. Stag tshang lo tsā ba shes rab rin chen relates this story and identifies Shākya Shambha with the father of Sucandra in *Dus 'khor spyi don bstan pa'i rgya mtsho,* reproduced by Trayang and Jamyang Samten (New Delhi, 1973), fols. 295–96. The Third Panchen Lama disputes this identification in *Sham bha la'i lam yig,* fol. 47b.

2. There seems to be no surviving copy of the basic or mūla-tantra. What we have been calling "the main Kālacakra text" —*Parama-ādibuddhoddhrita-śrī-kālacakra-nāma-tantrarāja,* trans. Somanātha and Śes-rab grags-pa in *The Tibetan Tripitaka, Peking Edition,* ed. D. T. Suzuki (Tokyo-Kyoto: Tibetan Tripitaka Research Institute, 1955) 1:127–74—is supposed to be a shortened version of the basic text written down by Sucandra.

3. See Sarat Chandra Das, *Contributions on the Religion and History of Tibet* (New Delhi: Mañjuśri Publishing House, 1970), p. 82.

4. From the Third Panchen Lama, *Sham bha la'i lam yig,* fols. 45a–46a. The Panchen Lama seems to have taken the story from the *Vimalaprabhā* (see n. 5 inf.). An English summary of the story from a Sanskrit text of the *Vimalaprabhā* appears in Biswanath Bandyopadhyaya, "A Note on the Kālacakratantra and its Commentary," *Journal of the Asiatic Society,* Letters 18, No. 2 (1952), pp. 74–75, where Mañjuśrīkīrti is called Yaśas.

5. The full reference for the *Vimalaprabhā* is *Vimalaprabhā-nāma-mūlatantrānusāriṇī-dvādaśasāhasrikā-laghukālacakra-tantrarāja-ṭīkā,* trans. Somanātha and Śes-rab grags in *The Tibetan*

Tripitaka, Peking Edition, ed. D. T. Suzuki (Tokyo-Kyoto: Tibetan Tripitaka Research Institute, 1958) 46:121–335. According to Klong rdol bla ma, the combined reigns of the tenth and eleventh Kulika Kings will be 403 years (*Sham bha la'i zhing bkod, Tibetan Buddhist Studies* 1:134–35). For a transliterated list of the seven religious Kings and twenty-five Kulika Kings see the Preface of Vira and Chandra, *Kālacakra-Tantra and Other Texts,* Pt. 1, pp. 5–6.

6. See Hoffmann, "Kālacakra Studies I," pp. 56–60. According to Hoffmann, Abraham appears as Varāhī, Moses as Mūṣa, Jesus as Īśa, and Mani as Śvetavastrin (the man with a white garment).

7. Through the Mongolians, the Manchus, and the influence of the Panchen Lamas, the Kālacakra even had an impact on China: A major landmark of Peking, the Pai t'a, a white Tibetan-style stupa on a hill overlooking the Forbidden City, bears the emblem of the Kālacakra teaching, "The Ten of Power" (see Fig. 7). Great Kālacakra initiations were also given in Peking.

8. On Aniruddha (Tb. Ma 'gag pa) see Hoffmann, *Religions of Tibet,* p. 125. For variations in the date of the Buddha's death see Alexander Csoma de Koros, *A Grammar of the Tibetan Language in English* (Calcutta, 1834; repr. ed., New York: Altai Press, Triad Reprints), pp. 199–201.

9. Klong rdol bla ma, *Sham bha la'i zhing bkod, Tibetan Buddhist Studies* 1:137.

10. Tibetan sources refer to the barbarian King as Byis pa'i blo (Childish Intellect) and Byed pa'i blo gros (The Intelligence of Doing). The confusion seems to have arisen from the corrupt Sanskrit name used in the original Sanskrit text, Kṛnmatī (see *Kālacakratantrarāja* in Vira and Chandra, *Kālacakra-Tantra and Other Texts,* Pt. 1, p. 339).

11. Adapted from K'am-trül Rinpoche, "Geography and History of Shambhala," p. 10.

12. On the Panchen Lama's version of where the final battle will take place see *Sham bha la'i lam yig,* fol. 46b. For Khamtul Rimpoche's version see K'am-trül Rinpoche, "Geography and History of Shambhala," p. 10. According to the *Kālacakratantrarāja* (Tibetan trans.), "At the edge of time, from the mountain of

Kailasha, from the city arranged by the gods will come the army of the Universal Emperor [Sk. *cakravartin*—i.e., Rudra Cakrin] . . ." (Vira and Chandra, *Kālacakra-Tantra and Other Texts*, p. 96).

13. From the *Vimalaprabhā*, quoted in Klong rdol bla ma, *Sham bha la'i zhing bkod, Tibetan Buddhist Studies* 1:138.

14. On the abbot of Reting (the "King" of Rva sgreng) see Stein, *Le Barde au Tibet*, p. 525. The prophecy of the Amdo lama, Jamyang Jepa, was told to me by Oleshe (Gechung Ngawang Leshe).

15. On the golden age see the Third Panchen Lama, *Sham bha la'i lam yig*, fols. 47a–b, and Klong rdol bla ma, *Sham bha la'i zhing bkod, Tibetan Buddhist Studies* 1:139. The sages who will come back to life include Nāgārjuna and Tsong kha pa—the latter according to Thubten Jigme Norbu and Colin M. Turnbull, *Tibet* (New York: Simon and Schuster, 1968), p. 344.

16. For the names of the Kings following Rudra Cakrin see Klong rdol bla ma, *Dus 'khor ming gi rnam grangs, Tibetan Buddhist Studies* 1:171. Klong rdol bla ma seems to have added three Kings to the usual list of eight following Rudra Cakrin. On the increase and decrease of human lifespan in the *Kālacakratantrarāja* see Vira and Chandra, *Kālacakra-Tantra and Other Texts*, p. 98 (Tibetan trans.).

17. There are various versions of the Maitreya prophecy. On Maitreya and one thousand Buddhas see E. Obermiller, trans., *History of Buddhism (Chos-ḥbyung) by Bu-ston* (Heidelberg, 1931; Suzuki Research Foundation, Reprint Series 5), Pt. 1, pp. 90ff.

18. Norbu and Turnbull, *Tibet*, pp. 344–45.

11: BEYOND SHAMBHALA

1. One of the best examples of this is the Revelation of John in the New Testament. Many myths seem to have their source in external events, such as the Battle of Troy. This does not preclude their actual origin in the unconscious: In such cases, we can argue

that the deeper mind has used historical events as concrete forms for expressing the essence of various myths—and it is because of this that the memory of these events has survived in epics such as *The Iliad* and *The Mahābhārata.*

Glossary

Names and terms are given as they are spelled in the text. Some of the Sanskrit and Tibetan entries are already in proper transliteration; transliterations of those that are not appear in parentheses. Unless otherwise indicated, the terms listed are in English or Sanskrit. Sk. and Tb. stand for Sanskrit and Tibetan, respectively.

Avalokiteshvara (Sk. *avalokiteśvara*) The Bodhisattva of Compassion.

Bodhgaya The place in northern India where Gautama Buddha attained enlightenment.

Bodhisattva (1) One who foregoes entry into Nirvana in order to help others attain liberation. (2) An enlightened being who embodies a spiritual force, such as wisdom or compassion.

Bon (Tb.) The pre-Buddhist religion of Tibet.

Buddha (1) Awakened or Enlightened One. One who has completely awakened to the true nature of reality. (2) Siddhartha Gautama, the historical person who attained enlightenment and founded Buddhism around 500 B.C.

Dakini (Sk. *ḍākinī*) Sky Goer. A female person or deity who inspires and helps a yogi to attain enlightenment.

Deeper level of mind A layer of the mind outside normal consciousness, characterized by purer energy and awareness.

Deeper mind See *Superconscious.*

Dhanyakataka (Sk. *dhānyakaṭaka*) The stupa in southern India where the Buddha was supposed to have preached the Kalacakra Tantra.

Ego A person's symbol or image of himself, which he takes to be himself.

Eight kinds of consciousness (Sk. *vijñāna*) The consciousness of sight, hearing, smell, taste, touch, thoughts, ego, and past impressions.

Ekajati (Sk. *ekajaṭī*) A female Bodhisattva who helps yogis overcome obstacles. A form of Tara.

Emptiness (Sk. *śūnyatā*) The ultimate nature of all things, devoid of all attributes.

Enlightenment (Sk. *bodhi*) The awakening to the true nature of reality.

Gautama Buddha See *Buddha.*

Guru A spiritual master or teacher.

Hidden valley (Tb. *sbas yul*) A country concealed, generally by Padma Sambhava, as a sanctuary for meditation, often stocked with treasures (Tb. *gter ma*).

Hinayana (Sk. *hinayāna*) The Lesser Way. A school or stage of Buddhism that aims at individual liberation.

Initiation (Sk. *abhiṣeka*) A ceremony or experience that confers wisdom and power—and in many cases permission to practice a mystical teaching.

Innermost mind The deepest and purest level of the mind, which is able to experience the true nature of reality.

Jambudvipa (Sk. *jambudvīpa*) The southern continent of the Mount Meru system of mythical geography, referring to the earth, Asia, or India.

Kalacakra (Sk. *kālacakra*) The Wheel of Time. The mystical teaching kept in Shambhala.

Kalapa (Sk. *kalāpa*)   The capital city and palace of the King of Shambhala.

Kalki (Sk. *kalkin* or *kalki*)   The future incarnation of Vishnu, who will bring in the golden age of Hindu mythology.

Karma (Sk. *karman*)   The effects of thoughts and actions that shape one's fate and character.

Khembalung (Tb. *mkhan pa lung*)   A hidden valley near Mount Everest.

Khumbu   The region of Nepal just south of Mount Everest.

Kulika (Tb. *rigs ldan*)   Holder of the Castes. Title of the second line of Kings of Shambhala.

Lama (Tb. *bla ma*)   Superior One. A term applied to a Tibetan monk or spiritual master, usually one considered to be the incarnation of a Bodhisattva.

Liberation   Freedom from the bondage of passions and illusions.

Mahayana (Sk. *mahāyāna*)   The Great Way. A school or stage of Buddhism that aims at the liberation of all beings.

Maitreya   The Buddha to come.

Mandala (Sk. *maṇḍala*)   A mystic circle used in meditation and initiations.

Manjushri (Sk. *mañjuśrī*)   The Bodhisattva of Wisdom.

Manjushrikirti (Sk. *mañjuśrīkīrti*, Tb. *'jam dpal grags pa*)   The first Kulika King of Shambhala, the one who unified the castes of the kingdom into a single diamond caste.

Mantra   Sacred sound—words and syllables used in meditation.

Meru   The mountain at the center of the world or universe according to Hindu and Buddhist mythology.

Nirvana (Sk. *nirvāṇa*)   The goal of Buddhism, the indefinable state beyond all suffering.

Nyingmapa (Tb. *rnying ma pa*)   The Ancient Ones. The followers of the oldest sect of Tibetan Buddhism, founded by Padma Sambhava.

Olmolungring (Tb. *ol mo lung ring*)   The place of origin of Bon, a mythical kingdom that followers of that religion equate with Shambhala.

Padma Sambhava   Also known as Guru Rimpoche. The Indian yogi who brought Buddhism to Tibet in the eighth century A.D. and concealed a number of treasures and hidden valleys.

Primordial Buddha (Sk. *ādibuddha*)　The essence of all Buddhas and the universe itself.

Psychic center (Sk. *cakra*)　A focal point of the psychic energy, or nervous, system, often symbolized by a wheel or lotus.

Pure Land (Tb. *zhing khams*)　A special kind of paradise for those on their way to enlightenment.

Rama (Sk. *rāma*)　An incarnation of Vishnu and the hero of the Hindu epic the *Ramayana*.

Rigden Dragpo (Tb. *rigs ldan drag po*)　See *Rudra Cakrin*.

Rimpoche (Tb. *rin po che*)　Great Precious One. Title of an incarnate lama.

Rudra Cakrin (Tb. *drag po 'khor lo can*)　The Wrathful One with the Wheel. The future King of Shambhala who will defeat the forces of evil and establish the golden age.

Shambhala (Sk. *śambhala*, Tb. *bde 'byung*)　The Source of Happiness. A mysterious kingdom north of Tibet where the Kalacakra teachings are supposed to be kept.

Sherpas　A people of Tibetan origin who have settled in Nepal, primarily in Solu Khumbu, a region south of Mount Everest. Some of them work on mountaineering expeditions.

Sita (Sk. *sītā*)　A major river on the way to Shambhala, tentatively identified with either the Tarim River or the Syr Darya.

Stupa (Sk. *stūpa*)　A sacred mound or monument for housing Buddhist relics.

Subconscious　The intermediate region of the mind between the surface consciousness and the superconscious.

Sucandra (Tb. *zla ba bzang po*)　Good Moon. The first religious King of Shambhala who received the Kalacakra from the Buddha.

Superconscious　The pure region of the deeper levels of mind together with the innermost mind.

Surface consciousness　The region of ordinary awareness, which includes the conscious thoughts, feelings, and perceptions of everyday life.

Tantra　A teaching or system of the Vajrayana. A practice that makes use of radical means for quickly attaining enlightenment.

Tantric Buddhism See *Vajrayana.*

Tara (Sk. *tārā*) The Savioress. A female Bodhisattva of compassion, counterpart of Avalokiteshvara.

Tengyur (Tb. *bstan 'gyur*) The second part of the Tibetan Canon, containing 225 volumes of commentaries on the Buddhist teachings.

Tutelary deity (Tb. *yi dam*) A visualized deity who guides a yogi in his practice and generally embodies some aspect of the deeper mind.

Unconscious All of the mind outside the ordinary awareness of the surface consciousness. Consists of the subconscious and superconscious.

Vajra Diamond. A thunderbolt or diamondlike substance that symbolizes the indestructible nature of emptiness.

Vajrayana (Sk. *vajrayāna*) The Diamond Way. A school or stage of Buddhism that aims at the fastest possible means of attaining enlightenment.

Vishnu (Sk. *viṣṇu*) The supreme deity of Hinduism in the role of preserver.

Yamantaka (Sk. *yamāntaka*) The Conqueror of the Lord of Death. A wrathful form of Manjushri, the Bodhisattva of Wisdom.

Yoga A practice leading to union with some usually spiritual objective.

Yogi (Sk. *yogin*) A practitioner of yoga.

Selected Bibliography

The bibliography contains works with references to Shambhala, the Kalacakra, and hidden valleys. For sources dealing with other topics discussed in this book, see the Notes.

SOURCES IN WESTERN LANGUAGES

Aris, Michael. "Report on the University of California Expedition to Kutang and Nubri in Northern Nepal in Autumn 1973." *Contributions to Nepalese Studies* 2, No. 2 (1975), pp. 45–87.

Bacot, Jacques. *Introduction à l'histoire du Tibet.* Paris: Société Asiatique, 1962.

———. *Le Tibet révolté: Vers Népémakö, la terre promise des Tibétains.* Paris: Hachette, 1912.

Bandyopadhyaya, Biswanath. "A Note on the Kālacakratantra and Its Commentary," *Journal of the Asiatic Society,* Letters 18, No. 2 (1952), pp. 71–76.

Bawden, C. R. *The Modern History of Mongolia.* New York: Frederick A. Praeger, 1968.

Bell, Sir Charles. *The Religion of Tibet.* Oxford: Clarendon Press, 1931.

————. *Tibet: Past and Present.* Oxford: Clarendon Press, 1924.

Bleichsteiner, Robert. *L'Église jaune,* trans. Jacques Marty. Paris: Payot, 1950.

Carelli, Mario E., ed. Introduction to *Sekoddeśaṭīkā of Naḍapāda* (*Nāropā*). Baroda: Oriental Institute, 1941.

Chandra, Lokesh. Preface to *Kālacakra-Tantra and Other Texts,* ed. Raghu Vira and Lokesh Chandra, Pt. 1. New Delhi: International Academy of Indian Culture, 1966.

Csoma de Koros, Alexander. *A Grammar of the Tibetan Language in English.* Calcutta, 1834; repr., New York: Altai Press, Triad Reprints.

————. "Note on the Origin of the Kāla-Chakra and Adi-Buddha Systems," *Journal of the Asiatic Society of Bengal* 2, No. 14 (1833), pp. 57–59.

Dargyay, Eva M. *The Rise of Esoteric Buddhism in Tibet.* Delhi: Motilal Banarsidass, 1977.

Das, Sarat Chandra. *Contributions on the Religion and History of Tibet.* New Delhi: Manjuśri Publishing House, 1970.

————. *Journey to Lhasa and Central Tibet,* ed. W. W. Rockhill. London: John Murray, 1902.

————. *A Tibetan-English Dictionary, with Sanskrit Synonyms,* rev. and ed. Graham Sandberg and A. William Heyde. Repr., Delhi: Motilal Banarsidass, 1976.

Dasgupta, Shashi Bhushan. *An Introduction to Tantric Buddhism.* Berkeley, Calif.: Shambhala Publications, 1974.

David-Neel, Alexandra. *The Superhuman Life of Gesar of Ling.* New York: Claude Kendall, 1934.

Dhargyey, Ngawang. "An Introduction to and an Outline of the Kalacakra Initiation," trans. Sherpa Tulku, Alexander Berzin, and Jonathan Landaw. *The Tibet Journal* 1, No. 1 (1975), pp. 72–77.

Eliot, Sir Charles. *Hinduism and Buddhism: An Historical Sketch,* Vol. 3. London: Edward Arnold, 1921.

Evans-Wentz, W. Y., ed. *The Tibetan Book of the Great Liberation.* New York: Oxford University Press, Galaxy, 1969.

George, James. "Searching for Shambhala," *Search,* ed. Jean Sulzberger. New York: Harper & Row, 1979.

Grünwedel, Albert, ed. and trans. *Der Weg nach Śambhala.* Abhandlungen der Königlich Bayerischen Akademie der Wissenschaften 29, No. 3. Munich, 1915.

Hoffmann, Helmut H. R. "Kālacakra Studies I: Manichaeism, Christianity, and Islam in the Kālacakra Tantra," *Central Asiatic Journal* 13, No. 1 (1969), pp. 52–75.

———. *The Religions of Tibet,* trans. Edward Fitzgerald. New York: The Macmillan Company, 1961.

K'am-trül Rinpoche, Gar-je. "A Geography and History of Shambhala," trans. Sherpa Tulku and Alexander Berzin, *The Tibet Journal* 3, No. 3 (1978), pp. 3–11.

Karmay, Samten G. "A General Introduction to the History and Doctrines of Bon," *Memoirs of the Research Department of the Toyo Bunko,* No. 33 (1975), pp. 171–218.

———, ed. and trans. *The Treasury of Good Sayings: A Tibetan History of Bon.* London: Oxford University Press, 1972.

Kawaguchi, Ekai. *Three Years in Tibet.* Benares and London: Theosophical Publishing House, 1909.

Laufer, Berthold. "Zur buddhistischen Litteratur der Uiguren," *T'oung Pao,* Ser. 2, Vol. 3 (1907), pp. 381–407.

Macdonald, Alexander W. "The Lama and the General," *Kailash* 1, No. 3 (1973), pp. 225–33.

Norbu, Thubten Jigme, and Turnbull, Colin M. *Tibet.* New York: Simon and Schuster, 1968.

Oppitz, Michael. "Shangri-la, le panneau de marque d'un flipper: Analyse sémiologique d'un mythe visuel," trans. Paule du Bouchet, *L'Homme* 14, Nos. 3–4 (1974), pp. 59–83.

Pelliot, Paul. "Quelques transcriptions apparentées a Çambhala dans les textes chinois," *T'oung Pao* 20, No. 2 (1920–21), pp. 73–85.

Prejevalsky, N. *Mongolia, the Tangut Country, and the Solitudes of Northern Tibet,* trans. E. Delmar Morgan. Vol. 1, 1876. Repr., Farnborough, Hants.: Gregg International Publishers, 1968.

Reinhard, Johan. "Khembalung: The Hidden Valley," *Kailash* 6, No. 1 (1978), pp. 5–35.

Roerich, George N., trans. *The Blue Annals*, 2 vols. Calcutta: Royal Asiatic Society of Bengal, 1949, 1953.

————. "Studies in the Kālacakra," *Journal of Urusvati Himalayan Research Institute of Roerich Museum* 2 (1931), pp. 11–22.

————. *Trails to Inmost Asia*. New Haven, Conn.: Yale University Press, 1931.

Roerich, Nicholas. *The Heart of Asia*. New York: Roerich Museum Press, 1930.

Rupen, Robert A. *Mongols of the Twentieth Century*, Pt. 1. Bloomington: Indiana University Press, 1964.

Snellgrove, David L., ed. and trans. *The Nine Ways of Bon*. London: Oxford University Press, 1967.

Stein, R. A. *L'épopée tibétaine de Gésar dans sa version lamaïque de Ling*. Paris: Presses Universitaires de France, 1956.

————. *Recherches sur l'épopée et le barde au Tibet*. Paris: Presses Universitaires de France, 1959.

————. *Tibetan Civilization*, trans. J. E. Stapleton Driver. London: Faber & Faber, 1972.

Tatz, Mark, and Kent, Jody. *Rebirth: The Tibetan Game of Liberation*. Garden City, N.Y.: Anchor Press/Doubleday & Company, 1977.

Tomas, Andrew. *Shambhala: Oasis of Light*. London: Sphere Books, 1977.

Tucci, Giuseppe. *Tibetan Painted Scrolls*, 2 vols. Rome: Libreria dello Stato, 1949.

Vira, Raghu, and Chandra, Lokesh. *A New Tibeto-Mongol Pantheon*, Pt. 20. New Delhi: International Academy of Indian Culture, 1972.

Vogel, Claus. "On Tibetan Chronology," *Central Asiatic Journal* 9, No. 3 (1964), pp. 224–38.

Wayman, Alex. *The Buddhist Tantras: Light on Indo-Tibetan Esotericism*. New York: Samuel Weiser, 1973.

Wylie, Turrell V., ed. and trans. *The Geography of Tibet According to the 'Dzam-gling rgyas-bshad*. Rome: Istituto Italiano per il medio ed Estremo Oriente, 1963.

————. "Was Christopher Columbus from Shambhala?" *Bulletin*

of the Institute of China Border Area Studies, No. 1 (1970), pp. 24–33.

SOURCES IN TIBETAN AND SANSKRIT

Blo bzang dpal ldan ye shes (Third Panchen Lama). *Grub pa'i gnas chen po sham bha la'i rnam bshad 'phags yul gyi rtogs brjod dang bcas pa* (known as *Sham bha la'i lam yig*). Block print, 50 fols., Bkra shis lhun po edition.

——. *Sham bha lar skye ba'i smon lam.* In *Tibetan Buddhist Studies of Kloṅ-rdol bla-ma Ṅag-dbaṅ-blo-bzaṅ*, ed. Ven. Dalama 1:150–51. Mussoorie: Ven. Dalama, 1963.

Kalāpāvatāra. P. 5908. In *The Tibetan Tripitaka, Peking Edition*, ed. Daisetz T. Suzuki 149:159–65. Tokyo-Kyoto: Tibetan Tripitaka Research Institute, 1957.

Klong rdol bla ma ngag dbang blo bzang. *Dus kyi 'khor lo'i lo rgyus dang sham bha la'i zhing bkod bcas.* In *Tibetan Buddhist Studies of Kloṅ-rdol bla-ma Ṅag-dbaṅ-blo-bzaṅ*, ed. Ven. Dalama 1:125–52. Mussoorie: Ven. Dalama, 1963.

——. *Rgyal ba tsong kha pa'i lugs dang mthun pa rnams phyogs gcig tu btus pa'i dpal dus kyi 'khor lo'i ming gi rnam grangs.* In *Tibetan Buddhist Studies* 1:152–81.

Padma gling pa, gter ston (discoverer). *Sbas yul mkhan pa lung gi gnas yig dang lam yig bcas.* Copied from a text at the monastery of Gsang sngags chos gling in Bhutan, courtesy of E. Gene Smith, 35 fols.

Parama-ādibuddhoddhrita-śrī-kālacakra-nāma-tantrarāja. P. 4. Tibetan text in *The Tibetan Tripitaka, Peking Edition*, ed. Daisetz T. Suzuki 1:127–74. Tokyo-Kyoto: Tibetan Tripitaka Research Institute, 1955.

——. Sanskrit, Mongolian, and Tibetan texts in *Kālacakra-Tantra and Other Texts*, ed. Raghu Vira and Lokesh Chandra, Pt. 1. New Delhi: International Academy of Indian Culture, 1966.

Rin spungs ngag dbang 'jigs grags kyis rang gi yab la phul ba'i zhu 'phrin rig pa 'dzin pa'i pho nya. Reproduced ms., 39 fols. Dharamsala: Library of Tibetan Works and Archives, 1974.

Rong tha blo bzang dam chos rgya mtsho. *Sham bha lar skye ba'i smon lam rig 'dzin grong du bgrod pa'i them skas zhes bya ba.* In *The Collected Works (Gsuṅ 'Bum) of Blo-bzaṅ-dam-chos-rgya-mtsho, Roṅ-tha Che-tshaṅ Sprul-sku,* reproduced by Ngawang Sopa 6:462–68. New Delhi: Ngawang Sopa, 1975.

Sa skya paṇḍi ta kun dga' rgyal mtshan (Sakya Pandita). *Sdom pa gsum gyi rab tu dbye ba.* In *The Complete Works of the Great Masters of the Sa Skya Sect of the Tibetan Buddhism,* ed. Bsod-nams rgya-mtsho 5:297–320. Tokyo: Toyo Bunko, 1968.

Sbas yul mkhan pa lung gi lam yig. Incomplete ms., 31 fols.

Stag tshang lo tsā ba shes rab rin chen. *Dus 'khor spyi don bstan pa'i rgya mtsho,* reproduced by Trayang and Jamyang Samten. New Delhi: Trayang and Jamyang Samten, 1973.

Thu'u bkwan blo bzang chos kyi nyi ma. *Grub mtha' thams cad kyi khungs dang 'dod tshul ston pa legs bshad shel gyi me long,* section 12. In *Collected Works of Thu'u-bkwan Blo-bzang-chos-kyi-nyi-ma,* ed. Ngawang Gelek Demo 2:483–519. Delhi: Jayyed Press, 1969.

Vimalaprabhā-nāma-mūlatantrānusāriṇī-dvādaśasāhasrikā-laghu-kālacakra-tantrarāja-ṭikā. P. 2,064. In *The Tibetan Tripitaka, Peking Edition,* ed. Daisetz T. Suzuki 46:121–335. Tokyo-Kyoto: Tibetan Tripitaka Research Institute, 1958.

Acknowledgments

I would like to begin by giving my deepest thanks to all the many people who gave of their time and knowledge to make this book possible. If *The Way to Shambhala* forms a complete whole, as I hope it does, then each person's contribution forms an essential part of it, to be appreciated and valued as such.

Lama Kunga Rimpoche (Ngor Thartse Sheptung Rimpoche) devoted a great deal of time and effort to helping me with the research for this book. He generously made available the resources of the Ewam Choden Tibetan Buddhist Center and did the snow lion's share of translating Tibetan texts on Shambhala. His deep knowledge of Tibetan religion and culture proved invaluable in helping me to place the myth in its proper context. Without his help and friendship, I could not have written a book of this scope and authenticity.

I am indebted to Raimundo Panikkar for his encouragement and guidance. Our conversations on the nature of myth and symbolism sparked many ideas and helped me to formulate my thoughts. In addition to going over the text and offering helpful criticism, he served the even more important function of continually reminding me that writing the book should be a part of my own journey to Shambhala.

I would also like to give special thanks to the person who set me on the path to writing about Shambhala—the Incarnate Lama of Tengboche. Through him I had my first contact with Shambhala and the living tradition of Tibetan Buddhism. By helping me to decipher the guidebook to Khembalung, he also enabled me to set my feet on the actual, physical path to a hidden valley. If ever I reach Shambhala, I would like to think that our friendship was the first step on the way.

Another person who contributed a great deal of time, skill, and effort was my cousin, Moira Hahn, who prepared the figures used in this book. Her special touch added a lightness and beauty that went far beyond my rather limited specifications. I am especially grateful for her vision, interest, and enthusiasm.

I am deeply honored that Garje Khamtul Rimpoche saw fit to confide his dream of going to Shambhala to me and this book. The beauty and freshness of this visionary dream, along with its human qualities, gives it an immediacy lacking in the more formal guidebooks to the hidden kingdom. Through it we get a living sense of what the journey to Shambhala can mean.

A number of lamas made major contributions to my understanding of the Kalacakra and the symbolism of Shambhala. Discussions with Samdong Rimpoche gave me a framework for explaining Tibetan Buddhism and relating the hidden kingdom to the hidden regions of the mind. I am still amazed at the clarity and precision of his explications. Chopgye Trichen Rimpoche spent a great deal of time explaining the world view of the Kalacakra and the history of Shambhala. He also provided a very useful summary of Rinpungpa's poetic guidebook to the kingdom. Khempo Noryang and Khempo Tsondu gave me many valuable insights into the nature of the Kalacakra and Shambhala. Without their help, this book would have lacked much of its depth and meaning.

I would like to thank the heads of three of the four major sects of Tibetan Buddhism for patiently answering my questions on Shambhala: H. H. the Dalai Lama, the Sakya Trizin, and Dudjom Rimpoche. Many other lamas and laypeople gave generously of their time, knowledge, and understanding. Most of them I have acknowledged in the text and the Notes, but some I have not. Doboom Rimpoche and Sherpa Tulku helped me find texts and shared what they knew about Shambhala. Jampa Gyaltsen Dakthon provided information on the myth and identified paintings of various Kings of Shambhala. Namgyal Wangchen gave me valuable background material on the Kalacakra and Shambhala—and cooked us a delicious dinner of Tibetan noodle soup. I am indebted to Kunga Yongten Hochotsang for his kind assistance at the Institute of Tibetology and to Karma Lhendup for his gift of a guidebook to the hidden valleys of Sikkim. I am also grateful for the help and information supplied by Tharik Tulku, Chatral Rimpoche, Chogyam Trungpa Rimpoche, Dongthog Rimpoche, Dungzhin Rimpoche, Lokesh Chandra, Tony Guida, Richard Mueller, Sechin Jagchid, Geshe Lobsang Tharcin, Wang Chu Lama, the Mendopake Lama, Ang Chumbi, Ngawang Samten, Dawa Tenzing, Tsewang Norbu, Tenzin Oser, and the teachers of the Tibetan Central School at Mussoorie.

Some of my deepest appreciation goes to those who interpreted for me. I wish to thank Kalsang Namgyal, in particular, for coming to Lumbini with us and enabling me to speak with Chopgye Trichen Rimpoche. Kalsang also provided valuable material on Shambhala and helped me to understand what I was learning. His wife, Kalsang Lhawang, and their two delightful daughters, Thinle and Yeshe, made the trip to Lumbini one of the most enjoyable parts of our research. In addition to interpreting and offering perceptive insights, Chophel Namgyal made an invaluable contribution by translating material central to this book. I cannot begin to thank him for all that he so generously did for me. Chope Paljor Tsering interpreted on a number of occasions and spent a great deal of time checking interviews I had recorded on tape. I am grateful to him not only for his assistance, but also for his friendship and astute observations. Matthew Kapstein helped with a number of interviews and contributed a great deal of valuable information from his extensive knowledge of Tibetan Buddhism and history. He also made a major contribution to a memorable New Year's Eve celebration in the Himalayas. Larry Hartsell and Nyima Dorje enabled me to interview Garje Khamtul Rimpoche and obtain some of the most valuable and unique material in this book. Ricardo Canzio helped me to speak with lamas and photograph art around Dehradun. Gyalse Rimpoche and Dorje Tsering helped me conduct some of my most important interviews—with Khempo Tsondu and Khempo Noryang. I would also like to thank the following people for their assistance in interpreting: Tenzin Geyche, Wang Chu Tsering, Sangye Dawa, Thubten Tsering, Tsering Dorje, Mingma Namgyal, June Campbell, and Jampal Kalden.

I am especially indebted to Gene Smith for his excellent suggestions on whom to interview and what texts to obtain in India and Nepal. His encyclopedic knowledge of Tibetan literature led me, in particular, to the most beautiful of all the guidebooks to Shambhala—the one by Rinpungpa. Giorgio Bonazzoli was of great help in digging up valuable references to the Hindu prophecy of Kalki—and pointing out relations between it and the Tibetan myth of Shambhala. Robert Thurman helped me to get an overall picture of the Tibetan myth and its significance. Sonam Gyatso (Ngor Thartse Khen Rimpoche) clarified a number of difficult points and kindly allowed me to photograph two of the most beautiful pieces of Tibetan art used in this book—the statues of Avalokiteshvara and Manjushri. Shozui Toganoo showed me the collection of paintings of Kings of Shambhala at the Boston Museum of Fine Arts and photographed them with me. James Bosson and Yasuhiko Nagano provided assistance in my research. Yolanda Gerritsen and Diane Ames helped me examine and translate German translations of two guidebooks to Shambhala. Alice Johnson sent a number of useful references my way.

I owe a great deal to Lois Greene for reading over early drafts of this book and making suggestions that initiated considerable improvements. Her criticism helped me to see the book from the reader's perspective and to make changes that led to greater clarity and conciseness of expression. My editor at Anchor, William Strachan, also helped with this process and contributed much-needed support and encouragement. I am particularly grateful to him for letting the book take its own form in its own, sweet time. Many thanks go to Lewis Lancaster for checking the chapter on Tibetan Buddhism and the Kalacakra, and for helping me in my research at the University of California at Berkeley. I would also like to thank Ann Buchwald for her faith in me and in this book. I am indebted to Faith Conlon for her editing and assistance at Anchor.

A number of people made it possible for me to go into the area where the hidden valley of Khembalung is supposed to be concealed. I am indebted to Urkien Sherpa for supplying essential information on its location. A good deal of credit must go to David Peterson for inviting me to join an expedition that he had organized to go into the general vicinity of the valley. I would also like to thank the *sirdar* of the expedition, Ngawang Samten, for all his *dukha*. Kalden Sherpa went to a great deal of trouble to help me make the necessary arrangements. I was fortunate to find a good companion for this venture in Kent Obee.

I wish to thank our Sherpa friends in Solu Khumbu for their generous help and hospitality. Some of my warmest memories are of sitting around Kunjo Chumbi's hearth in Khumjung, munching boiled potatoes and talking about hidden valleys. In addition to helping with our research, Ngawang Gendun and Kipa Lama entertained us with songs and *raksi* at their teashops in Junbesi—surely the merriest teashops this side of Mount Everest. I would also like to thank Katsering for guiding us up to the Amphu Labtsa Pass and for putting us up in his home in Khumjung. His stepmother, Nyima Putti, also provided warm hospitality—and tasty potato pancakes. Pasang Thondup and the monks of Tengboche Monastery could not have treated us better.

Finally, I would like to express my love and appreciation to my wife, Diane. By listening patiently as I read and reread portions of this book out loud, she gave me much-needed support and helped me to clarify my thinking, in addition to supplying valuable criticism. She also photographed our research in India and Nepal, participated in interviews, and followed the guidebook to Khembalung with me up to the glaciers beneath the Amphu Labtsa. In many ways, this book is a product of our joint efforts. Without her constant help and support, I doubt that I would have been able to complete *The Way to Shambhala.*

Index